Beyond the Anti-Group

Beyond the Anti-Group: Survival and transformation builds on the success of Morris Nitsun's influential concept of the anti-group, taking it into new domains of thought and practice in the current century. 'A historical and ideological breakthrough' (Tuttman 1991), the concept focuses on anxiety and hostility within, towards and between groups, as well as the destructive potential of groups. In *Beyond the Anti-Group,* Morris Nitsun continues his inquiry into the clinical implications of the anti-group but also explores the concept beyond the consulting room, in settings as wide-ranging as cultural and environmental stress in the twenty-first century, the fate of public health services and the themes of contemporary art.

Groups are potentially destructive but also have the capacity for survival, creativity and transformation. Focusing on the interplay between the two, Morris Nitsun explores the struggle to overcome group impasse and dysfunction and to emerge stronger. Why does this happen in some groups and not others? What are the conditions for group transformation? How does this affect individuals, groups, organizations and societies? By tracking this process in a range of cultural settings, the author weaves a rich tapestry in which group psychotherapy, organizational process and the arts come together in unexpected and novel ways. The author draws on group analysis and the Foulkesian tradition as his overall discipline but within a critical frame that questions the relevance of the approach in a changing world, highlighting new directions and opportunities. Questions of group and organizational leadership and their contribution to anti-group processes are a further theme.

Readers of *Beyond the Anti-Group* will be stimulated by the depth, breadth and creativity of the author's analysis and by the excursion into new fields of inquiry. This book offers new scope, new ideas and new impetus for psychotherapists, group analysts and group practitioners in general, students of group and organizational processes and those working on the boundary between psychotherapy and the arts.

Morris Nitsun is a consultant psychologist in Camden and Islington NHS Trust, psychotherapist at the Fitzrovia Group Analytic Practice, Training Analyst at the Institute of Group Analysis, and Convenor, Diploma in Innovative Group Interventions, Anna Freud Clinic. His books *The Anti-group: Destructive Forces in the Group and their Creative Potential* (Routledge, 1996) and *The Group as an Object of Desire* (Routledge, 2006) have been described as 'classics in the field'. He has lectured and run workshops in countries across the world. He is also a practising artist who exhibits regularly in London.

Beyond the Anti-Group

Survival and transformation

Morris Nitsun

Routledge
Taylor & Francis Group

LONDON AND NEW YORK

First published 2015
by Routledge
27 Church Road, Hove, East Sussex, BN3 2FA

and by Routledge
711 Third Avenue, New York, NY 10017

Routledge is an imprint of the Taylor & Francis Group, an informa business

British Library Cataloguing in Publication Data
A catalogue record for this book is available from the British Library

Library of Congress Cataloging in Publication Data
Nitsun, Morris.
Beyond the anti-group : survival and transformation / Morris Nitsun. –
First Edition.
pages cm
ISBN 978-0-415-68736-2 (hbk) – ISBN 978-0-415-68738-6 (pbk) –
ISBN 978-1-315-73945-8 (ebk) 1. Social interaction–Technological
innovation. 2. Great Britain. National Health Service. 3. Group
psychotherapy. I. Title.
HM1111.N58 2014
302–dc23
2014023386

ISBN: 978-0-415-68736-2 (hbk)
ISBN: 978-0-415-68738-6 (pbk)
ISBN: 978-1-315-73945-8 (ebk)

Typeset in Times New Roman
by Saxon Graphics Ltd, Derby

MIX
Paper from
responsible sources
FSC
www.fsc.org   FSC® C013056

Printed and bound in Great Britain by
TJ International Ltd, Padstow, Cornwall

To Shirley,
With love and deep thanks

Contents

PART IV
Group analysis and the arts

Foreword

I welcome this third book by Morris Nitsun on group analysis. Unlike the first two, it covers a wide range of themes, reflecting the range of interests and experience of its author. In the Preface, he comments on the book being a product of his varied career as a psychologist, psychotherapist and manager in public services, as a group analyst in private practice and as a practising artist. Each of these would be a full career for most people, but he has pursued them simultaneously and has inhabited each fully, making contributions that have been important to people in all three worlds. The book is permeated by all three worlds. While the content of each chapter may reflect more one or another and the lens he focuses on each is that of group analytic thinking, the book overall reflects his own "coherence of experience" and is in this way a distinctly personal book. In terms of group analytic thinking, the book is unified by the concept of the anti-group, his important and original contribution to the field, and the sub-themes of survival and transformation, which are particularly relevant at the present time. But in this Foreword, I shall take as my theme the three worlds that the author represents.

For over 40 years, since 1969, Morris Nitsun has worked in the National Health Service, initially as a psychologist, psychotherapist and manager of NHS psychological therapy services, and latterly as a trainer and group consultant. The NHS is an extraordinary national icon, established with a visionary mission of providing free healthcare for all and continuing to enjoy unrivalled public support, but subject to enormous political and financial pressures and internally prone to schisms – clinicians vs managers, doctors vs nurses, psychologists vs psychotherapists, psychoanalytic psychotherapists vs cognitive behavioural therapists, health commissioners vs hospitals, government of the day vs the NHS. An important contribution of this book is the understanding it brings to these schisms, most directly in the chapter on NHS change, but also in other chapters. In the vast organization of the NHS, this is difficult territory to see clearly and write about when inside and a part of the process. What Morris Nitsun brings personally and in his analysis is an ability to embrace the full emotional impact of these schisms while keeping in mind the strengths and positive ambitions of each NHS tribe to contribute to the mission of the NHS. With increasing pressures expected on all healthcare systems from public expectations and ever better but more costly healthcare technologies, never has this been a more important message.

The chapter on the contribution of group analysis to cognitive-behavioural therapy (CBT) is also indirectly about schisms, with unfortunate splits and lack of mutual understanding between different approaches to psychological therapy. I have to declare an interest as fifteen years ago, as head of psychological services in Camden and Islington, I invited Morris Nitsun to come and work as part-time trainer and consultant in group work when he retired after 30 years as Head of Psychological Therapies in Redbridge, outer London. There is a rich tradition of psychoanalytic psychotherapists providing consultation to enhance the work of other health professionals, not just in mental health but through Balint groups for general medical practitioners, but not as yet much from group analysts. With over 500,000 NHS patients a year in England seen in CBT and other brief therapies, around 100,000 in brief group CBT, there is a huge need for training and consultation in group work. Public health is improved through small impacts on large numbers of people as well as intensive impacts on a few, and Morris Nitsun sets out how group analysts can contribute to helping many more people than they could possibly help directly. His sympathy for and real interest in the dilemmas and difficulties of people running groups with little or no prior group training shines through his descriptions and are without doubt key to the success of this work.

How to help people with significant mental health problems at the margins of society is a challenge for publically funded health systems. Psychotherapy and group therapy in the NHS is sometimes viewed as being just for the more articulate and psychologically minded, with many being called but few chosen. In the inner London NHS group therapy service Morris Nitsun coordinates, the surprise to referrers is that most are chosen, despite the patients' multiple difficulties, and that many groups are run by trainee group therapists. In the chapter on the Group as a Refuge, he describes how being open to the possibilities of such patients, while addressing the challenges and anxieties of running such groups, can bring benefits. The benefits may be different and in some ways more limited than those obtained by patients without such difficulties, but no less important. This combination of travelling optimistically with people, whether patients or supervisees, while being attentive to and embracing the difficulties, is the hallmark of his approach and of this book.

In the Introduction, Morris Nitsun describes how some of his thinking about groups and a reconsideration of his ideas about the anti-group, have come from conducting groups in private practice. Retiring from full-time NHS work in 2001 afforded him the opportunity to increase his private group work while continuing part-time in the NHS. The chapter about these groups is a delightful read, full of warmth, life-affirming and optimistic about the possibilities of group analytic therapy helping people with difficulties forming intimate relationships. It should end up on any shortlist of best reads to encourage a friend or colleague with doubts about entering group therapy.

As a young man in South Africa, Morris Nitsun studied art as well as psychology and in 1966 was a prize winner in the South African Artists of Fame and Promise Competition. While psychology and psychotherapy won out as his employment career choice, he has continued to paint, exhibit and sell his paintings, which with their vibrant colours and rich textures bring pleasure to the homes of many colleagues, friends and lovers of fine art. Until now, this aspect of his life has been separate from and not directly reflected in his writing. So an added interest of this book is two chapters on the arts, albeit performance art and film rather than visual art per se, but richly informed by his own experience as an artist.

While this Foreword has highlighted the different worlds of experience that Morris Nitsun has brought to this book, his chapter on being a group therapist includes directly autobiographical sections. Among other illustrative examples, he draws on his own experience, looking backwards to past influences, to the present and forward to the future: all this in relation to the development of his ideas and person as a group therapist. While these sections are explicitly personal, as he writes in the Preface, the book overall is 'the culmination of a long career and the life that went with it'. Looking forward, with the originality, freshness and importance of his ideas in this book, many of us will hope that there is still more to come.

Professor John Cape
Director of Psychological Therapy Programmes University College London

Preface and Acknowledgements

A book has an historical context as well as a current context in which the writing of the book has taken place.

On the historical front, the world we inhabit today is a very different world from that in which S. H. Foulkes (1900–76) made his mark in the new field of group analysis. Foulkes emigrated from Germany to Britain in 1932 where he re-established himself as a psychiatrist and psychoanalyst through the years of World War II and the post-war decades. Most of his writing was produced in this period, his publications stretching from the late 1930s to the early 1970s. I have previously commented on the contradiction of Foulkes generating a positive, optimistic vision of groups at a time when Europe was engulfed in a world war of unprecedented proportions, and even in peacetime England the ruins of war were painfully etched across the landscape of the country. The concept of the anti-group was an attempt to address this gap in history and theory, emphasizing aggression and its disruptive consequences as a major component of group behaviour in human beings. Coming up to the present time, at a very different point in history, many of the questions remain, raising an overarching question about the relevance of group analysis in the current age and how it is positioned in the more pluralistic society of the twenty-first century with its advances in many fields of the arts, sciences and humanities: its pressing concerns about environmental, technological and ideological change; and the turmoil of political change which promises to redraw the world as we know it. How relevant still is the concept of the anti-group and how does it reflect current concerns?

I aim in this book not to attempt a comprehensive or heroic vision of the twenty-first century but to delve into particular areas of interest that I believe have relevance to the group analytic endeavour. There remain questions about the force of aggression between human beings, with nagging fears that the lessons of the past have not been learned. But I come to my task by no means with a purely pessimistic outlook. The twenty-first century world is also a world of creative ferment in which progress has been made on many fronts, not least in the social domain, where greater freedoms than ever before exist, where the value of human diversity is more recognized and where damage to both the physical and the social environment is the subject of reflective processes aimed at greater personal and social responsibility. Yet, progress in all these spheres is continually resisted and undermined and it is this oscillation to which this book is addressed.

....

Closer to home, the book started as a collection of my published papers, with the possibility of one or two additional chapters. But as the writing progressed, new ideas and other ideas that had previously woven in and out of thought began to seek expression. Before long, I realized that I was writing an entirely new book. Some themes, particularly regarding group analytic psychotherapy, will be familiar to those who know my work. But I have also taken the opportunity to delve into several new areas. Because of the range of themes, I became concerned early on that the book would lack coherence. My developmental psychologist mentality demanded a logical sequence, chapter building on chapter, all moving steadily to a grand and convincing conclusion. Friends and colleagues (many of whom are both) were very helpful in relation to this dilemma. Some who heard my ideas for the book and others who read early drafts of the chapters expressed enthusiasm and a measure of excitement. Not only did they feel that the book had thematic coherence but that it had the coherence of experience – through my long career in psychology, psychotherapy and group analysis, including decades of work in public health services, as well as private practice. The fact that I am a practising artist and was for the first time writing seriously about art (in Chapter 8) was also welcomed.

This feedback added ballast to my journey and provided a framework within which I could go forward. It helped me to galvanize my efforts over the months and years of writing and to struggle with the periods of doubt and impasse.

Several friends/colleagues stand out for their particular support with the book, reading and commenting as the manuscript progressed, and contributing from different countries: Phil Schulte, Sylvia Hutchinson, Graham Fuller, Sue Einhorn, David Vincent and Peter Wilson in the UK; Bertha Lewitton in South Africa: and Bracha Hadar in Israel. They gave generously of their time, read chapters and helped me to stay on track. Several close friends also put up with my writing neuroses and valiantly supported the project: Tony Fagin, Marc Kingsley, John Schlapobersky, Jenny Stolzenberg and Howard del Monte, to name just a few. Thank you all. Since the book increasingly became the culmination of a long career and the life that went with it, it has made me aware of the riches that I have been fortunate to garner over the years. I count your friendship amongst these.

Since the book covers a number of work contexts in time and place, I want to thank my many colleagues in the different settings for their enormous support and appreciation. Without them, I could not have written this book. In the National Health Service, my thanks go to John Cape, Jeff Halperin and Alastair Bailey in

Camden and Islington NHS Foundation Trust, and to the many clinicians past and present who have worked in the Islington Group Psychotherapy service I convene. My experience of groups in the NHS, running, organizing and supervising them, coupled with the great colleagueship I have known, has been grounding and affirmative in many ways. In the private sphere, I want to thank my partners at the Fitzrovia Group Analytic Practice, Bonnie Gold, Roberta Green, Sara Scott, Peter Wilson and David Wood, who bring professionalism, warmth and humour to our work together and have provided a stimulating work setting in which to develop my interests. Thanks also to Nexus, my loyal, loving and formative eighteen year-long peer supervision group, including members old and new – Geraldine Festenstein, Graham Fuller (under a different hat), Diana Kinder, Alan Larney, Carmen O' Leary, Amelie Noack and Phil Schulte (also under a different hat).

Finally, I owe a great debt to the many patients I have worked with over the years, in both NHS and private practice settings. Their trust me in and our work together has made this "impossible profession" not just possible for me but meaningful and rewarding – a privilege indeed. Their singular contributions, honesty and courage, and the richness of their narratives, is present symbolically through the pages of this book.

Morris Nitsun
London 2014

Introduction

I write this book primarily as a clinician, having spanned public and private psychological and psychotherapeutic services over a long career. I make this point to distinguish myself from writers/readers who have had limited contact with the turbulent, demanding reality of clinical services. I do so partly to support the arguments in the book that emerge from the psychotherapeutic matrix, reinforced by wide experience with many patients in many different contexts. I do so also because of the value I place on clinical services and the urgency to find the best possible solutions for the people I see, the most congruent and effective approaches, recognizing at the same time the considerable limitations of what we can offer. I am keen on theory but not without continuing recourse to what happens in the consulting room. Equally, I am very interested in applied group analysis and its relevance to organizations, wider social processes and contemporary cultural forms – which is reflected in several chapters – but the clinical remains a passionate point of reference.

Revisiting the anti-group

In a typical week as a group analyst and consultant in group work, I might encounter the following situations. In a course I am running on group psychotherapy for NHS staff, we are discussing participants' previous experiences in groups. A psychologist shares his negative experience of a reflection group he attended while training. He says the group was tense, uncomfortable and unsafe and there was no positive development in the group. Students' dissatisfaction with the experience contributed to a strong mistrust in groups that became part of a group-resistant culture on the overall course. The student has avoided participating in and running groups ever since. Another student tells me that her first attempt at running a group was a complete failure. The group was very difficult to establish, there was dissatisfaction from early on amongst participants, and there was a chain of drop-outs: the group collapsed within weeks. In my NHS role as group consultant, a clinical psychologist tells me that, following her completing a group for depression, her manager decided not to permit further similar groups in the service because the group she ran was too problematic and patient outcomes rather poor. The manager's conclusion was that this kind of group was neither clinically- nor cost-effective. The psychologist argued that this was their first attempt at such a group and that it merited re-running, with greater planning and support than she previously had, but the manager was unconvinced. In a peer supervision group of group analysts of which I have been part for many years, a senior, trusted colleague shares her anxiety that her one remaining private practice group is disintegrating. There have recently been several unexpected departures, she is getting no new referrals and the group membership is down to four, with yet another member saying he wants to leave. My colleague struggles with painful feelings of failure and loss. These are the sorts of situations I encounter routinely in my work. Although of course there are also success stories, and higher levels of satisfaction, there is a shadow of doubt and anxiety that hovers around group work, particularly in public services – often an anxiety about whether the group will *survive* – and it is this concern that is a major theme of this book.

  I hope in writing the book to convey something of the world of *real* groups, the groups we live in, work in, belong to, delight in, puzzle over, flee from. While I make excursions towards the end of the book into the world of the arts, my main focus is on psychotherapy and organizational groups, and in exploring these groups I hope to convey a sense of their quality and immediacy: our lived experience of them. I contrast this with the *theoretical* world of groups, by which I refer to the growing literature on the theory of groups in the field of group analysis, which provide impressive insights into the metapsychology of groups but in which I miss a sense of what groups are really like. So, I come to this book with excitement and enthusiasm for groups, especially psychotherapy groups, which have increasingly become a rich and rewarding aspect of a long career. But I also come to the task with a sense of the difficulty that can be experienced in groups, the anxiety and hostility that can be felt in groups and towards groups, the implosive and disintegratory tendencies in some groups, and the struggle many groups have to survive and thrive in challenging environments. While the richness and creativity of groups is familiar to me, so are the darker and disruptive aspects. This is summed up in my concept of the anti-group, the subject of my first book in this field (Nitsun 1996). I return to the subject in the present book, seeking opportunities to revisit, explore and extend the concept. In a series of chapters on diverse groups in different contexts and settings, I focus particularly on questions of survival underlying group difficulties – and their relation to the anti-group: and further, in the process of survival, the potential for transformation.

What is the anti-group?

The anti-group is a term that describes different manifestations of anxiety and hostility towards the group that can undermine its constructive and collaborative potential (Nitsun 1991, 1996). It is a process, varying in expression from group to group: it has latent and manifest forms; and it occurs at different levels – individual, sub-group and group as a whole (although it is always understood as a group process).

My original writing on the anti-group was in the spirit of a challenge to Foulkesian group analysis and this is where I would like to pick up a thread that links the two books. When I originally took issue in the 1980s and 1990s with the under-emphasis in group analysis on the problematic and potentially destructive aspects of the psychotherapy group, I was coming from an experiential rather than a theoretical position. Much of what I saw in groups in my roles as a group analytic psychotherapist, convenor of an NHS group service, consultant to groups, and head of overall NHS psychology and psychotherapy services for many years, was different from the picture of groups conveyed in the well-known group analytic literature of the time. I encountered more gaps, unpredictability, chaos, fall-out, dissatisfaction and group disintegration than was recognized, hostility and a sense of damage sometimes sustained (rather than repaired) groups, and an overall suspiciousness of groups in both the patient population and the service organization, which could undermine the group project. This prompted me to formulate the notion of the anti-group largely as a corrective to what I saw as the sometimes blinkered optimism of group analysis. This resulted in a series of publications (e.g. Nitsun 1991, 1996, 2000, 2005) that developed the concept primarily as a *critical principle* but also explored the actual manifestation of destructive and self-destructive tendencies *in* groups and *towards* groups Although I believe my writing made an impact, and I have now given talks on the subject in many countries across the world, the problems I refer to are still, in my view, to some extent denied or concealed in the complex theoretical culture surrounding group work practice. Hence, although much of the recent theoretical writing has added to an overall understanding of group process, particularly in highlighting the social as an ontological frame, this still in my view ignores the real, day-to-day problems of clinical practice, which for many group analysts remain a major concern. Additionally, as I emphasize in later sections of the book, this is at a time of considerable anxiety about the survival of long-term analytically orientated psychotherapies in public services, groups included, a time when a robust theory–practice link is more urgently needed than ever.

One of the objections to the concept I have sometimes encountered is that the formulation of the anti-group unnecessarily distinguishes and *names* an aspect of the group that is intrinsic to the group process. With this usually goes a concern that the concept is subject to reification. I have argued myself against its reification, emphasizing repeatedly that it is a process (Nitsun 1996). At the same time, although I agree that it is embedded within the group, I am sufficiently concerned about the impact of potentially group-destructive processes and their marginalization and obfuscation in theory and practice, to argue the continued need for a concept that signals the ever-present potential for group disruption and, at worst, disintegration.

I am not advocating pessimism as a virtue in itself. Rather I seek realism, in which doubt and a degree of pessimism are necessary ingredients, akin to what

Thompson (1991), in an appreciation of Freud's later writing, called 'corrective pessimism'. Apart from the advantage of maintaining a balanced clinical perspective, this approach is a way of avoiding ideological splits, where the idealized and devaluing versions of the same phenomena are all too readily apportioned between different theoreticians and their followers. This includes what I consider to be the unhelpful schism between the approaches of Foulkes and Bion – a theme explored in my 1996 publication and that I describe in Chapter 3 as an aspect of the contradictory nature of group psychotherapy theory.

Reformulating the anti-group: survival and transformation

While keen to delineate the problematic aspects of the anti-group, I have throughout my writing (Nitsun 1991, 1996, 2000, 2005) emphasized the interplay of destructive and constructive processes and the paradoxical function of the anti-group in stimulating the creative progress of the group. In various ways, I see the anti-group as a catalyst for group development, a stimulus for the creative unfolding of the group. This, I suggest, is linked to the all-important issue of survival as fundamental to any group undertaking. William McDougall (1871–1938), the early social psychologist and group theoretician, identified 'continuity of existence' as the prime requirement of the group (in Foulkes and Anthony 1967, p. 138). Although the importance of survival is self-evident, I believe it is yet another concern that can be concealed in group discourses but that merits close attention in itself.

I suggest a two-fold perspective of survival as a group principle: 1) survival as a systemic issue concerning the continuity of the group as a living system; and 2) psychological survival in the face of anxiety and hostility in and towards the group. The first perspective has an evolutionary aspect. How does the group survive as a temporary social system in its particular environment?

This entails questions of co-operation and competition, in a way that is congruent with an evolutionary perspective of why some individuals/groups/ species survive and others do not (Holland 1975). It assumes the presence of adaptive agents, the group members, who together interact, exchange information and support each other's presence in a way that reinforces the purpose and value of the group and its survival.

In its manifest form, the anti-group takes the form of challenges to the group, expressing doubt about the integrity and purpose of the group, including behavioural expressions of dissatisfaction, such as late-coming, irregular attendance and drop-outs. It also entails potentially destructive conflict and competition in the group in which the lack of compromise or resolution renders the group vulnerable to implosion. While the anti-group, seen in these ways, appears to threaten rather than enhance survival, it is at the same time vital in challenging and testing survival capacity, emerging naturally in the complex, ambivalent relationships between members and their relationship to the group and the conductor. Rather than constituting separate, contradictory states, the cooperative and the competitive, the pro-group and the anti-group, these tendencies usually emerge in a mutually generating, dialectical fashion, together creating the fabric of the group as a complex living entity. I have previously suggested (Nitsun 1996, 2005) that, as long as the anti-group is part of the dialectical flux of the group, it has a developmental function, challenging and paradoxically confirming group survival. It takes a pathological turn, however, when the dialectic breaks down and the conditions for group stasis or disintegration deepen.

The second, linked, survival perspective of the group concerns the psychological relationship between members and with the conductor and group as a whole. The psychological dimension reflects the personal and interpersonal problems members bring to the group, against a background of emotional trauma in the context of family/social history in which the issue of survival is key. One of the consequences is the transfer into the group of anxiety and hostility towards group membership itself, the therapy group becoming the object of negative projections of varying intensity. This places a demand on group endurance, particularly if there is a predominance of unmetabolized destructive and self-destructive fantasies and impulses. There is then a sense that the group might fragment and disband – and survival is once more in question.

In good enough group development, these tensions are contained and sometimes transformed. A situation akin to Winnicott's (1968) notion of *the use of an object* emerges. The capacity of the group, the conductor and all the members to survive the attacks is strengthening. It reinforces trust and hope in the group. In this way, the anti-group, variously expressed through members and the group as a whole, has both tested and deepened the capacity of the group to survive. While this formulation of group therapy process arises in a group analytic frame, it veers towards complexity theory in its depiction of the group on the edge of chaos, continually constructed and deconstructed through members' responses and interactions (Stacey 2003).

Beyond the anti-group

While maintaining my position on the anti-group potential of all groups, at the same time I acknowledge a change in my experience and understanding of groups. Since my original writing on the concept in the 1990s, I have spent more time working in private practice in central London. As the concept of the anti-group arose in the context of my work in the NHS over several decades, reflecting the very high level of psychological disturbance in typical NHS populations referred for psychotherapy, it has been illuminating to see the rather different picture in private practice. As described in Chapters 5 and 7, people attending groups in the private sphere are generally less disturbed, better resourced economically and educationally, and usually motivated to join a psychotherapy group. Overall, they seek psychotherapy voluntarily and pro-actively and come with positive expectations of group psychotherapy. This contrasts with the typical NHS psychotherapy patient who has a complex and long-standing history of mental health problems, has usually been referred for psychotherapy rather than initiated it and tends to have a limited understanding of what to expect, especially from group psychotherapy. Not surprisingly, in the NHS setting there is a large preference for individual therapy over group, a finding that Bowden (2002) documented and linked directly to anti-group attitudes. Psychotherapy groups in private practice, by contrast, function more consistently and constructively. The group is usually not as preoccupied with its own survival as NHS groups, and the work of the group can proceed more smoothly. In this setting anti-group attitudes and enactments are less apparent, although they are by no means absent and the group still has to deal with significant periods of group disruption, disorganization and sometimes threatened if not actual disintegration.

The relatively easier experience of conducting groups in private practice, while continuing my NHS work, is in part the stimulus for a reconsideration of the concept under the title *Beyond the Anti-group*. The book embarks on a journey that explores differences between groups in a range of clinical settings. But it also reaches beyond the clinical to examine organizational and environmental processes, as well as cultural phenomena ranging from the visual arts to the group as reflected in the world of film. In all these contexts, I follow the thread of the anti-group, trying to understand its manifestation in a variety of cultural and clinical domains, and to evaluate its usefulness in making sense of group process. I retain my stance of 'corrective pessimism', and note the struggle groups have to cohere, to survive and to thrive. But I hope that the creative and transformative aspects of both group and anti-group emerge in this book with sufficient clarity to generate as balanced and realistic a vision of analytic group work as is possible at the present time.

Further perspectives

Apart from the anti-group, my main vantage point in the group analytic encounter is what I have referred to as the *group as an object of desire* (Nitsun 2006). The thrust of this notion concerns what it is that makes groups, including but not only therapy groups, meaningful and rewarding enough for people to want to join and contribute to the group process. I have previously described these two vantage points – the anti-group and the group as an object of desire – as representing thesis and antithesis in a dialectical journey. Neither exists on its own but rather in a complementary relationship in which each may generate the other in an ongoing cycle. This perspective of a mutually generating relationship between the constructive and potentially destructive aspects of the group led me to propose the *dialectical perspective* as a way of understanding groups in their own right, suggesting that this may add coherence to our understanding of groups. In my 1996 book I included the dialectical perspective as one of *three* interlocking perspectives that offer avenues of further exploration in group analysis: *the dialectical perspective, the ecological perspective* and *the aesthetic perspective.*

The *ecological perspective*, as noted above, is important in relation to questions concerning survival at many levels of the group and the complex interaction between group systems and sub-systems. It will be found weaving through most chapters in the book. Whereas a number of questions arise within the ecological framework, there is an underlying question that informs the early part of the book: will the world as we know it, the environment that hosts life in its existing forms, survive? This question, at one level seemingly removed from the immediate preoccupations of the psychotherapist, nevertheless resonates at deeper levels of concern about existential issues and the fear of annihilation (Weintrobe 2013). Throughout this book, I will highlight the concern about survival as a major theme in understanding groups and organizations. My hypothesis is that the anti-group is organized around a fundamental anxiety concerning annihilation. In this view, groups generate anxiety on several levels: anxiety about the survival of the individual group member, anxiety about the survival of the group and anxiety about the survival of the environment containing the group.

The *aesthetic perspective* reflects expressive and symbolic forms in the group, their transformative potential and their link with cultural processes. This perspective emerges more clearly in later sections of the book exploring contemporary art and the world of film.

A further perspective is the *organizational*. While the concept of the anti-group originated in the clinical field, I have also sought to relate it to the broader organizational field. As a head of psychology services in the NHS for several decades, I had considerable contact with the managerial context of the health service and followed the remarkable course of organizational change in the NHS in the late twentieth century and early twenty-first century. In the 1996 book and in two subsequent papers (Nitsun 1998a, 1998b), I introduced the notion of the organizational mirror as an attempt to formulate an understanding of organizational process that emphasized mirroring processes, and especially dysfunctional mirroring, as a core dynamic of organizations under stress. This perspective appears in several parts of the book.

No attempt to understand the fate of the group in the twenty-first century can ignore the profound *technological advancement* that marks the progress of the century. We are only beginning to grapple with the complex questions concerning a shift from the material world of relationships and groups to a virtual world in which face-to-face participation in groups may be eclipsed by the power of social networking and Internet groups. The positive advantages of this are evident: it considerably opens up the communicating world and encourages connection at very wide levels. But what balance will emerge between the virtual and actual domains of social relating? Will virtual and real come together in generating new forms of relating? Does the virtual revolution reflect a turning away from conventional physical/social groupings and what lies behind such withdrawal? Will the accelerating spread of virtual networks reinforce the retreat from actual groups? And further, what are the destructive aspects of technology and the Internet? While the fruits of technological progress open up before us, we also know that this progress has a shadow side, that the Internet harbours the potential for damage, at both social and individual levels. How do we understand these aspects of the Internet?

Outline of the book

This book is divided into four parts and the following outlines the chapters:

In *Part I of the book, The wider context*, I look at the social, cultural and organizational context of contemporary group processes.

Chapter 1, The question of survival in the twenty-first century: challenges to group analysis, explores current changes in the wider environment that touch on concerns about survival and the impact this has on group processes in a variety of domains. Several areas of concern are delineated – the accelerating rate of change, the social impact of technology, climate change, the collapse of time, the loss of society, the notion of immortality and crises of authority. It is suggested that these phenomena are already having a significant impact on the fabric of social life and will do so increasingly in the continuing twenty-first century. Given the group analytic emphasis on the 'colossal' influence of the social, there are important questions about how the theory embraces these changes, since fundamental group analytic principles such as communication, the group matrix and nodal points in a network will take on different meanings in a universe transformed by technology. In parallel, there are questions about the relevance of group analytic psychotherapy in a radically altered universe. Throughout, I consider the anti-group aspects of twenty-first-century progress.

Chapter 2, An anti-group perspective of organizational change: the case of the National Health Service (NHS), examines the pattern of repeated restructuring in the NHS and the destructive impact this can have on services, groups and individuals. The NHS is one of the most revered institutions in the UK. But political and social influences are at play, the NHS serving as the pawn of successive governments in the UK. Additionally, health service organizations also have to deal with the considerable anxiety aroused by illness, both physical and mental, by death and madness, and the dynamic processes triggered by these anxieties contribute crucially to the culture of services. What is emphasized here is the way in which organizational restructuring, while aiming to increase efficiency and claiming to safeguard and strengthen services, usually exacerbates anxiety and undermines group functioning. The anti-group aspects of this process are interpreted in part as the shadow side of care, suggesting that the delivery of care can be understood as a paradoxical process that reflects both reparative and destructive tendencies.

Part II, The clinical setting, focuses on the clinical application of group analysis – the aspect that most group analysts consider their core occupation. This is set against the tense background of psychotherapy services in the National Health Service in the UK where the dismantling of psychotherapy departments raises questions about the survival of all psychotherapy.

Chapter 3, Group psychotherapy on the edge, explores the status of group psychotherapy in the problematic context of UK public mental health services and the anti-group culture that complicates the situation. I also highlight problems in the theory–practice link in group analysis, creating a field that is therapeutically powerful but lacks clinical rigour and empirical grounding. I take issue with aspects of the social perspective in group analysis. While recognizing the importance of this perspective and how it has become a group-analytic focus in recent years, I argue that this is insufficiently reconciled with clinical practice and that it leads to what I call 'the decentering of the clinical subject'. I suggest that the notion of 'the individual' is problematized in a way that may make sense theoretically and ideologically but is at variance with the focus on the individual that is the hallmark of responsible clinical practice. This, in my view, makes it more rather than less difficult to meet – or challenge – current criteria in healthcare that emphasize evaluation and accountability in clinical practice. I also address what I regard as a vein of continuing idealization in group analysis that may render dealing with the challenges all the more difficult.

Chapter 4, Group analysis and cognitive-behavioural therapy (CBT), draws a comparison between two very different psychotherapeutic approaches. I embark on this comparison in order to challenge the polarization that exists in the field of psychological therapies, resulting in stereotyping and prejudice that I believe is unhelpful to the overall credibility and status of the psychotherapies. I contrast group analytic psychotherapy and CBT on various grounds, particularly their scientific and clinical traditions, which reflect highly divergent influences and value systems. But I go on to suggest areas of perhaps unexpected overlap between the two. I describe a new course I convene on NHS group work and how, in a supervisory capacity, I have used group analysis as a way of addressing process issues in CBT groups. I also suggest, conversely, that knowledge of CBT helps the group analytic practitioner to see that a group conducted according to analytic principles does not preclude therapeutic developments that may be explained by other approaches, including CBT. I also ponder whether the judicious use of CBT principles in the psychotherapy group might add clinical ballast.

Chapter 5, The group as refuge: group psychotherapy in inner London, describes the challenges of a group analytic psychotherapy service in an inner-city NHS mental health trust in London. A key component of the service is the changed demographic of the inner city, reflecting an increased influx of immigrants in the last 50 years, a far more diverse population generally and a greater incidence of serious mental health problems, particularly borderline conditions and complex forms of multiple psychopathology. The difficulties of psychotherapy groups catering for such populations are described, highlighting the social and cultural tensions that exacerbate anti-group developments, the impingements of severe emotional disturbance and the lessened capacity of the groups to use processes based on verbal communication and empathic resonance. The chapter argues that in such instances the group functions more as a refuge than as a fully fledged psychotherapy group. It provides a shelter from an inhospitable world. This does not diminish the value of group therapy but requires a re-evaluation of aims and technical considerations.

Part III, Developmental perspectives, deals with themes in life-span development that relate to both the conductor and group members.

Chapter 6, Being a group therapist: a journey through life, focuses on the person of the group practitioner, what draws him/her to the field and what past influences are at play in this development. Some of the positive motivations for undertaking group work are explored, such as a positive belief in groups and their potential to transform personal narratives, as well as the value placed on community and the democratic process. Problematic aspects of the group therapist's personal development are also highlighted, including difficult family processes and the struggle with identity and belonging. There is a search to repair the symbolic family group. While the group therapist strives to create a healing group, the journey is not straightforward, given the problems encountered in groups. Part of the journey is the group therapist's confrontation with the anti-group, including his/her own ambivalence. The conductor needs to reconcile his/her reparative urge with the frustrations of dealing with sometimes antagonistic and intractable group processes. This can lead to a personal crisis in group leadership.

Chapter 7, Falling in love: a group analytic perspective, is perhaps the most optimistic chapter in the book. Based on a sample of patients who completed long-term group psychotherapy, it documents the significant gains patients made in the area of close interpersonal relationships, specifically the establishment of a primary emotional attachment. While falling in love is usually understood from an individual or couple perspective, the chapter highlights the important role the group played in supporting individuals' development of close relationships. This applies both socially and clinically. A large part of the group's influence emerges directly in the psychotherapy group: the interpersonal learning and socializing techniques that Yalom and Leszcz (2005) has emphasized, the reshaping of life narratives in the group, and the function of the group as a witness to the formation of intimate relationships that I highlighted in *The group as an object of desire* (Nitsun 2006). "Pathologies" of love, and how they are dealt with in the group, are also highlighted.

Part IV of the book, Group analysis and the arts, sets out to look at the world of contemporary arts, exploring possible areas of creative overlap with group analysis.

Chapter 8, Group analysis and performance art, considers recent developments in contemporary art and how these at times converge with the content and process of psychotherapy. Two aspects of this development are relevant to group analysis. The first is an increasing emphasis in performance art on the social influences on human behaviour. This includes not only the exploration of social relationships in the performance itself but also the engagement of the audience as part of the performance, aiming to challenge the boundary between inner and outer and promote a wider social consciousness. The second aspect is the representation of self as a performative act reflecting the way people present themselves in social and interpersonal interaction. These performance modes highlight aspects of human identity and interaction. The chapter illustrates how these perspectives may be utilized beneficially in group psychotherapy and how anti-group processes may be viewed in this light.

Chapter 9, Rebel without a cause: authority and revolt as themes in the cinema, is an excursion into the world of film. Film is a rich repository of themes revealing many aspects of the human and cultural narrative, often touching on social and group processes. Rather than attempting a comprehensive review of the films illustrating this theme – a huge and overwhelming task – this chapter focuses on the particular ways in which authority, rebellion and revolt are represented in film, the theme of my Foulkes Lecture in 2009 (Nitsun 2009). The four films chosen illustrate universal aspects of authority relations and the conflict with authority, an aspect of anti-group formation. The films dramatize the struggle with authority not only as personal and individual but as reflecting wider social and political processes in which inter-generational differences come to the fore and aspects of culture undergo transformation. It is suggested that group analysis could add meaningfully to the study of film by bringing a group perspective and a deeper appreciation of context.

Summary and conclusions aims to re-evaluate group analysis as a discipline in the twenty-first century, focusing on the key themes of survival and transformation. There is a considerable challenge to group analysis in redefining its understanding of the social and in adapting to change in many areas, including the ethos and culture of psychotherapy. Gaps in the recognition of destructive and self-destructive processes remain a concern and the need for a critical perspective is highlighted. At the same time, there is considerable potential for group analysis to contribute to the all-important debate on human communication in an increasingly global but fragmented and virtual universe.

A brief addendum to the book, *Postscript*, considers two themes: 1) Bion's theory of the basic assumptions; and 2) violence and mass murder, to which I give little attention in the rest of the book but which merit further comment.

References

Bowden, M. (2002) Anti-group attitudes at assessment for psychotherapy, *Psychoanalytic Psychotherapy*, 16, 246–58.

Foulkes, S. H. and Anthony, E. J. (1967) *Group Psychotherapy: The Psychoanalytic Approach.* London: Penguin.

Holland, J. H. (1975) *Adaptation in Natural and Artificial Systems.* Ann Arbor: University of Michigan Press.

Nitsun, M. (1991) The anti-group: destructive forces in the group and their therapeutic potential, *Group Analysis*, 24, 7–20.

Nitsun, M. (1996) *The Anti-group: Destructive Forces in the Group and their Creative Potential.* London: Routledge.

Nitsun, M. (1998a) The organizational mirror: a group-analytic approach to organizational consultancy, part 1 – theory, *Group Analysis*, 31, 245–67.

Nitsun, M. (1998b) The organizational mirror: a group-analytic approach to organizational consultancy, part 2 – application, *Group Analysis*, 31, 505– 18.

Nitsun, M. (2000) The future of the group, *International Journal of Group Psychotherapy*, 50, 455–72.

Nitsun, M. (2005) Destructive forces, in Motherwell, L. and Shay, J. (eds) *Complex Dilemmas in Group Psychotherapy*. New York: Brunner-Routledge.

Nitsun, M. (2006) *The Group as an Object of Desire: Exploring Sexuality in Group Psychotherapy*. London: Routledge.

Nitsun, M. (2009) Authority and revolt: the challenges to group leadership, *Group Analysis*, 42, 1–23.

Stacey, R. D. (2003) *Complexity and Group Process*. Hove: Brunner-Routledge.

Thompson, A. E. (1991) Freud's pessimism, the death instinct, and the theme of disintegration in 'Analysis Terminable and Interminable', *International Review of Psychoanalysis*, 28, 165–80.

Weintrobe, S. (2013) *Engaging with Climate Change*. London: Routledge.

Winnicott, D. W. (1968) The use of an object and relating through identifications, in *Playing and Reality*. London: Pelican.

Yalom, I. B. and Leszcz, M. (2005) *Theory and Practice of Group Psychotherapy*. New York: Basic Books.

Part I

The wider context

Chapter 1

The question of survival in the twenty-first century[1]

Challenges to group analysis

Survival has been a preoccupation since the beginning of civilization, taking different forms in the evolution of time. This chapter poses the question of survival in the twenty-first century as a framework within which to consider the potential of group analysis to make a contribution in the continuing century. While physical survival is likely, given the overall positive thrust of civilization, this is less true of 'life as we know it', including our changing social configurations. It is suggested that the quality and speed of change, in technological, environmental and social spheres, is of such an order that some revision of group analytic theory is necessary, including the need for a more robust understanding of anxiety about 'real' group and social processes as opposed to virtual connections through the Internet. This may include a greater awareness of the anti-group and its manifestations at different levels. At the same time, the group analytic emphasis on human connection and dialogue in groups is a valuable medium through which to uphold the value of direct relationships and communication and to counterbalance the increasing drift towards the virtual world of the Internet. These are vast themes to which I can do scant justice in a brief chapter but I present some preliminary thoughts.

The individual is permeated to the core by the colossal forces of society. This belief, formulated by S. H. Foulkes, the founder of group analysis, distinguishes group analysis from most other psychotherapies by its emphasis on the social as a primary force in individual development. At its most committed, it states not simply that social factors are important and influential but that all that is human, including paradoxically the individuality of individuals, is a reflection of the pervasive impact of social processes (Stacey 2003). That group analysis as a methodology was born at the Northfield Experiment, in the throes of World War II, is itself significant, given the profound impact of war on society (Harrison 2000). Subsequent to this, however, Foulkes himself did not pay much attention in his writing to wider social processes. Once group analysis was established on firmer footing in the UK, the focus became more directly clinical, with theory and practice development emerging in the setting of group psychotherapy. Later group analysts, such as Dalal (1998) and Stacey (2003), have focused more directly on the social, both recognizing and challenging group analysis as a foundational theory, but not confronting the overall and profound tide of cultural and social change that is a feature of the twenty-first century.

In this chapter I explore the social and technological changes that are presently occurring in society at a time of rapid transformation and that augur a future world that looks very different from anything we have previously known. To what extent is group analysis able to address these changes from within the existing theory? Since in principle all that we are is constructed within the social domain, this would presuppose that our theories are also affected by social change. A theory that is relevant in one era may not be relevant in another. An example is Freudian theory that had to undergo considerable revision in the face of social change over the twentieth century and that was required to respond to challenges about its relevance and viability in an altered social and psychotherapeutic universe. As we know, the 'modernization' of psychoanalysis has been controversial, some would argue unsatisfactory, and there are important questions about the survival and continuity of psychoanalysis in the emerging culture, with differing viewpoints on the issue (Chessick 2007). I suggest that we face a similar question about the future of group analysis and whether in its present form it can accommodate the significant social change that we see all around us. Further, what does group analysis have to offer in a positive sense to a developing social world that promises to redraw many personal and institutional boundaries?

Much of what I say will be familiar, since most of the changes I am describing are already part of our lives. We must all be aware of the speed and turbulence of change in many areas of our lives. The points I will make about subjects such as environmental change, globalization, technological advancement, crises of leadership and authority and so on, will come as no surprise. Equally, the overall framework within which I consider these changes will be familiar, since the question of survival has been uppermost in the minds of environmentalists and other commentators on the state of the world for many decades (Weintrobe 2013). In parallel to the universal anxieties about survival there have been increasing concerns about whether psychotherapy in general in its present form/s will survive into the future of this century (Norcross *et al.* 2007; Burch and Campbell 2013). So, my territory will be familiar, except perhaps for the specific questions about group analysis and its relevance and value in the continuing century. I will draw loosely on my concept of the anti-group, since, in my view, much of the debate about the future hinges on the principle of social cohesion and group belonging vs group destruction and alienation.

Although I believe that there are good reasons to be anxious about the future, even in our lifetimes, I am cautiously optimistic and will suggest areas of group analysis that are open to review and development, as well as areas of social change to which group analysis could make a continuing and valuable contribution. The overall challenge to us in general and to group analysis in particular could be described in ecological terms. Many of the changes that are now altering the world we live in can be seen as changes in the global ecological balance, in both environmental and social terms. Ecology emphasizes the interdependencies of processes within a larger environment and the extent to which existing structures can continue to survive and co-exist. We are all part of an evolutionary process that sometimes seems too fast for some of us, yet we recognize as inevitable and unstoppable and to which we have to adjust if we choose to live in the world.

The subject matter of this chapter has been popularized by the media, newspapers, books and films. The problem with popularization is the loss of proportion, with a tendency to distort, magnify or trivialize issues, fantasy sometimes becoming decoupled from fact, creating cultures of rumour and speculation that acquire a life of their own. However, there is also a respectable literature on most of these themes and I draw on some of this literature to develop my arguments. The theme takes several forms. Will we survive as a species? Will the world survive? Will our way of life, the societies and communities in which we live, survive? Will psychotherapy survive? There are no ready answers to these questions but at least we can raise the questions.

Current preoccupations about the twenty-first century

While the overall framework of this chapter is the issue of survival in its broadest sense in the twenty-first century, I will focus on changes that are most relevant to social processes, while leaving a fuller consideration of what we might consider a 'group analytic future' to a later section of the chapter. I consider the following:

- the accelerating rate of change;
- the social impact of technology;
- the loss of society;
- the collapse of time;
- climate change and environmental chaos;
- the question of immortality;
- crises in authority.

The accelerating rate of change

One of the most common experiences of the 'man in the street' at the present time is a sense of rapid and escalating change in the cultural and technological milieu (Stapley and Rickman 2009, 2012). There is a sense of feeling overwhelmed, baffled and ill-prepared to deal with the avalanche of change. Although there has presumably never *not* been change in the inexorable march of civilization, the impression is that change is now experienced as exponentially faster and qualitatively different from anything that has previously been encountered. The reasons for this are generally attributed to the relentless advances of technology and, in particular, the power and ubiquity of the Internet, which has become a primary mode of connection in a changing world and which itself is subject to galloping change.

Interest in the notion of accelerating change, although felt acutely at present, goes back at least several decades. Toffler (1971), in his famous treatise *Future Shock*, highlighted the overwhelming nature of change to come, a view that remains as, if not more, pertinent than ever. Hawkins (2002) in his book *Mindsteps to the Cosmos*, formulated the notion of 'mindsteps' as cataclysmic changes to existing paradigms which bring us closer to 'reality', seen as our understanding of the human relationship to the cosmos. Whether the changes or mindsteps take us closer to 'reality' is, in my view, debatable, since much of current technological change, especially as mediated by the Internet, is associated with the production of new and different realities. At the same time, the 'reality' of our relationship to the cosmos is also deepening, as science brings us closer to the mysterious and the unknown.

Vinge (2003) created a vision of accelerating technological progress in which more and more sophisticated technologies are separated by shorter and shorter time intervals, until they reach a point beyond human comprehension. In 1992 he formulated the evolution of a super-intelligence developing through an exponentially accelerating process and ending in a transcendent, almost omnipotent power unfathomable to mere humans. Kurzweil (2001) proposed 'The Law of Accelerating Returns', predicting a dramatically transformed universe:

> An analysis of the history of technology shows that technological change is exponential, contrary to the common-sense 'intuitive linear' view. So we won't experience 100 years of progress in the 21st century – it will be more like 20,000 years of progress (at today's rate) ... Within a few decades, machine intelligence will surpass human intelligence, leading to ... *technological change so rapid and profound it represents a rupture in the fabric of human history*. The implications include the merger of biological and non-biological intelligence, immortal, software-based humans, and ultra-high levels of intelligence that expand outward in the universe at the speed of light.
>
> (italics added)

For most of us who have lived long enough, certainly dating back to the post-world war period and beyond, the world has in some respects already changed beyond recognition. There is little doubt that this process will culminate in unimaginable technological change in the twenty-first century and that the change will spawn yet further change in an accelerating way.

The social impact of technology

'Technological change is social change' (Harris and Sarewitz 2012, p. 29). These authors describe the intensification of complexity and uncertainty in the current world, produced largely by dramatic advances in science and technology. Recognizing the progressive aspects of technological change, they at the same time highlight the enormous social and cultural disorganization this generates, with the loss to many of familiar social beacons, including employment, community and our assumptions about social relationships – all resulting from the 'complex and tragic essence of our commitment to technology' (p. 31). They also describe the narratives people use to make sense of prodigious change and suggest that 'we make sense of complexity via notions of progress that celebrate the creative and sweep aside the destructive aspects of innovation' (p 32). This leads these authors to use the term 'creative destruction' and its converse 'destructive creation' as defining the paradoxical impact of progress and change.

This is by no means the only century in which there has been techno-logical growth: every century has been powered by its own forms of technological innovation. One of the distinguishing and far-reaching effects of techno-logical progress in the current century, however, is its impact on human connectedness. The Internet has spawned multiple forms of communication that dispense with face-to-face or voice-to-voice contact – or that entrain facial and verbal communication in altered ways – providing dense systems of communication that transcend time and space in previously unimaginable ways. There are great advantages here of which we are all aware and take daily advantage of, considerably extending our fields of social interaction, our access to knowledge and our opportunities for creative enterprise. But the advent of social networking has also contributed to the demise of local communities and social groups, creating an obsession with the virtual universe and in many ways a retreat from the 'ordinary' relationships that for most of us have been the foundation of our social and personal lives. Sherry Turkle (2011), in the last part of a trilogy dealing with technological development in the past few decades, concludes her studies with a sober, concerned and sometimes dystopian account of the social distancing and alienation that is as much a part of technology as the forging of expanded networks. But if there are already problems in the present, an unbalancing of actual and virtual relationships in our accumulating networks, what does this tell us about the future and the nature of society in decades to come?

Turkle, amongst others, comments on the ambivalence about human intimacy implied in the rush to technological connectedness. Technology appeals through the alternatives it provides to human vulnerability. Ensconced in a networked life, we can hide from the demands of others and the challenges of intimacy. The satisfactions of wider connectedness supplant the riskier pleasures of face-to-face, body-to-body contact. If the 'ordinary' verbal communication that underlies all our personal and social relationships, that through symbol and language has mediated the social world for millennia, remains difficult because of the anxiety and ambiguity associated with such communication, the computer offers us compelling alternatives. 'Cybersex', for example, in various forms provides sexual stimulation and release in place of sex with real others – or provides shortcuts to intimacy. It also opens up avenues for searching and realizing divergent desires and preferences, in various ways liberalizing desire but at the same time limiting the need and the capacity to find solutions to sexual and other difference in actual relationships. The proliferation of pornographic sites and virtual worlds such as Second Life further provide opportunities for exploration beyond given identity and orientation while increasingly blurring the boundary between the virtual and the real. Commentators on the future of technology are very clear that virtual and real will increasingly become merged in a 'new' composite reality. Who we are individually and collectively, how we negotiate identity and belonging, have already changed and will change exponentially.

The attraction of the different forms of technological communication, including mobile phones, texting, Twitter, social networks, email, instant messaging and online games, to name just a few, is reflected both in the massive amounts of time people spend on these devices and the literal closeness of these devices to the body and person of the individual. People on the pavement, in shops, restaurants, in all public and private places, carry their mobile phones everywhere, as if no longer a separate object but an extension of themselves, an indispensable device that links them continually to others and the wider world. The mobile phone, so frequently cradled in the owner's hand, represents the seemingly indispensable technological link to the communicable universe, at once an integral part of the self and at the same time an alias in a vast expanding social network. Two aspects of this configuration bear scrutiny: the intense dependence on these forms of instant connection, often occasioning significant distress and disorganization if the device is lost or malfunctions; and the very intimacy of contact between device and owner, as if it is part of the body, another limb, an intimate object that condenses all other personal objects into the shape of a small machine. Research on communication in the near future foretells even closer concordance between body, mind and computer: the computer lodged in the brain, scrolling and texting happening through simply looking and thinking, as if increasingly man and machine become one. 'Technology', comments Turkle (2011, p. 1), 'proposes itself as the architect of our intimacies'. Technology increasingly becomes us, rules us, *is* us.

Turkle also ventures into a phenomenon that already exists but is destined to become a powerful commodity in the future: the robot. Surveying the scene, she describes everything from robots in the form of domestic factotums to cherished pets that bring solace to the lonely, to robots as sexual partners who provide safer intimacies than people. Robots, she suggests, may be sought after as more reliable, more predictable and more controllable than human partners. She quotes the author David Levy (2007) as advocating marriage to robots as a better bet, or at least a useful practising ground. But Turkle also reveals her discomfort with these developments, questioning the unconscious way we may be seduced more and more by the temptations of technology and the promises of a better existence than we have known. Human beings are already prone to conformity, but it may be increasingly difficult to hold out against the majority when it comes to new technology – assuming there are those who would prefer to do so. Already we see the obsession with the latest gadgets, iPhones and beyond, queues of people waiting for many hours to secure the latest models of ever-new technologies. While buying into the diverse pleasures of the Internet, and the access to different worlds, we paradoxically become increasingly conformist and homogenized.

These are mere glimpses of the technological changes that are already part of our lives and that will intensify in an accelerating way in the decades to come. The main question for us here is how this will affect human groups and the ordinary communication processes that bind people into 'real' social groups at the wider level and 'real' intimacy at a more personal level. Can we see a time when human groups as we know them will dwindle and even die? Will the power and appeal of the social network eventually eclipse the group? Will the value we place on human groups and authenticity in close relationship become passé, discarded, a figment of the past?

Weinberg (2014), in an excellent account of Internet groups, and their link to the wider culture of the Internet, largely concludes on the positive, growthful and enriching aspect of these groups, but, in my view, minimizes the dark side. His positive statements include, "The Internet is successful in transforming ... losses and broken hearts, into a world of support and connection' and 'In our modern world typified by immigration, relocation, alienation, and isolation, the Internet provides the perfect answer to these problems' (p. 15). While there is some truth in these views, what is left out is the *loss* of connection, the retreat from groups, and the loneliness and alienation that fester in people's lives while the computer becomes a more and more dominant presence. The anti-group aspects are hidden in the vision of a perfect world generated by the Internet. Even within seemingly supportive Internet groups or forums of seemingly well-adjusted people, I have seen examples of marked splitting, intense idealization of chosen figures, rapid escalation of feelings and opinions, scapegoating, voyeurism and exhibitionism, the excitement of envy, the exclusion and marginalization of those on the outside, and an often unacknowledged tension between the private and the public. These are not altogether unusual phenomena in groups. They are part of the dynamic power of the group but become problematic when unacknowledged and unmanaged.

More generally, there are the increasing problems arising from Internet preoccupation: addiction to harmful and destructive sites, porn addiction, severe self-harm. In my own clinical practice, especially in the NHS, I see a growing number of people whose lives have become derailed by Internet activity, producing different forms of obsession, depersonalization, alienation and catastrophic disappointment interlinking with the more familiar conditions of depression, suicidality, mania, panic and overwhelming anxiety.

Loss of society

Implied in technological change is the vision of a radically altered social universe. We may be looking at a social world that is very different from what we know. One of the frequent themes reported by Stapley and Rickman (2003, 2009, 2012) in their listening posts across countries is the sense not just of social change but the loss of society as a whole. As Stapley and Rickman point out, this is the product of globalization and the diffusion of cultural boundaries, on the one hand, and individualism, viewed as a reaction to the decentring of cultural life, on the other. Much commentary on the financial recession of the years 2008–13, highlights the culture of individualism associated with the bank and borrowing crises as a major feature of the recession. Capitalism ran riot in the late twentieth century with it rampant consumerism and relentless acquisition, the spoils of greed and waste becoming all too apparent in the meltdown of the early twenty-first century. But if globalization continues, and it is hard to see how it will not, and at the same time individualism paradoxically survives, even thrives, society as a cohesive and meaningful entity may fall through the net. Already there is a tangible loss of community, of belonging, of the familiar social reference points that structure human life, as well as the more complex social symbols that add depth and subtlety to the experience of living. When Margaret Thatcher in 1989 famously proclaimed that 'there is no such thing as society', her statement (in part taken out of context) provoked a near universal outcry. Her words were seen as an attack on society, reflected in the aggressive individualism that she herself sought to inculcate in the economics of the day. Yet, her statement has had a disturbingly prophetic aspect. What she said largely preceded the rise in globalization and technology: how much more is this the case now and in the emerging future?

Globalization at one level shrinks the world and brings people closer but at another level homogenizes culture and society in a way that diffuses traditional social difference. Defensive reactions to this include aggressive nationalism and fundamentalism in which faith, ideology and rigid conformity become the principles of society. 'Ordinary' society is increasingly challenged. What we so much fear about fundamentalists is not just that they wish to attack 'our' society but that they seek to replace it with theirs.

Population trends in the present century add to the picture of an imploding society. Increased longevity and expanding numbers of older people, uncontrolled population growth in the less developed world, greater levels of migration across countries and continents, all add to swelling but fragmented societies, unable to contain the diverse needs of the many. Add to this the appeal of a seemingly more cohesive, in some respects more manageable, Internet society, available by pressing a button or flicking on a screen, and we can see the increasing redundancy of a grounded society, of communities that need time, patience and commitment to cohere.

The collapse of time

I use the term 'collapse of time' to describe the way technological progress has radically challenged our notions of past, present and future. Norbert Elias (2007) formulated notions of 'social time', describing how the representation of time varies historically according to different sorts of societies and how the organization of work and similar systems influence the construction of time in a particular age. Elias' analysis preceded the digital age and we can assume that time perception and manipulation is undergoing further massive transformations in the face of ever-expanding digital technology. Sievers (2009) presents a cogent analysis of the way our relationship to time – past, present and future – is undergoing change in the cultural ethos, in part under the sway of corporate life and its programme of mastery over the conventional domains of space and time.

One aspect, in line with the previous section, is the accelerated speed of communication via the Internet and associated technologies such as mobile phones and other rapid transmission devices. These processes eliminate virtually any gap in time between the sent and the received, producing the instant communication that Sievers (2009, p. 33) refers to as 'instantaneous timelessness'. Communication now happens in 'real' time, messages of every sort transcending pre-existing limits and boundaries. There can be no doubt that with the explosion of Internet technology, communication in real time will increasingly become the order of the day. Highlighting the predominance of organizational culture and its manipulation of time, he quotes McKenna (1997, p. 3) as noting that real time is lauded as 'a world in which time seems to vanish and space seems completely malleable'. 'Real' time paradoxically is no time. Yet again, the power of technology overwhelms human capacity: computers can think and act more quickly, more effectively and more comprehensively. Instantaneity challenges not only our experience of the present but disrupts and undermines the past, since the past recedes ever more quickly into a black hole of vanished memories as the future rushes headlong to meet us in an onslaught of the new and the unexpected.

Sievers elaborates the picture of time-collapse by examining the management of the future in organizational life. Through striving to control the environment, organizations transform the ineffable nature of the future into an object, a commodity, a thing that is meant to be foreseeable, controllable and able to be reinvented as an extended present. Industrialization and investor-capitalism emphasize the calculation of time in relation to money, efficiency and profit, and from this arises the negation of time as an experience that is more nuanced and complex. This includes a denigration of the past, seen as irrelevant and expendable, except for clues as to what capricious processes need to be controlled and suppressed. In this vision, there is little sense of what may be called the 'shadows of the past' or the 'shadows of the future'. These shadows, which may be insubstantial as matter, nevertheless are an integral part of human experience and memory and deepen our sense of personal and collective identity and continuity.

We may speculate that, concealed by the objectification of time, in particular the negation of the past and the control of the future, there are unconscious strivings towards immortality. Hence in the absence of recall and reflection, the non-remembered remains 'socially immortal' (Sievers 2009, p. 33). Organizational future tends to conceal a longing for infiniteness, immortality. These strivings in turn encode fears of death and annihilation and contribute to the illusion that death can and should be conquered.

The collapse of time is further reinforced by the factor of obsolescence, which is so much a consequence of the speed of change. This happens particularly in the world of material goods, technological and otherwise, in which the proliferation of the new, new models, new systems, new processes, eclipses the old in an unstoppable frenzy. Technology demands that we keep up, that we adjust to rapid change, that we acquire the latest devices and that we learn and master new systems. Consumerism aids and abets the process, pressuring us into buying and owning, keeping up, matching others. 'Keeping up with the Jones's' is more pressing than ever, with more goods to purchase, more choice and more anxiety about being left behind. In the process, the 'old' is rapidly outdated, anachronistic and disposable. Although this applies to goods, to material possessions, it implies a loss of valuing what came before and by implication, our values, our memories and our understanding.

Climate change and environmental chaos

Of the various changes presented here, climate change constitutes perhaps the greatest and most visible threat to survival in the twenty-first century. It is also the change that is most widely represented in the media, with a proliferation of books, articles and films gaining considerable public attention. There are two overriding preoccupations about climate change. The first is with the accumulating evidence of change, mounting statistics revealing a rise in global temperatures set to increase within the century to levels well beyond what are regarded scientifically as safe. The statistics are reflected in part in chaotic weather conditions across the world in the last few decades, a greater incidence than ever of earthquakes, tornadoes, hurricanes and floods in vulnerable areas, unprecedented droughts in some areas and prolonged rainfall in others. Although a recent report suggested that climate change may have temporarily plateaued (Gillis 2013), in overall terms climate change is occurring more rapidly in this century than expected.

The other preoccupation is the *denial* of climate change. I suggest that there may be two types of denial. One is a form of passive denial, which is what most of us are guilty of, where denial is more like inertia or the wish to turn a blind eye, possibly out of a sense of helplessness (Hoggett 2013). The other is a more aggressive form of denial in which a substantial and influential body of sceptics challenge factual evidence of climate change as exaggerated and misleading (Weintrobe 2013). Further, they accuse the climate change movement of being a hoax, of exploiting the population for their own profit, scientists and the media alike. Hamilton (2013) uses the term 'denialism' to describe an entire culture geared to denial of the facts through processes of disavowal and dissociation, which generates 'an industry' of its own, so powerful is the determination to refuse acceptance of the evidence.

Climate change and the linked phenomena mentioned above, particularly the destruction of the natural environment, are perhaps more than any other change associated with a destructive trend in human nature (Keene 2013; Steiner 2013).

It is well-recognized that most of these disasters or near-disasters are man-made, the spoils of capitalism, commercialism and greed, and there is a not altogether far-fetched notion of retribution, of inevitable consequences. The Gaia hypothesis (Lovelock 2000), well-known in eco-psychology, draws the analogy of the rape of the earth and its moral and environmental consequences. I (Nitsun 1996) have previously postulated an anti-group process at social and cultural levels that can be seen as the widest expression of the anti-group and that is transmitted successively to groups within the cultural container, such as family, work and organizational groups. I further suggested that at the root of the cultural anti-group is the fear of insufficiency leading to destructive greed and rampant control that paradoxically create the very conditions that are feared: the loss of resources and supplies that are essential for living. I made the case for a link between survival fears at an individual species level, inhabiting the human psyche as the shadow of annihilation, and the collective fears of annihilation that are reflected at the wider level of environmental destruction and the fear of ultimate catastrophe. In sum, I stated:

> In this way, the deepest internal and the widest external forms of disintegration interpenetrate at the point of environmental failure. At the dark heart of the anti-group is the dread of insufficiency and, beyond that, of extinction.
>
> (Nitsun 1996, p. 270)

The question of immortality

The nature of change is usually paradoxical (Watzlawick *et al.* 1974) and it is worth highlighting some of the paradoxes that apply to the question of human life expectancy. On the one hand, as noted above, there is a struggle for survival against the odds and the fear that we may be doomed: on the other, the possibility, through medical advances, of individuals surviving far longer than anything we are used to or can even imagine. On the one hand, there is the ever-present threat of disease and death, especially in third world countries: on the other, in affluent countries, the escalating medical and cosmetic procedures that promise eternal youth, if not eternal life. In this section I highlight the scientific and medical projects that are impacting on our preconceptions of the life-span and the inevitability of death. While immortality as such remains for the most part a fantasy, what is incontrovertible is the dramatic impact of science on longevity and the swelling proportions of older people within the world's population. The United Nations Population Fund (UNFPA) predicted in 2012 that by the year 2050 one in five of the global population would be aged 60 or older, nearly double the one in nine at the present time. The UNFPA further warned that nearly every government is unprepared for the massive demographic shift. There is a need to redesign amenities for older people, including parts of cities, and to consider the life-style, occupational and relational aspects of increased longevity. In the UK and other countries retirement age has been extended to allow older people to work for longer: some countries have introduced anti-discrimination legislation in order to strengthen the chances of older people getting jobs. These positive initiatives, however, are still in the minority and leave open a huge area of untapped anxiety in the older-age population. While ageing carries with it the inevitable fears of decline and disintegration, there may be commensurate fears about living longer than expected and the requirement to find meaning and purpose in an extended existence.

From a clinical perspective, the fact of people getting older more slowly and surviving for longer creates considerable pressure on medical and psychological services. With enhanced longevity, there is a greater demand for medical, psychological and social support in health systems, which are already sagging under the weight of need and demand. With limited funding in virtually every country, there are painful questions about prioritization and to what extent to focus on older people, possibly at the expense of others, raising ethical concerns about health planning and treatment decisions. Social concerns about isolation and exclusion in older age groups add further poignancy. How to strengthen communities in which older people live, whether in hospitals and supported living or 'outside' in people's homes, is a major concern.

As for immortality itself, although this is in the nature of fantasy rather than fact, the vision of immortality grows less far-fetched as medical science progressively finds cures for illness and age decline. As a result, the idea of immortality appears to have gained greater ground in the popular imagination in recent years (Moorstein 2010). This is increasingly fed by technological and medical reports. Jarrett (2013) calls this the age of the superhuman, citing the advance of the so-called cyborg, the creature who merges human and technological and can overcome the ordinary fallibility of the body and brain. He cites the so-called *2045 initiative*, which predicts that by that year, approximately, it will be possible to upload our minds into a non-biological body, thus making us immortal. And if indeed fiction becomes fact, through some extraordinary, undreamt of change, the psychological and social consequences are more profound than anything that can be envisaged at the present time, as are, more immediately, the ecological implications of populations in which people live much longer than ever before.

The point about an increasing contingent of older people is what it implies not just for the individual him/herself but for the network of people supporting them: family, friends and carers. It is not just about the elderly but the way they signify social change at a wider level and the way medical progress impacts on both the individual life-span and the society that contains individuals. But, having looked at the deconstruction of society itself in the wake of expanded Internet communities, we may wonder whether fragile societies can provide adequate containment not only for older people but also for the many other dependent and vulnerable members of our communities, the non-included and the marginalized (Scanlon and Adlam 2011). Again, the paradox may become accentuated in the twenty-first century: the 'immortal' and the 'superhuman' in one version of reality, and the weak, the dispossessed and the deeply vulnerable in another, the two realties probably becoming more divided by the access or non-access to wealth (although notions of transcendence and immortality are inscribed in different ways in different cultures and belief systems).

Crises of authority

Many of the changes outlined above – and others – presage a world that is plunging into a maelstrom of change, with hugely unpredictable consequences, a world potentially spinning out of control. These situations will require constructive and purposeful leadership at various levels: leadership to deal with natural disasters, with population explosion, with failures at systemic levels of government and civic life, with emergent new illnesses and contagious diseases, with terrorism and threats of violence, and with the harnessing and management of spiraling technological change. The difficulty is that as the twenty-first century progresses, there is a deep disillusionment with authority and leadership. Against a background of increasing disenchantment with leadership in the western world in the preceding decades, the financial crisis of the years 2008–13 exposed in an unprecedented way the corruption of leaders and companies mediating the world economy. The loss of trust in leadership deepened in these years and, with this, a sense of great uncertainty and anxiety about facing, rudderless, a world in upheaval.

Given the decentring impact on social life in the early twenty-first century and the disillusionment in embodied leadership, there is an emerging sense that the new authority is the Internet and the powers behind it. There is increasing public concern about the uncontrollable development of the Internet, its intrusion into social life and personal boundaries – the sense of a twenty-first-century version of Big Brother, but a Bigger Brother than we have ever known. Is it possible that in the absence of effective human leadership, some form of superintelligence mediated by technology will claim leadership? Is it possible that the science-fiction vision of a world ruled by machines could come true?

Challenges to group analysis

In this section I consider the impact on group analysis of the changes I have described, how the theory may have to adapt, what implications there are for practice and what group analysis can contribute to a rapidly changing universe. When Foulkes (1990, pp. 151–2) says 'the individual is pre-conditioned to the core by his community, even before he is born', this invites consideration, however speculative, of how the transforming world of the twenty-first century can influence human development and, by implication, group analytic theory and practice.

I propose doing this under the following headings, which to some degree mirror the headings of the previous section:

- The group matrix
- Communication
- The problematic of time
- Human destructiveness
- The future of the group
- Human connectedness.

The group matrix

The concept of the group matrix is a key consideration in confronting our changing universe. Described by Foulkes as 'an invisible web of communications', this concept embraces a transpersonal network in which the individual is conceived of as a nodal point, as if suspended in that network (Foulkes 1964). The concept has been used extensively as a framework for group psychotherapy as well as for society as a whole. The question now is to what extent expanding Internet networks will transform the group matrix as we understand it. The whole process of society becoming globalized, yet more virtual and fragmented – and yet more linked up in new technologically based ways – changes the boundaries of the group matrix in fundamental ways. Foulkes' (1948) seminal ideas about the individual as a nodal point in the social network acquire new meanings when the social network is one that so radically redraws the lines of contact and communication. When the wider matrix is now as extended as it is – and will become more so – can we rely on our old assumptions and sets of explanations to make sense of wider social relationships? I suggest not – and that the notion of the group matrix requires revision. Group analysis will need both to assimilate and accommodate to a changing social order and this will require an expanded version of the matrix, one that takes account of the many new and emerging forms of communication and the vastly expanded networks with diverse and intricate groupings contained within the networks.

   Will the matrix in any case be a sufficient concept in the face of a universe with increasingly different levels and types of reality, both actual and virtual? Sociological thinkers have begun to propose alternative models to describe the human environment, such as Sloterdijk's (2011) notion of *spheres*. This concept has a more spatial emphasis than the invisible matrix and may be contested by those who argue for a purely social perspective but ideas of this sort may need to be considered in debates about the nature of transforming matrices, trying to make sense of myriad nodal points connected in far more dense networks than ever before.

Communication

When Foulkes (1948) and his followers gave major weight to communication, particularly verbal communication, in their understanding of groups and their appreciation of the psychotherapeutic process, this was in a world that was not yet exposed to the new and very different potentials of the Internet. We now see how Internet connection has in many ways surpassed conventional interpersonal communication. Not only is the overall sphere of communication considerably expanded but new forms of communication – email, Twitter, Skype, 'selfie', to name but a few, all with their particular idiosyncrasies, shortcuts, codes and rituals – have proliferated and diversified contact between people.

While subscribing to the importance of communication in group analysis, I have also expressed reservations about the emphasis on the coherence of verbal communication (Nitsun 1996, 2006). In line with a range of commentators on the flawed nature of verbal communication, from Lacan to Daniel Stern, I have sought to give weight to the underlying limitations of language: the incommunicable: the misattuned; the division of the self through verbal communication (Stern 1985); and what I refer to as 'contaminating communication' (Nitsun 1996). I have argued that these problems of communication are associated with anti-group developments, as both antecedents and consequences, and suggested that they are deserving of greater attention in theory and practice. The question arises now of the extent to which it is not just the ambivalence about groups in general but the specific problems inhering in face-to-face communication, with all its frustrations and ambiguities, that drives people to embrace the Internet. Given the increasing ascendance of the Internet, will there be an exponential withdrawal from ordinary social communication in the decades to come? Will we find people becoming more averse to human communication in its foundational sense and less and less able to communicate, whether in day-to-day interactions with others or in the closer encounters of intimate relationships?

Group analysis faces an important challenge here. Attention needs to be focused on both a) the anxieties and inhibitions concerning 'conventional' communication in a way that helps people to manage their 'ordinary' non-virtual interactions with greater trust and confidence and not have to resort to the more remote world of the Internet as a defensive strategy, and b) the challenges of communication in the newer world of the Internet itself. There is a whole new Internet language that we are still in the process of constructing and that may have fundamental and far-reaching effects on systems of human communication. These new systems have their potentials as well as problems and, in so far as they affect the social fabric of communication, may be an important focus for group analysts: groups are constituted not just by the people who inhabit them but by the nature of conversations that occur in the group, including the forms of the conversation (Stacey 2003) and the words that constitute them. These are changing all the time.

The problematic of time

Several factors – the breathtaking speed of technology, the instrumental nature of business and the overall acceleration of change, amongst others – are altering the parameters of time. Although chronological time continues, the emphasis on the immediate and the short-term is intensifying the dominance of present time at the expense of the past and the future. Some group analytic concepts, such as the foundation matrix and the dynamic matrix (Foulkes 1964), which are variants of the group matrix described above, assume a relationship in time: the foundation matrix is what came before, in place, history and ancestral transmission, while the dynamic matrix is what happens subsequently, as time unfolds and elides into future. Some revision of these concepts is needed in the light of time's 'collapse'. There are a number of questions that need attention. What relationship will past, present and future have in a speeded up and increasingly virtual reality? How will group analysis understand the emergence of group matrices in this altered time zone? How will the nuances of time be symbolized in a different temporal framework? In the altered vision of time outlined above, there may be less regard for the foundational and more emphasis on dynamic change, but within a time-scale that is radically altered. Whatever the outcome, the collapse of time will in various ways compromise existing psychotherapeutic premises and may require a reorientation of theory and practice.

These views are consistent with Elias' (2007) notions of social time, giving time a central place in social theory. According to Elias, 'dominant time' varies historically in relation to different forms of society, reflecting both organizational functions and value-based processes. Tabboni (2001), commenting on Elias' views, notes that social time always results from a choice: even if formulated in quantitative terms, it is inherently qualitative. Time, in this view, is also a norm, perhaps the most pervasive of social norms. Given this description, I suggest that the conception of social time in the twenty-first century will change according to transforming organizational processes as well as altered value systems linked to new forms of communication, business, work and ethics, and that this transformation will reach into the deepest recesses of culture.

Linking this issue more closely to psychotherapy, how does the accelerating speed of change and altered perception of time affect the function of psychotherapy in a transforming universe? Will psychotherapy survive, be relevant in the future and what will happen to the conventional notions of change espoused by most traditional psychotherapy? Change is key in psychotherapy but the change we aim at as psychotherapists is generally at a much slower, more human rate than anything promised by the technological 'avalanche'. How will we reconcile notions of ordinary biological and psychological change with the escalating speed of change of technological progress? It is no coincidence, in my view, that the cultural acceleration of change, combined with the contraction of time, parallels the dramatically increased emphasis on shorter-term, solution-focused psychotherapies in mental health services. These therapies serve a useful purpose (see Chapter 4 on group analysis and CBT) and, backed up by a seemingly strong evidence base, are likely to retain their place in the continuing century. They address current cultural expectations of the 'quick fix'. By contrast, long-term psychotherapy is under considerable attack in public services (as outlined in Chapters 4 and 6). Unless there is a return to the value system of longer-term therapy – which seems unlikely – the situation is likely to deteriorate. Group analysis as a long-term method is likely to suffer, unless the advantages of patients coming together in conjoint therapy for a substantial period can be argued successfully – and unless group analysis can respond more actively to the demands of current services. Fortunately, group analysis lends itself to alternative forms of practice, ranging from shorter-term therapeutic intervention (Lorentzen *et al.* 2014) to consultation in a variety of settings, and I suggest that these approaches will increasingly gain ground.

The issue about psychotherapy, though, is not one purely of pragmatics. There are important philosophical and existential considerations. The problematic of time in the contemporary world challenges some of our fundamental assumptions about loss and the need for mourning. The centrality of loss and mourning in the progress of civilization and society – as well as in the living of an individual life – has been emphasized by writers from many different schools of philosophy and psychotherapy (Dollimore 1999). But what role will there be in the future for psychotherapeutic approaches that value continuity and emphasize the human significance of loss, when faced with the commodification and repudiation of time? Armstrong (1999) considers the contribution of psychoanalysis in a changing world, which often seems beyond human comprehension, to be one of containing the confusion: 'to understand the future' in the sense of helping us 'to understand our not understanding'. I suggest that group analysis can make a similarly important contribution: how we understand and grapple with rapid change and perhaps how groups can assist this process.

The future of the group

Within the broad spectre of the loss of society is the whole question of group survival. Given the shift to Internet groups and social networks, group analysis will need to address the question of what constitutes a group in the coming world, how much it is an actual physical group and how much a virtual group: further, what the motivations are for belonging to either sort of group (Weinberg 2014). There is much commentary suggesting that the enormous, often addictive, attraction to Internet networks is a retreat from social groups as we know them (Turkle 2011). How do we understand this? Does Bion's original view that human beings are deeply ambivalent about groups – the 'group animal at war' with himself for 'his groupishness' (Bion 1961, p. 131) – come to the fore in this age? My own view is that we cannot understand the group-in-the-future without some notion of the anti-group (Nitsun 2000). I have argued that the resistance and hostility we find to groups in the clinical setting is an expression of a deeper anxiety about groups in western society and that there is a danger in maintaining a too optimistic, universalizing approach to groups, an understanding which emphasizes constructive factors and de-emphasizes group resistant or disruptive factors.

It may be necessary to view the future of the group from an ecological perspective – *the ecology of the group*. This perspective, which has dominated thought about the environment, both physical and social, in the last few decades (Weintrobe 2013), has in my view hardly been embraced by group analysis but has considerable potential. Psychoanalytic psychotherapy has attempted to forge a link with ecological thinking but this has been mainly in relation to climate change (Randall 2013), which is a crucial consideration but only one amongst many other concerns. I referred to this earlier in the chapter and want to return to it as a relevant if not essential line of thinking. In essence, the ecological standpoint considers the interdependencies of systems in their quest for survival within the greater whole of environmental and social change. This perspective is highly compatible with group analytic thinking in its emphasis on the overall context. It seems to me well nigh impossible not to embrace these considerations if group analysis is to keep pace with the rapid transformations that are already a feature of the twenty-first century. Understanding groups then becomes even more contextually bound, more linked to economic, social and environmental influences as they accelerate and fluctuate in their complex progress. Equally, understanding psychotherapy groups at close quarters – the group in the consulting room – is illuminated by an understanding of interdependencies in the group as they bear on issues of survival and transformation in the group – and *of* the group. The notion of *group ecology* may be a way of understanding the complex and uncertain trajectory that awaits the group in its emerging forms.

Human destructiveness

This book started with questions about the marginalization of aggression and destructive behaviour in group analysis, restating my position that Foulkes and his followers to a large extent avoided this challenge. This issue takes on added significance in the face of concern about survival in the twenty-first century. Actual survival of course is impossible to predict one way or the other but it is not, in my view, an idle question. The leading astronomer and cosmologist Martin Rees (2003) has made survival the key consideration of his treatise, *Our Final Hour*. Describing himself not as a prophet but as an informed and concerned member of the human race, Rees emphasizes concerns about human destructiveness, reflected particularly in the depredation of the natural environment, and what this will mean in a century in which there is a fragile balance of economy and ecology. There is also the paradox of how progress, particularly technological progress, goes hand in glove with regressive or destructive processes. There are two ways of looking at this phenomenon. One concerns the social disruption created by technological progress, highlighted by Harris and Sarewitz (2012). These authors describe how the advance of complex technological systems, now a defining aspect of human progress, creates 'ever-expanding domains of uncertainty and unpredictability ... an inescapable incoherence at the heart of modern society' (p. 29). This includes marked societal and economic disorganization, with the loss of community, employment and agency, as ever-increasing technological innovation requires new skills and new social configurations. The other perspective emphasizes the paradox by which progress in the positive sense, including technological progress, is linked to destructive or regressive processes. Harris and Sarewitz (2012) use the terms 'destructive creation' and 'creative destruction' interchangeably to describe the inherent contradictions in progress. These contradictions have always existed in some form but take on added significance in an age of particularly rapid change.

The question is how conscious we are of these changes, whether we can stand aside sufficiently to consider the social meaning of sometimes destructive change or whether we are ourselves so overwhelmed by change that we become passive victims, sometimes enthralled by change, sometimes exhausted, increasingly resigned.

Human connectedness

I come now to my final consideration of a group analytic future. I have suggested throughout this chapter that in an age that is dominated by technology, with the vision of a future that is increasingly subject to the mechanization of communication and relationships, the fate of the human group as a field of direct face-to-face interaction, hangs in the balance. Yet, the importance of safeguarding the interactive human element and of strengthening communication within and between face-to-face groups is widely recognized as a necessary aspect of the survival of the human race (Sennett 2012). This is where, I believe, group analysis has an important role to play in the developing century. If we are experts at all, it is within the sphere of group relationships, of communication processes within small, median and large groups. The preceding 80 years approximately of group analytic development have witnessed great commitment to the study of the group in these forms and it is on this basis that we can go forward into the wider arena of a challenging century.

Various commentators on the state of society highlight the potential for new forms of connectedness, collaboration and leadership. Capra (1996), Scharmer (2009) and Sennett (2012) all call for social evolution through creative leadership. These are inspiring visions but they require the tools to make them work, to bring people together in ways that build on relatedness at direct levels of contact – and to move from ideology to action. These initiatives will require people to meet in groups and these groups will require facilitation and guidance, aiming to keep alive the spirit of face-to-face, person-to-person communication. There is an important project here, helping to safeguard human communication in its non-technological form, while accepting that technological change will bring myriad opportunities and rewards. But it is a project that needs momentum, given the speed of change that challenges the survival of the communicating subject.

Note

1 A modified version of this chapter was presented at a conference "Gesellschaft und Gruppe" in Bonn, Germany, 14–16 June 2013. The abridged paper was subsequently published in the journal *Gruppenpsychother Gruppendynamik*, 2013, 49, S.298–315.

References

Armstrong, D. (1999) The recovery of meaning, in French, R. and Vince, R. (eds) *Groups, Management, and Organization.* Oxford: Oxford University Press, pp. 145–54.

Bion, W. R. (1961) *Experiences in Groups.* New York: Basic Books.

Burch, N. and Campbell, M. P. (2013) Blue skies or dinosaurs: the future of psychoanalysis, *New Associations*, 10, 15.

Capra, F. (1996) *The Web of Life. A New Scientific Understanding of Living Systems.* New York: Anchor Books.

Chessick, R. D. (2007) *The Future of Psychoanalysis.* New York: SUNY Press.

Dalal, F. (1998) *Taking the Group Seriously.* London: Karnac.

Dollimore, J. (1999) *Death, Desire and Loss in Western Culture.* London: Penguin.

Elias, N. (2007) *An Essay on Time*, Loyal, S. and Mennell, S. (eds). Dublin: UCD Press.

Foulkes, S. H. (1948) *Introduction to Group Psychotherapy.* London: Maresfield Reprints.

Foulkes, S. H. (1964) *Therapeutic Group Analysis.* London: Maresfield Reprints.

Foulkes, S. H. (1990) *Selected Papers of S. H. Foulkes* (ed. E. Foulkes). London: Karnac.

Gillis, J. (2013) What to make of a warming plateau, *New York Times* (Environment), 11 June.

Hamilton, C. (2013) What history can teach us about climate change denial, in Weintrobe, S. (ed.) *Engaging with Climate Change.* London: Routledge.

Harris, P. and Sarewitz, D. (2012) Destructive creation and the new world disorder, *Science: Global Trends*, 111, 29–33.

Harrison, T. (2000) *Bion, Rickman, Foulkes, and the Northfield Experiments.* London: Jessica Kingsley.

Hawkins, G. S. (2002) *Mindsteps to Cosmos.* New Jersey: World Scientific Publishing.

Hoggett, P. (2013) Climate change in a perverse culture, in Weintrobe, S. (ed.) *Engaging with Climate Change.* London: Routledge.

Jarrett, C. (2013) The age of the superhuman, *The Psychologist*, 26, 720–3.

Keene, J. (2013) Unconscious obstacles to caring for the planet: facing up to human nature, in Weintrobe, S. (ed.) *Engaging with Climate Change.* London: Routledge.

Kurzweil, C. O. (2001) The law of accelerating returns, Kurzweil Accelerating Intelligence Essays. Online: www.kurzweilai.net/the-law-of-accelerating-returns (accessed 13 August 2014).

Levy, D. L. (2007) *Love and Sex with Robots: The Evolution of Human-Robot Relationships.* New York: Harper Collins.

Lorentzen, S., Ruud, T., Fjeldstad, A. and Hoglend, P. (2014) Comparison of short-term and long-term dynamic group psychotherapy: a randomized clinical trial, *British Journal of Psychiatry*, 203, 280–7.

Lovelock, J. (2000) *Gaia: A New Look at Life on Earth.* Oxford: Oxford University Press.

McKenna, R. (1997) *Real Time: Preparing for the Age of the Never Satisfied Customer.* Boston, MA: Harvard Business School.

Moorstein, M. (2010) *Super-Ageing: The Moral Dangers of Seeking Immortality.* Bloomington, IN: iUniverse Books.

Nitsun, M. (1996) *The Anti-Group: Destructive Forces in the Group and Their Creative Potential.* London: Routledge.

Nitsun, M. (2000) The future of the group, *International Journal of Group Psychotherapy*, 50, 455–72.

Nitsun, M. (2006) *The Group as an Object of Desire: Exploring Sexuality in Group Psychotherapy.* London: Routledge.

Norcross, J. C., Hedges, M. and Prochaska, J. O. (2007) The face of 2010: Adelphi poll on the future of psychotherapy, *Professional Psychology: Research and Practice*, 33, 316–22.

Randall, R. (2013) Great expectations: the psychodynamics of ecological debt, in Weintrobe, S. (ed.) *Engaging with Climate Change.* London: Routledge.

Rees, M. (2003) *Our Final Hour: A Scientist's Warning.* New York: Basic Books.

Scanlon, C. and Adlam, J. (2011) Defacing the currency: a group analytic appreciation of homelessness, dangerousness, disorder and other inarticulate speech of the heart, *Group Analysis*, 44, 131–48.

Scharmer, O. (2009) *Theory U: Leading From the Future as It Emerges.* San Francisco, CA: Berrett-Koehler.

Sennett, R. (2012) *Together: The Rituals, Pleasures and Politics of Co-operation.* London: Allen Lane.

Sievers, B. (2009) Pushing the past backwards in front of oneself: a socio-analytic perspective on the relatedness of past, present, and future in contemporary organizations, *Organizational and Social Dynamics*, 9, 21–42.

Sloterdijk, P. (2011) *Bubbles: Spheres 1.* Cambridge, MA: MIT Press.

Stacey, R. D. (2003) *Complexity and Group Processes.* Hove: Brunner-Routledge.

Stapley, L. F. and Rickman, C. (2003) Britain and the world at the dawn of 2003, *Organizational and Social Dynamics*, 3, 165–9.

Stapley, L. F. and Rickman, C. (2009) Global dynamics at the dawn of 2009, *Organizational and Social Dynamics*, 9, 109–37.

Stapley, L. F. and Rickman, C. (2012) Global dynamics at the dawn of 2012, *Organizational and Social Dynamics*, 12, 81–105.

Steiner, J. (2013) Discussion: Climate change in a perverse culture, in Weintrobe, S. (ed.) *Engaging with Climate Change.* London: Routledge.

Stern, D. (1985) *The Interpersonal World of the Infant.* New York: Basic Books.

Tabboni, S. (2001) The idea of social time in Norbert Elias, *Time and Society*, 10, 5–27.

Toffler, A. (1971) *Future Shock.* New York: Bantam Books.

Turkle, S. (2011) *Alone Together: Why We Expect More from Technology and Less from Each Other.* New York: Basic Books

Vinge, V. (2003) Technological singularity, *Whole Earth Review*, Spring.

Watzlawick, P., Weakland, J. H. and Fisch, R. (1974) *Change.* New York: Norton.

Weinberg, H. (2014) *The Paradox of Internet Groups: Alone in the Presence of Virtual Others.* London: Karnac.

Weintrobe, S. (ed.) (2013) *Engaging with Climate Change.* London: Routledge.

Chapter 2

An anti-group perspective of organizational change

The case of the National Health Service (NHS)

Concern about the mounting problems of the NHS is attracting increasing commentary from socially minded thinkers and writers who describe the coercive yet chaotic organizational culture of the NHS (Campling and Ballatt 2012; Rogers 2009; Fischer 2012). The crisis came to a head in 2013 in a series of high-profile scandals involving an unprecedented number of unexplained deaths in hospital services, blatant cover-ups and whistle-blowing controversies at all levels of clinical and organizational management. This was against the background of a far-reaching and unpopular NHS restructuring instigated by the existing Conservative–Liberal Democrat coalition government, with an escalating fear that the demise of the NHS was nigh. Writers such as Campling and Ballatt (2012) recommend ways of understanding and ameliorating the troubled situation. This chapter adds to that literature by emphasizing group processes in the NHS as requiring greater elucidation, drawing on the concept of the anti-group as a critical principle that addresses group conflict and fragmentation as a major factor in the anxious and turbulent atmosphere of the NHS. The anti-group is linked to overwhelming survival fears at all levels of the NHS, ranging from political and economic panic, to staff survival in a threatened workplace, to questions of life and death at the heart of healthcare. Reorganization, a frequent and debilitating occurrence in the NHS, is seen as both generating and reinforcing these fears. Seeking a way forward, I suggest that a solution might lie in a better understanding of the negative consequences of NHS organizational change as well as the increased education of health professionals and policy makers in the psychosocial awareness of healthcare.

Introduction

The National Health Service is one of the most revered institutions in Britain. It has a dominating presence in the lives of millions of people, providing the vast bulk of healthcare across all ages of the population. Yet it is an organization that is almost constantly under siege. The reasons for this are complex and accrue partly from the politicization of the NHS in which the major policy and funding decisions are made at ministerial levels, subject to the vicissitudes of governmental policy, hence creating an unstable context for the management of the NHS. The translation of these decisions into the day-to-day reality of healthcare is fraught with ambiguity and tension. This is just one aspect of a multi-determined state of ongoing uncertainty and conflict that impinges on the delivery of a very complex healthcare programme.

The spread of anxiety about the survival of the NHS raises questions about the containment of anxiety in an organization whose primary task is the diagnosis and treatment of illness, itself a generator of anxiety. In the tense, uncertain world of the NHS, there is a tendency to polarize groups along persecutor–victim lines: the managers often seen as brutal and unthinking, imposing change in line with destructive governmental policies, and the staff the victims of managerial raids on structures and resources. The nexus of change is usually NHS organizational restructuring, almost always a painful and confusing process that aggravates the clinician-manager split and confirms fantasies of attack and annihilation.

What predisposes the NHS to such divisions? Are there inherent processes within the structure, function and dynamics of a large healthcare organization, such as the NHS, that need to be understood in order to make sense of the near constant state of attrition? Without such understanding, there is likely to be an ongoing war, changing in form with the different governments and policies that preside over the NHS, but nevertheless corrosive of the confidence needed to provide comprehensive health services to as large a population as that of the UK. Understanding may not itself change anything, but provides a perspective on the traumatic patterns that so frequently beset the NHS. This chapter aims to unravel some of the underlying anxieties and defences that reside in the delivery of health services and that may influence the deeply problematic relationships between managerial and clinical levels of the service. Although my approach does not shrink from attributing crass and sometimes destructive actions to those at policy and managerial levels, it attempts to look at the overall matrix of health services in such a way that we can see the protagonists on all sides not necessarily as good or bad but as enacting profound dilemmas in the provision of healthcare.

The background

In my long association with the NHS as a clinician, manager and consultant, I have been witness to an extraordinary amount of change. Working mainly in mental health services, perhaps the most dramatic change I have seen was the complete reorganization of services for the mentally ill in the late 1960s and 1970s, with the widespread closure of psychiatric hospitals and the spread of community mental health services across the country. The change was very controversial – and remains so – with differing views about the motivation for change, the necessity and meaning of change and the impact on thousands of vulnerable patients who had to make their lives in the cut and thrust of the outside world. Ostensibly the main generator of change was the advent and widespread use of psychotropic medication, ushering in a seemingly brave new era in psychiatry. There were those who saw the change as a great liberation: the release from institutional care for many, the normalization of psychological disturbance, and the gift of 'freedom' for institutionalized patients. There were others who adopted a more cynical view: the driving force for change was essentially financial, to cut down the cost of care, to dismantle institutions and to withdraw from patients the valued provision of asylum, increasingly rare in a pressured, uncaring society – all of this aided and abetted by the powerful pharmaceutical companies.

The change described above is just one example of the change I have witnessed in several decades of association with the NHS. Inevitable changes have come about through the natural process of evolution in healthcare, requiring new systems and structures. But the change I am particularly concerned with in this chapter is the 'top down' organizational change instigated at managerial levels and usually implementing governmental policies dictated by ministers of health. There are usually both ideological and financial reasons for the reorganization and not unusually the two are conflated, the ideological often concealing the real financial reasons. Even if some degree of financial savings is achieved, it is widely agreed that these changes are implemented at great cost – in human terms – to the organization. Far from achieving greater efficiency and effectiveness of services, the reorganization usually has a highly disruptive impact on services. The proposed changes are usually presented with patients in mind, as reflected in the organizations' mission statements – 'our patients come first'. But, if there is some attempt at protecting patients' interests – or appearing to do so – staff are usually targeted in a direct and often undisguised fashion. Cuts in posts, cuts in salary and cuts in entire services are the Damoclean sword waiting to fall. Under the rubric of greater efficiency, the process of organizational change often leads to redundancies, the closure of entire departments and a typically protracted restructuring process in which there are crippling anxieties and uncertainties for staff, all the while hugely disrupting clinical services. There is a marked neglect of staff well-being as a corollary of patient care. If some concern is displayed about patients, there is very little if any about staff, as if they are dispensable, superfluous and usually at fault for bad or inefficient services. Not surprisingly, this usually leads to deep demoralization and resentment amongst staff and a pervasive culture of mistrust. Staff become so preoccupied with their own survival in these circumstances, are so caught up in the protracted uncertainty and feel so bruised by the treatment they receive, that the energy and goodwill left for patients deserts them. These periods of change are associated with considerable staff stress, illness and disorganization so that the very task of care, which is at the heart of the NHS, is undermined.

A typical example is an NHS trust in which a large-scale reorganization disrupted children's psychological services. In the prior service the waiting list for treatment had been building up for some time but the majority of children (and their families) were offered some form of therapeutic intervention. In the reorganization, the children's service was completely taken over by a new provider. There followed a long period of confusion and staff disorganization, most staff suspended in terms of future employment and then either losing their jobs or resigning. During this period, the waiting list grew considerably larger, without any clarity of management and direction. Eventually, when the restructuring was complete, a policy was instituted that all children on the waiting list should be assessed but not offered treatment, at least partly because there were now far fewer members of staff, and partly because the service model was being revised. This led to drastically cutting treatment options, so that there was nowhere to refer patients who had been assessed and often desperately needed help. The few remaining staff felt overwhelmed at the prospect and despairing about the value of the service.

repetitive

The most striking, and perhaps most disturbing, aspect of all is the *recurring nature* of NHS reorganization. If this was a one-off process that would be one thing. But the repeated nature of NHS reorganization in a way that is relentless and sometimes ruthless, irrespective of the state of the organization, with seemingly no reflective stance at the heart of the process, is what makes the process so alarming. In an indictment of a merger process of three acute hospitals in which she herself held a senior position, Rogers (2009) at several points asks, 'Why don't we learn from our evidence and experience?' This is an all too familiar question in our understanding of psychopathology, at both personal and organizational levels. Freud (1936) formulated the repetition compulsion and many subsequent writers have described repeated trauma in individual lives as well as recurring trauma inflicted by one group on another in the wider social sphere (Volkan 2001, 2014). The NHS often appears as the helpless victim in a recurring process of destabilization and attrition.

The NHS as group and anti-group

A perspective on group function and dysfunction, I suggest, is crucial to the NHS. Some writers (Campling and Ballatt 2012) view the NHS ideologically as a large community in which compassion and collaboration create a containing framework for the exacting daily responsibilities of clinicians across a wide range of services. While I agree with the community perspective of the NHS, and the goals of care and compassion, I see these as ideals that are realized with considerable difficulty. The ideal is seldom achieved or maintained as the healthcare community is so frequently disrupted by the tensions and conflicts that pervade the NHS. How does the concept of the anti-group apply?

Adopting an interlocking group and anti-group perspective, I include the NHS organization as a whole, but with sub-organizations and groups in which notions of group integrity and functionality are implicit in the effective performance of the primary task. While health service units vary considerably in size, from small clusters of staff at the periphery of services to large and comprehensive teams at the epicentre, they all consist of a group or groups of some kind, large or small. Hence, I use the generic term 'group' to describe the overall configuration of groups within the organization. 'Anti-group' refers to phenomena that undermine or disrupt the group process, which threaten the health environment and impair functional groups within it. The concept is elastic, allowing for the inclusion of a range of explanatory concepts to make sense of how conscious group tensions, as well as unconscious and mythical components, contribute to the problem. As well as the anti-group, I draw later on my concept of the organizational mirror (Nitsun 1998a, 1998b), which emphasizes mirroring processes at different levels of the organization in ways that may contribute to group dysfunction.

A brief history of NHS restructuring

The NHS was established in 1948 in post-war Britain, in a spirit of hope about the health and well-being of the entire population. It was the climax of a visionary plan generated to provide healthcare to all 'free at the point of delivery'. For the first time, hospitals, doctors, nurses, pharmacists, opticians and dentists came together under a single framework to provide services. The NHS aimed to diagnose and treat the full age range. 'From cradle to grave' became a popular motto. The vision, in line with Campling and Ballatt's perception noted above, was of a large community of doctors, nurses, allied staff and their patients, the intention being a caring and continuous service that would deal effectively with problems through life.

In many ways the NHS fulfilled its purpose, becoming indispensable in the lives of millions of people. Newspaper and journal articles in the UK frequently refer to the British population's love of the NHS. The NHS is also often cited as a model for health services in other countries. The future of the NHS became a matter of national concern from early on, increasingly intertwined with the politics of the day and a major focus of influence and controversy at times of election. The dependence on government, with a remote system of ministerial responsibility and policy-making controlling all-important NHS funding levels, is a major factor in the tension surrounding the NHS. As noted by Butler (2010), few governments could resist imposing their own blueprint for 'reform' on the NHS, with the consequence that for decades health service staff have had to endure 'almost endless upheaval'. Butler refers to this, the history of NHS reform, as a state of *permanent revolution.*

Originally the product of a Labour government and inspired by egalitarian values, the NHS increasingly became a political pawn as British politics swung from Labour to Conservative and back again in fluctuating cycles of government. Part of the problem from early on was the inevitable gap between supply and demand. With the advance of medical and related sciences, the cost of healthcare increased dramatically while at the same time the average user became more and more aware of patients' rights and the issue of choice in healthcare. With this came the increased longevity of the population, creating a larger and larger group of frail older people. All of this added to NHS pressures and exacerbated the debate about effective forms of treatment and management to contain and facilitate the explosive growth of health services.

The decades of the most pronounced NHS change, from the 1970s until the present, are marked by an uneasy attempt to address the financial pressures of the NHS while generating reforms that were consistent with political ideology and ambition. Each time this happened, it meant not just change in the NHS, but reorganization of major systems and services, sometimes within the life-span of a particular government but more dramatically in the switch from one government to another. Entire management systems and service arrangements, which might have just bedded in following an earlier reorganization, had to be dismantled and new ones established, with massive implications for both staff welfare and patient provision.

Bringing NHS changes up to the present time, the Conservative–Liberal Democratic coalition elected in 2010 was responsible for the most far-reaching reorganization in NHS history. A new Health Bill in 2012 announced major new structural changes at a time of severe economic recession in the country. Austerity measures, which included cuts across the entire public sector, were rapidly instituted. This ushered in a period of crippling uncertainty in the NHS. As well as the draconian programme of service cuts and realignments, there was now growing anxiety about the future impact of the new bill. Staff were left with prolonged uncertainty about whether they had a job or not – and, moreover, if the bill was passed, whether there would be an NHS at all.

Anxiety mounted in spite of the government saying 'Never again' – never again will there be the same level of disruption to services and staff as created by previous reorganizations (Timmins 2012). The present reorganization, it was promised, would put paid to the depredations of the past. Both the architect of the bill, Andrew Lansley, and the prime minister were seemingly signed up to this. But, a radical and exacting new health bill was pushed through against widespread opposition. Almost without exception, in my experience, NHS staff regarded the current level of cuts and realignments, combined with the anxious anticipation of a new NHS system, as the worst period they had ever known in the NHS.

The impact of restructuring: a recent example

The restructuring of any organization is likely to be a controversial and difficult process but the size and complexity of the NHS, and the often urgent nature of health services, almost certainly add gravity to the chaos. It may be instructive to consider some of the effects of NHS restructuring and how this may play out at an everyday level. This example builds on the previous one about the children's service. Although focused on a particular health trust, the description could fit many NHS trusts at the time of writing.

The children's service previously described was part of a large mental health trust in a semi-urban environment. The trust had been through difficulties for some years – near bankruptcy, failing targets, poor user feedback – which the trust attributed to decades of underfunding. The 2012 NHS reorganization with its swinging cuts was therefore on top of existing serious budget deficits. The reorganization further exposed the trust's difficulties and, following a Department of Health inquiry, it was decided to establish an external managerial presence in the trust that would assist the implementation of restructuring while also monitoring the progress of the trust as it attempted to improve services. This presence, a deputy chief executive on secondment from another trust, was regarded as intrusive and persecutory by most of the trust staff and a number of incidents confirmed people's fears.

Within weeks of the new manager taking post, several people in top posts were fired – the chief executive, one of the clinical directors and two divisional leads. A new trust executive management team was hurriedly put together, with little consultation locally, using some existing post-holders and some external recruitment. The new management team swung into action on the reorganization agenda, instituting a sweeping change management process in an atmosphere of zero trust, aiming to rationalize services, create new service lines and dramatically reconfigure and reduce the staff component of services. The approach confirmed the worst perceptions of the new organization as punitive. The change management process became agonizingly protracted, rounds of apparent consultation and preparation leading nowhere, decisions delayed over and over again, with staff feeling directionless and unsupported. Jobs were deleted and downgraded and existing post-holders were required to compete with colleagues in an atmosphere fraught with anxiety about survival and fears of annihilation. The thin layer of staff who survived this process felt that they had escaped by the skin of their teeth. The trust witnessed an exodus of staff, some of its most talented and influential clinicians fleeing to safer territory. Remaining staff were left with shrunken services struggling to meet more demanding performance targets than ever. The children's service was one example of this attrition.

The trust executive team was perceived as remote and authoritarian. They brooked no criticism and appeared to require unquestioning loyalty to the as-yet fragmented organization. Yet, viewed at close quarters, they had an impossible task, while trying to cohere as a group themselves: struggling to repair a deeply wounded organizational identity, battling to make ends meet in the context of continuing financial raids, anxious to shore up hope in the face of deep demoralization and resentment at all layers of staff.

There were several serious casualties of the process. One was the mental breakdown of a respected senior consultant pediatrician. Nearing retirement, the consultant was caught in the crossfire between management and clinicians and, under the strain of conflicting demands within his embattled service, compounded by domestic difficulties of his own, he suffered an acute bi-polar illness. While still at work, he committed a serious clinical error that led to his suspension. Following an inquiry, but without full regard for his psychiatric condition, he was sacked. The event stoked great local controversy, with opinion sharply divided, though mainly in favour of the consultant and against the trust executive.

It was clear that the trust as a whole was in the grip of massive anxiety. A sharp vein of insecurity united personnel at all levels. Ironically, in a splintered health community the unifying factor, if any, was the shared dread and moral disorganization. This is one version of the anti-group – a disunited group bound together though fear and rage. The trust, some years later, did eventually strengthen but not without considerable fallout.

In addition to illustrating the dramatic impact of restructuring on group cohesion and morale, the example describes the often corrosive effect of outside NHS investigatory teams, which in this case triggered a very difficult organizational process. I have previously written about the persecutory impact of such teams (Nitsun 1988). The example also illustrates how individuals, in this case the consultant pediatrician, can become victims of organizational dysfunction. Although the reorganization was part of a wider NHS process, there can be no denying its destructive impact and the anti-group process it generated at several levels.

The shadow side of healthcare

Much of this paper is concerned with the wider context of healthcare and the way economic and political processes can destructively infiltrate the workings of the NHS. But how much is this also a mirror of 'internal' problems, processes within the psychology of healthcare itself, perhaps a deeper, more elusive aspect, more difficult to name? This perspective contrasts with the more common narrative of health services as purely benign and altruistic. There is of course immense altruism, goodwill and unselfish caring at many levels of the NHS, but it is important to consider that a shadow side may exist in which the benign impulse may conceal something darker and more destructive. This is an aspect of the caring role that, in my view, is under-theorized. We may refer to the psychoanalytic literature which suggests that altruistic acts may be a sublimation of aggressive impulses, particularly in the Kleinian literature which generates the notion of reparation, seen as a healthy expression of the wish to do good in the face of guilt about destructive impulses (Klein 1975).

I raise this theme in order to make sense of the destructive enactments that are often seen in the NHS context. I suggest that in the health service there may be a largely – but not entirely – unconscious destructive constellation that exists side by side with the constructive caring impulse and that interacts with it – and that this shadow side may become entangled in the damaging tensions that arise in NHS environments. Not only is it awakened in a passive sense, I suggest, but destructive fantasies and impulses, often the product of intense with- and between-group rivalry and animosity, may actively contribute to organizational enactment. It is not only 'bad' politicians, commissioners and managers who are responsible for the ills of the NHS but clinical staff themselves, either consciously or unconsciously, may contribute in various ways to this process. I suggest, in line with the above, that the shadow is not so much an individual shadow but an organizational shadow that renders the NHS particularly vulnerable to the infiltration of destructive influences from 'without' when these resonate with destructive impulses 'within'.

I hesitate to pathologize so much of what is good in healthcare. I am not singling out health professionals as any more destructive than others. Most clinicians I know work unstintingly hard to protect services and safeguard patients. But the influence of the shadow side of caring, I suggest, operates at a deeper level and reflects primordial aspects of the 'wounded healer' (Groesbeck, 1975). I offer this speculatively as a hypothesis, since it can hardly be verified, but it may amplify understanding of why there is so much destructive collusion at various levels of the NHS.

The competitive environment

Shifting back to the environment of services, it is noteworthy that in the 66 years since the NHS was established it has gone from an idealistic Labour-inspired institution to a highly competitive culture. This probably reflects the sharp increase in competitiveness in society at large, with more people and organizations competing for fewer resources, competition in the NHS driven by commercial interests and the capitalist orientation of governments that encourage privatization. This has introduced a very different culture from that in which the NHS was born. Campling and Ballatt (2012) refer to the industrialization of the health service and the corrupting effect on services and people. In this vision, a manufacturing model of production tends to mechanize healthcare: commodification encourages an obsession with fragmented units of service delivery. This approach eschews the complex human aspects of illness and staff behaviour. Performance management, targets, payment by results and various other organizational manoeuvres to maximize output are products of this culture – and are implemented in a way that is consistent with such a culture. This can be seen in NHS tendering processes aimed at contracting services which are financially competitive ('value for money') but set impossibly high standards for patient throughput, creating an ongoing system of contract making and breaking that can be hugely disruptive to ongoing services. In the outer-city trust described above, an entire service was held in thrall for months while the commissioners embarked on an inexcusably protracted tendering process. In the end, the existing contract was renewed but by this time staff were exhausted. Little thought is given to the impact of repetitive cycles of tendering on existing services, as if the staff involved are mechanical beings producing mechanical outcomes rather than people struggling to do their best in the face of massive clinical demand and undermined by the constant uncertainty about their jobs. Continuity, the bedrock of clinical services, is often totally disregarded.

Governance in these circumstances, instead of providing a sensitive system of evaluating healthcare or of considering staff's well-being, becomes a stultifying system of quantification and measurement that adds to the burden required of clinicians to perform their work, painfully squeezing available time for what clinicians are mainly interested in – seeing and treating patients. All too often NHS staff say that they are prevented from doing their jobs by their administrative loads, while at the same time pressures are heaped on them to meet further targets. These demands are among the main sources of frustration and resentment amongst clinicians, reflecting more and more the bureaucratization of clinical services. Rogers (2009) links this to a major ethical shift in the public sector's role from the delivery of public services to the management of scarce resources. She sees leadership as also contaminated by this process. Leadership becomes not so much the support and direction needed by staff in the performance of difficult duties, or the negotiation of priorities for healthcare in relationship with the community, but a bureaucratic organizational mode which strips leadership of its relational and social responsibilities.

This is a situation in which instrumental relationships come to the fore, staff seen as a means to an end rather than as human beings in their own right. It is a short step to a culture of domination and submission, a master–slave dynamic (Hegel 1807) in which those with the power and the funds can control and punish those who deliver the goods. The field is open to a sadistic turn and it is not surprising, as noted above, that in the first decades of the twenty-first century words such as 'brutal', 'draconian', 'toxic', 'corrupt' and 'perverse' became a commonplace in discussions about health service culture (Fischer 2012; Long 2008).

But the worst effect by far of the obsession with performance and targets concerns patients themselves and the risks the competitive culture poses to life itself. In 2013 one of the most serious scandals in the history of the NHS dominated the news. In the mid-Staffordshire health trust an estimated figure of about 1,000 patients died as a consequence of poor care and neglect in the general medical hospital. The Frances Report, the outcome of a public inquiry, published findings strongly suggesting that the imposition of rigid targets – and consequent neglect of non-targeted but crucial areas – caused the majority of the deaths. This led to the conclusion that the widespread implementation of NHS targets can distort judgement, disempower professionals and radically impair rather than improve treatment. Caulkin (2013) argued that mid-Staffs was not alone: the problem was endemic to the NHS.

Adding to the picture of draconian management was the attack on information about poor services being reported to the outside world. In mid-Staffordshire two-thirds of nurses raised concerns about patients receiving inadequate care but were told *not to pursue them* because this would give a bad impression of the service. The prevalence of 'gagging orders' has been echoed in numerous other trusts, prompting increasing comment on the NHS's 'culture of fear and intimidation' (Hughes, 2013; Campbell, 2013).

Between the paranoid-schizoid and depressive positions

Current writers on the atmosphere of the NHS typically describe a paranoid environment in which there is a pervasive fear of attack in some form, whether from within or without (e.g. Fischer 2012). This fear would seem to be a natural response to the threat of annihilation arising from financial raids, sweeping cuts and impossible targets. It reinforces the so-called paranoid-schizoid position (Segal 1973), not only in the expectation of attack but in the split between good and bad objects, usually projected onto outside figures. Although there is a benign form of splitting that can mediate differences between individuals and groups – and possibly protect group identity – splitting becomes vicious when other individuals and groups are repeatedly identified as the enemy. In the anxious, threatened atmosphere of the NHS, this happens all too easily. At all levels of the NHS, there is the potential for deep mistrust and suspicion, not unusually erupting into open antagonism. This contributes directly to anti-group developments in the organization and the sense of an organization at war with itself. This is intensified by organizational restructuring. In the trust example I gave above, reorganization unleashed powerful differences and splitting between groups.

In the depressive position, there is an attempt at reconciling the disturbed internal world with the outer world, the good with the bad, in such a way that a greater sense of wholeness can be achieved. But this is painful, opening up areas of guilt and agonizing responsibility. Psychoanalytic writers describe the oscillation between the paranoid-schizoid and depressive positions as a normal state of affairs but note that regression occurs to the paranoid and schizoid state when the depressive anxiety becomes unbearable (Steiner 1987). In the NHS, although a paranoid mentality is widespread, the depressive position is near the epicenter of the organizational psyche. As previously suggested, the sense of loss in a damaged world of self and other fuels the striving for reparation, the wish to make good, and from this emerges the caring impulse common to most health service staff. But holding onto the sense of personal responsibility that is the hallmark of the depressive position is difficult in the face of the disruptive developments that can occur. The health service community is therefore in a constant state of vulnerability and expectancy and can easily regress from the healthier depressive position to a more persecuted state of mind. When threats from outside arise, as in the case of reorganization, the spiral of projection is triggered again and the organization slides back into a paranoid mode.

Between idealism, idealization and denigration

As is often the case in organizational life, the NHS is subject to considerable tension between an idealistic perception of its aims and achievements and a denigrated view of its defects and failings. This polarity has been described more generally as an aspect of organizational identity (Schwartz 1990). Much of the idealism of the NHS can be seen as healthy and necessary. Idealism is intrinsic to the spirit of a national health service, congruent with a hugely ambitious programme to provide comprehensive health services from cradle to grave. The NHS could not, would not, have been born without a large element of idealism. It probably would also not continue without idealism. The enormously demanding work of treating illness and disease and of saving lives could not be sustained minus a large degree of hope and idealized belief in the service and the staff who provide the service. But we need to distinguish between idealism and idealization. Idealism reflects a spirit of hope and faith in the good that is possible, whereas idealization verges on an illusory belief in the absolute rightness and goodness of things and people. Idealization seldom exists without the shadow of attack and denigration.

One aspect of the idealization is the veneration of clinical staff. This may be especially true of doctors and nurses, the largest group of staff with the most direct patient contact and in whom profound hopes and expectations of care are often vested. They are often perceived as powerful: medical consultants regarded as the 'gods' of the service, attracting huge projections of omnipotence; nurses commonly seen as 'angels' dispensing care and nurturance. Allied professionals attract similar projections. But this respect and reverence can quickly turn sour in the face of misunderstanding and disappointment. Frustrated dependence is a feature of NHS treatment and provokes reactions varying from subdued anger to rage. The shadow of disappointment and discontent lurks in the background of every NHS corridor, ward and clinic. When doctors' and nurses' real limitations are revealed, their misjudgements and mistakes often the product of ordinary human error, their fallibility can seem shocking and unforgivable. Idealization then quickly turns to denigration. In the denigrated version, doctors and their colleagues are not to be trusted. They are uncaring and indifferent to patients' needs and sufferings. They are prone to egregious error. There is a powerful propensity for the twin processes of idealization and denigration to be mobilized in an intense and unstable fashion.

On a different note, how much does the heroic aspect of health services attract envy? There is a popular version of doctors and nurses as contemporary heroes, reflected in many films and television programmes that dramatize the daily life and work of this brave but beleaguered species. Is the shadow side of this heroism the envy of the caring role, of the power to heal? Such envy may be akin to envy of the parental function, symbolized by the envy of the feeding breast or phallus (Klein 1975). Stein (2000) emphasizes envy, rather than anxiety, as triggering social defences, a view that accords with Kreeger's (1992) notion of envy pre-emption. It is highlighted here as an aspect of the organizational rivalry that ripples through the NHS. It is sometimes argued that managers are in competition with clinicians. If this is the case, does this reflect envy of doctors' and other clinicians' power and privileges, the importance of their jobs, their higher salaries, their public recognition, their seeming self-aggrandizement through work, when managers have to keep things running, to pick up the pieces, to keep order and sanity – with very little thanks or recognition?

The NHS has often been described as having significance at deeper symbolic levels. There is the analogy of the NHS as an 'environmental mother' (Winnicott 1960). This metaphorical mother, as in the 'dual nature of mothering' (Prodgers 1990), has paradoxical qualities: on the one hand a containing mother who harbours and nourishes all; on the other, a cold, rejecting mother or a devouring mother in its huge consumption of goods and people, its insatiable hunger for resources. These contradictory views are not unusually evoked by the NHS. The expectation of refuge and care has been dashed in recent decades by the pressure on basic facilities such as hospital beds and the culture of rapid patient turnover in hospital and out-patient settings. Here, too, idealization quickly turns to disappointment and anger. The dream of safe harbour gives way to the nightmare of abandonment in crammed waiting rooms and overfull hospital wards.

I emphasize this oscillation of idealization and denigration partly as a way of understanding the adverse aspects of group life and relationships in the NHS. This polarization may exist in any human service but becomes especially problematic in healthcare, where disillusionment undermines the trust so crucial to effective healthcare.

Death anxiety and denial

Questions of survival and extinction are common themes in the debate about the future of the NHS. There are frequent predictions of doom, usually on the grounds that the NHS is unsustainable in its present form, that its scale is too large and that the ever-increasing cost of services makes it unviable. Plans to privatize the NHS have been key criteria in the election of new governments and have appeared to sway voters in one direction or another. Although the NHS has survived most of these threats, it is subject to continuing rumours about its probable demise.

The issue of organizational survival vs extinction parallels the same preoccupations at the patient level. Death is the shadow of all healthcare. While services are generally geared to saving and prolonging life, the spectre of death is never far away. It is the bottom-line existential reality that haunts our lives and that provokes painful questions about the meaning and purpose of life. Various writers have highlighted death as a problematic theme in healthcare, from people writing directly on death and dying (Kubler-Ross 1997), to those who regard death anxiety as the source of social defences in NHS settings (Menzies-Lyth 1959; Obholzer and Roberts 1994). The significance of death in the present context is that it underscores the survival anxiety and fears of annihilation that I posit as an organizing theme in the turbulent dynamics of the NHS. Few if any institutions have to deal at such close quarters with the reality of death. Although human survival and organizational survival are different domains, there are unconscious resonances between these levels, creating an environment that is shot through with a sense of fragile existence. Staff may operate at some distance from the site of death, but ultimately healthcare is concerned with the protection of life against the ailing body and mind, struggling against the time-line of each individual existence.

Holding the conscious awareness of such resonances is painful and it is not surprising that the denial of death is an intrinsic aspect of western culture. Ernest Becker (1973) has written illuminatingly about this dilemma – that we all die but live as if we will *not* die. In Becker's vision, it is not only death itself but our animal vulnerability, the messiness and decay of our bodies and our lack of control of our physical selves, that is so painful and difficult to accept. This is the stuff of the NHS – human vulnerability and mortality. But since Becker's writings, society has, if anything, become more inured to the reality of death, manically seizing any opportunity to stave off ageing, to prolong life at all costs, to beautify ourselves through surgery and cosmetics, to remain forever young. Although this is the cultural expression of the denial of death, organizations that deal with illness such as the NHS are prone to their own denial. Death and loss are often concealed under the hurly-burly of over-stretched services, administrative tasks and bureaucratic demands (Menzies-Lyth 1959), yet the anxiety can never go away.

Various writers have described a narcissistic trend in organizations, either at the individual level of self-enhancement (Pfeffer and Fong 2005) or a corporate level of grandiosity (Schwartz 1990). The individual drive to self-enhance, to see oneself and be seen favourably, reflects personal striving and ambition which may override the recognition of uncomfortable truths. Organizational narcissism is associated with the transcendence of the organization as a whole and this striving for transcendence may conceal a fantasy of immortality. In the NHS, both these narcissistic trends, the individual and the corporate, may be marshalled in the unconscious strategy to deny or dissociate death. Rogers (2009, p. 241), similarly trying to make sense of NHS anxieties, puts this succinctly: 'What could be more

powerful in the quest for ultimate narcissistic fulfillment than to vanquish, or appear to vanquish, death?'

NHS reorganization exacerbates survival anxiety. Is this why, in situations like mid-Staffordshire, the incidence of death rose out of all proportion, since the organization was in the grip of its own anxiety about survival? People die like flies and no one seems to notice until an untoward death comes to light and suddenly a whole cycle of neglect and decay is revealed, sometimes mirroring the plight of the organization facing its own demise.

I have put some emphasis on physical, actual death but what of the loss and disorder associated with psychological breakdown or 'psychic death'? Whereas death anxiety is not uncommonly cited as a source of organizational anxiety, particularly in the NHS, it is noteworthy that 'madness' (a term I use generically to describe states of mental chaos and breakdown) is seldom recognized as a factor in the genesis of NHS organizational turbulence. Yet, mental illness is as much part of NHS services as physical illness. We also know that staff are subject to high rates of psychological disturbance themselves, and it seems to me not far-fetched to suggest that anxiety about madness has its place in the organizational psyche. I suggest that these are the two great overriding fears in the NHS: death *and* madness. Death is the more obvious, given its corporal reality, while the fear of madness is more hidden, more elusive. But both, I suggest, are stirred up in the cycles of reorganization.

The organizational mirror

Throughout this chapter I have highlighted parallels between different levels of NHS organizations in the grip of a restructuring process. This applies in particular to survival anxiety as a theme that emanates from the inner workings of hospitals where matters of life and death are in the forefront of consciousness, to the outer layer of policy making and funding decisions, where decisions are driven by anxieties about the sustainability of services in the face of mounting costs. I have also suggested that these parallels are not coincidental, that they are related dynamically and interpenetrate in ways which intensify organizational turbulence, particularly at times of significant change. In my concept of the *organizational mirror* (Nitsun 1998a, 1998b), I attempt to provide a conceptual framework within which to make further sense of these parallels.

The focus of the organizational mirror is the process of mirroring that occurs between different levels of the organization. I differentiate between functional and dysfunctional mirroring, the former describing a process of communication and information-giving that, allowing for considerable anxiety at times of stress, is nevertheless sufficiently coherent to give the recipients the opportunity to form judgements and make realistic decisions. It is facilitated by clear, meaningful information coming from the top level of the organization and it strengthens appropriate boundary differentiation at different levels of the organization. Dysfunctional mirroring, by contrast, occurs when unclear information is transmitted in a way that exacerbates anxiety and deregulates boundaries between the different levels of the organization, so that there is a sense of pooled anxiety verging on panic. This is aggravated by rumour and ambiguity. Rampant projection and a paranoid-schizoid mentality are rife in situations of this sort.

I highlight this way of seeing things in order to suggest that NHS restructuring tends to be implemented in ways that generate dysfunctional mirroring. The communication process, in my experience, is usually blatantly flawed, rumour confused with fact in a process that is guaranteed to raise anxiety levels. Decision-making is often unreasonably protracted, with no sense of a clear authority at the centre of operations. The organization then tends to crumple, languishing for months in a state of suspended animation. By the time the decisions about cuts are finally made, the organization is already a shadow of itself, weakened and fragile. Delays and indecision are endemic in NHS reorganization and are rationalized as part of a necessary 'change management process'. The term 'change management' is ironical, however: recipients commonly experience the process as seriously unmanaged.

In addition to addressing communication and boundary processes across the organization, the organizational mirror reflects the fantasy level of the organization: the subjective aspect of what lies at the heart of the organization. This is akin to the organization in the mind (Armstrong 2005) and hypothesizes a set of unconscious beliefs and fantasies that drive the organization. I have suggested (Nitsun 1998a,b) that in the NHS this usually draws on primordial themes to do with life and death, cure or kill, the ideal and the denigrated, guilt and redemption. Throughout this chapter I have attempted to identify narratives of this sort, both conscious and unconscious, and the way they are configured in the process of NHS reorganization. I also suggest that this configuration is a source of anxiety that itself can influence the organization's dysfunctional response to the challenge of restructuring. It is reflected in the tension and ambiguity around boundary levels of the organization, anxiety from the 'internal organization' meeting the anxiety aroused in the 'objective' process of restructuring and combining to create an organization under duress.

I refer to the example of the suspended children's service earlier in this chapter. Here, the construct at the deeper level of organizational represent-ation might be characterized as one concerning the hope of providing care for vulnerable children, coupled with the fear that this is insufficient to repair the damage the children have suffered. The primordial dilemma is construed as one concerning the love and care of children vs their abandonment or neglect. When organizational restructuring threatens and reduces the available therapeutic care, the fear of abandoning the children is exacerbated. Staff identify with this in two ways: as the adults abandoning the children and as the abandoned children themselves. Anxiety and resentment about this grow as the change management process takes hold and the relationship between managers and staff becomes fraught with mistrust. Information about the reorganization is poorly communicated: staff are neither consulted nor informed; they feel bewildered and helpless. This is what I describe as dysfunctional mirroring. Eventually, when the dust has settled, what remains is a virtually destroyed service, very little left for therapeutic work with the children and their families. There is a sense amongst staff, and in the service, of an emotional wasteland: the image of a neglected child lurking in the minds of all who have been affected by the process. In this process, the fantasy of a traumatized child has been dysfunctionally mirrored organizationally across several levels of the service with little consciousness of how this might have been exacerbated by the change process, how it might have affected people working in the service, and, of course, how it would affect the children themselves.

I have previously written about how the dysfunctional organizational mirror feeds into the anti-group and in the next section I pick up on this theme.

The anti-group in the NHS: further thoughts

How does all the above come together in the perspective of the anti-group? Why is the group/community/organization so easily derailed in NHS settings, when the safety of the group is such a crucial aspect of the containing aspect of the NHS?

In my original formulation of the anti-group I drew heavily on the concept of *the group as object*, suggesting that the anti-group is a negative construct of the group in which anxieties and fantasies of loss and fragmentation are uppermost. Derived largely from Bion's (1961) emphasis on group mentality and Anzieu's (1984) formulations of the group as a projection screen, it, in my view, helps to explain the intense and problematic group configurations that occur in organizations under stress. The group as object can have containing and nurturing functions but these are corrupted by hostile group projections in states of heightened anxiety. Anti-group configurations are a particular version of the group as object. They derive from both paranoid-schizoid and depressive positions but may also contain the reparative potential that can transform the group into a more benign group object. The capacities for reparation and integration are inherent in the human psyche and social relationships and, with sufficient support and working through, the group can be re-invested with its constructive potential.

In the NHS, in times of stress such as restructuring, the group is infused with particularly anxious and destructive themes. This emanates from both the 'outside' in the form of attacks on the group and 'inside' in the form of fear, hatred and a loss of faith in the collaborative function of the group, all in the grip of dysfunctional organizational mirroring. This means that the containing function of the group weakens: as the 'real' group of everyday interactions becomes more fraught and divided, so the group as object is contaminated and weakened and no longer provides a safe, containing frame within which to conduct the business of work and relationships.

Anzieu (1984) takes the analogy further by suggesting that the group has an underlying bodily representation. The group in symbolic terms is a body, or is represented unconsciously as a body. The overriding unconscious fear in the group is of bodily dismemberment: the group itself might become dismembering and devouring. This not only reflects fears of fragmentation that I have alluded to above but suggests in NHS groups a possible unconscious association with the patient's body, the body that is ill, suffering, perhaps dying.

Another analogy is that of the group as womb. Both Bion and Foulkes have at different times described the group as a womb. The core group analytic term, 'group matrix', means mother or womb (Roberts 1982; Elliott 1994). It is relevant that in organizational reconfiguration we usually have not just a death but also a *birth*. However unwanted the change, it usually takes the form of something new: a new structure, a new service, a new contract. In ontological terms, a birth may be as traumatic as a death. Something new in a vulnerable matrix may be unwelcome, an intrusion, a threat. This may explain the great resistance that restructuring often generates in clinical staff: the new idea, the 'new baby', is fraught with anxiety (Pincus and Dare 1978).

In sum, much of what I describe is mediated by the anxiety about survival that is endemic in the NHS: organizational survival, service survival, group survival, patient survival and staff survival. The compounding of survival fears underlies the genesis and maintenance of an anti-group culture.

What can we do?

In the turbulent, deeply uncertain world of the NHS, with its many imponderables and unclear future, there are real questions about how we can manage the difficult processes of change in a constructive way. While the concept of the anti-group is meant to reflect the destructive aspects of groups and attacks on groups, I have many times pointed out that this is with a view to understanding and amelioration (Nitsun 1996, 2005), hence my usual epithet: 'destructive forces in the group *and their creative potential*'. How can we use our insights constructively in the NHS, in the midst of so much fear and resentment?

I have three suggestions, none of which are necessarily new but merit consideration. The first concerns organizational mirroring, as outlined above. I made the point that NHS organizational chaos and resentment is exacerbated by the poor quality of communication down the line and the unreasonable delays in decision making, creating an environment in which rumour and fantasy run riot and add to dysfunctional mirroring at all levels of the organization (Nitsun 1998a,

1998b). If trusts are serious about developing an effective 'change management process', this requires far greater attention to the communication process and the timing of decisions in such a way that staff are not suspended in a chasm of anxiety for longer than is absolutely necessary. This applies similarly to *the way* decisions are communicated. There are many examples of crude, unthinking and insensitive forms of communication about vital changes in the NHS. The fact that these are difficult decisions does not mean that they have to be presented in an inhuman way. Awareness training for staff who have responsibility for communicating decisions is an important requirement.

The second suggestion concerns the level of psychosocial awareness in NHS staff at large. So often staff get caught up in unproductive and destructive interactions, as if helplessly drawn into conflict and angry enactments that add to the environment of the anti-group. There often seems to be a lack of basic insight about the psychosocial implications of healthcare, the existential preoccupations and anxieties that link us universally and the psychodynamics of relationships with patients and colleagues in a pressured healthcare setting. Highly trained specialists in their own fields often seem not to have a smattering of psychosocial insight, as if their jobs are carried out in a psychological vacuum and their relationships with colleagues and patients have no meaning beyond the immediate task and the concrete realities of space and time. It is not surprising then that there is so much inter- and intra-professional tension in the NHS. This is not to say that all tension and conflict is unnecessary and unproductive – much of this concerns ordinary day-to-day tensions that are an inevitable part of working relationships in the NHS, and there are of course many examples of collaboration and resolution – but where the tensions get out of hand, there is a need for greater insight. Calling in organizational consultants may be a way of achieving this but often produces disappointing results. Another way is a wider programme of education in psychosocial relationships that is part of all staff curricula and not consigned to a few 'experts'. So, staff would have components in their training that are geared to an enhanced psychosocial awareness of healthcare: methods might include didactic and practical teaching in a way that is 'experience-near' (Kohut 1977) and touches the human factor in healthcare more closely than currently is the case.

Finally, I make a plea for working towards a more supportive, compassionate NHS environment. I am not at all alone in this. Following the series of high-profile scandals in 2013, particularly mid-Staffs (see above), there is a renewed move to develop a more humane environment. The pull of regressive and antagonistic forces will always be there but can be offset by active attempts to support staff, amongst themselves and in their relationship with patients. We now have working models aimed at such development (e.g. Hartley and Kennard 2009), highlighting the tradition of staff support and reflective groups in some NHS services. But this tends to happen randomly and in limited settings. I suggest that the more structured, educational approaches noted above are needed in combination with reflective practice groups and that this should be a built-in part of organizational development. Supporting staff is about finding ways of inculcating a culture of 'intelligent kindness' (Campling and Ballatt 2012) with the kind of leadership that values compassion and support across the organization. I believe that approaches of this sort would help to mitigate dysfunctional mirroring. At the same time, I suggest that these approaches will lack impact if they do not take account of the anti-group dynamics I have outlined in this chapter – the shadow side of healthcare, the oscillation between paranoid and depressive positions, the interplay of idealization and denigration, and the paradoxical denial of death and madness in an organization that exists in order to grapple with matters of life and death.

References

Anzieu, D. (1984) *The Group and the Unconscious*. London: Routledge and Kegan Paul.

Armstrong, D. (2005) *Organization in the Mind*. London: Tavistock Clinic Series.

Becker, E. (1973) *The Denial of Death*. New York: The Free Press.

Bion, W. R. (1961) *Experiences in Groups*. London: Tavistock.

Butler, P. (2010) History of NHS reforms: a state of permanent revolution, *The Guardian*, 9 July 2010.

Campbell, D. (2013) NHS 'culture of fear' stops nurses raising patient safety concerns, *The Guardian*, 23 April 2013.

Campling, P. and Ballatt, J. (2012) Intelligent kindness – reforming the culture of healthcare. *Forum: Journal of the International Association for Group Psychotherapy and Group Process*, 5, July 2012, 19–37.

Caulkin, S. (2013) Mid Staffs shows everything that's rotten in the house of management, *The Guardian*, 1 March 2013.

Elliott, B. (1994) The womb and gender identity, in Brown, D. and Zinkin, L. (eds) *The Psyche and the Social World*. London: Routledge.

Fischer, M. D. (2012) Organizational turbulence, trouble and trauma: theorizing the collapse of mental health settings, *Organization Studies*, 33, 1153–73.

Freud, S. (1936) Inhibitions, symptoms and anxiety, *Psychoanalytic Quarterly*, 5, 415–43.

Groesbeck, C. J. (1975) The wounded healer, *Journal of Analytical Psychology*, 20, 122–45.

Hartley, P. and Kennard, D. (eds) (2009) *Staff Support Groups in the Helping Professions*. Hove: Routledge

Hegel, G.W.F. (1807) *The Phenomenology of the Spirit*, trans. by Miller, A V. (1977). Oxford: Clarendon Press.

Hughes, D. (2013) NHS hospitals spend £2m on gagging orders, *The Independent*, 12 June 2013.

Kohut, H. (1977) *The Restoration of the Self*. Chicago: University of Chicago Press.

Klein, M. (1975) *Envy and Gratitude*. London: The Hogarth Press.

Kreeger, L. (1992) Envy pre-emption in small and large groups, *Group Analysis*, 25, 391–412.

Kubler-Ross, E. (1997) *Questions and Answers on Death and Dying*. New York: Touchstone.

Long, S. (2008) *The Perverse Organization and its Deadly Sins*. London: Karnac.

Menzies-Lyth, I.E.P. (1959) A case-study in the function of social systems as a defense against anxiety, *Human Relations*, 13, 95–121.

Nitsun, M. (1988) The effects on the organization of hospital visiting teams, *Psychiatric Bulletin*, 12, 3, 83–8.

Nitsun, M. (1996) *The Anti-group: Destructive Forces in the Group and their Creative Potential*. London: Routledge.

Nitsun, M (1998a) The organizational mirror: a group-analytic approach to organizational consultancy, part 1 – theory, *Group Analysis*, 31, 245–67.

Nitsun, M. (1998b) The organizational mirror: a group-analytic approach to organizational consultancy: part 2 – application, *Group Analysis*, 31, 505–18.

Nitsun, M. (2005) Destructive forces in group therapy, in Motherwell, L. and Shay, J. J. (eds) *Complex Dilemmas in Group Therapy*. New York: Brunner-Routledge.

Obholzer, A. and Roberts, V. Z. (1994) *The Unconscious at Work: Individual and Organizational Stress in the Human Services*. London: Routledge.

Pfeffer, J. and Fong, C. T. (2005) Building organization theory from first principles: the self enhancement motive and understanding power and influence, *Organization Science*, 16, 372–88.

Pincus, L. and Dare, C. (1978) *Secrets in the Family*. New York: Pantheon Books

Prodgers, A. (1990) The dual nature of the group as mother: the uroboric container, *Group Analysis*, 23, 17–30.

Roberts, J. P. (1982) Foulkes' concept of the matrix, *Group Analysis*, 15, 111–26.

Rogers, A. (2009) Organizational reconfiguration in health care: a life and death struggle, *Organizational and Social Dynamics*, 9, 225–48.

Schwartz, H. S. (1990) *Narcissistic Process and Organizational Decay: The Theory of the Organizational Ideal*. New York: New York University Press.

Segal, H. (1973) *Introduction to the Work of Melanie Klein*. London: Karnac.

Stein, M. (2000) After Eden: envy and the defences against anxiety paradigm, *Human Relations*, 53, 193–211.

Steiner, J. (1987) The interplay between pathological organizations and the paranoid-schizoid and depressive positions, *International Journal of Psychoanalysis*, 68, 69–80.

Timmins, N. (2012) *Never Again: The Story of the Health and Social Care Act*. London: King's Fund Publications.

Volkan, V. D. (2001) Transgenerational transmission and chosen trauma: an aspect of large group identity, *Group Analysis*, 34, 79–97.

Volkan, V. D. (2014) *Animal Killer: Transmission of War Trauma from One Generation to the Next*. London: Karnac.

Winnicott, D. W. (1960) The theory of the parent-infant relationship, *International Journal of Psychoanalysis*, 41, 585–95.

Part II

The clinical setting

Chapter 3

Group analytic psychotherapy on the edge

As a senior group analyst, practising, teaching and supervising group methods across the private and public healthcare sectors, I struggle with how to address what I perceive as the difficulties in my field while at the same time imparting hope and enthusiasm for what I consider to be a powerful psychotherapeutic approach. In this chapter I look at group analysis in the wider context of mental health services in the UK and consider its struggles, like many psychotherapeutic approaches, to find ballast in a changing and demanding environment. Highlighting the clinical agenda – how group analysis is practised in psychotherapeutic groups – I explore several linked themes: the status of group psychotherapy in the turbulent world of mental health services; theoretical drifts in the development of group analysis; the schisms in the field, the tension between idealization and denigration; the impact of post-modernity; the neglect of science; the problematic theory–practice link; and questions about the social perspective in group analysis. My aim is to map this territory with a view to strengthening the clinical application of group analysis and to make suggestions for the way forward.

The situation to some extent parallels that in the USA where there are similar challenges to all in-depth psychotherapy but where, in my view, there is a more pragmatic approach to these problems, reflected for example in the writing of Gans (2010), who addresses practice difficulties more openly and directly than is usual in the UK.

The crisis in public services

I write this chapter in the midst of a major crisis about the future of psychotherapy services in the United Kingdom. Psychotherapy departments (largely psychoanalytic or psychodynamic in approach) in the National Health Service (NHS), which for decades have held sway over the psychological therapies in this country, have been the targets of severe financial cuts in the last few years. The result is the widespread and unprecedented closure of entire psychotherapy departments and a marked reduction or fragmentation of resources in those departments that have survived. The NHS has for decades not only been an important provider of jobs in psychotherapy but as the largest provider of health services in the UK has strongly influenced the pattern of overall mental health services in the country, including psychotherapy. The allocation and withdrawal of funding therefore has serious implications for the survival and integrity of the psychotherapeutic professions and the clinical services they offer.

The position of group psychotherapy within this crisis is fragile. As part of psychotherapy services, long-term group analysis has already suffered losses, resulting in a diminution and disruption of services. However, group analytic psychotherapy represents a different tradition to individual psychoanalytic psychotherapy and tends to be viewed in a different light in the NHS, mainly because it is considered to be cost-effective given the number of people who can be treated at any one time. Hence group analytic psychotherapy is generally seen as more compatible with present-day service priorities than individual psychotherapy and has possibly fared better in the overall unraveling process. However, the writing is on the wall. We face a very different world of funding and service prioritization from that of even a year ago and no psychotherapeutic form can take for granted its survival, let alone development, in mainstream services in the UK. In any case, funding of group psychotherapy services has historically been on a smaller scale than individual psychotherapy, with meagre services often buttressed by trainees and other honorary staff. This reflects the struggle group analytic psychotherapy has had to establish its place in the NHS – a point I explore more fully below. The question is to what extent this limited funding will be sustained in the future and, if not, what will happen to group psychotherapy provision in the next ten to twenty years and beyond.

The status of group psychotherapy – 'the yo-yo effect'

Group therapy still enjoys a dubious status in public services in the UK and is subject to considerable ambivalence in the minds of both patients and staff. A study by Bowden (2002), influenced by anti-group considerations, found that by far the majority of patients, if given the choice, preferred to have individual therapy, citing as the main negative factors fear of groups and disbelief in the idea that a group could be therapeutic. Healthcare staff, in my experience, reveal similar ambivalence. Working in the NHS, I frequently see evidence – across the professions – of staff members' anxious and ambivalent if not hostile attitudes to groups. An example is the recent meeting of a large number of psychologists in an IAPT service (Improving Access to Psychological Therapies) in a London NHS trust who had come together to discuss a strategy for meeting the challenge of providing more services with reduced funding – a widespread current preoccupation. At the meeting there was strong agreement that the way forward was to develop a comprehensive programme of group treatments. It was noted that group work was geared to a variety of clinical conditions and that there was a growing evidence base for its efficacy. However, when it came to the question of who amongst the staff would undertake to run groups, no one came forward. This, in my experience, is not unusual and is often linked to lack of confidence about running groups as well as the aforementioned ambivalence about groups as a primary psychotherapeutic medium. It reflects, in part, the conspicuous lack of training in group methods across all the mental health professions in the UK, leaving practitioners very unsure of their group skills and anxious about putting them to the test. In clinical psychology training, for example, there is a great emphasis on individual psychotherapy, with many courses emphasizing CBT and other individual approaches, but practically no training – at most a session or two over three years – in group therapy. Yet, NHS mental health staff generally are increasingly required to run groups. This aggravates the difficulty, maintaining fear of running groups and perpetuating a culture of ambivalence and avoidance.

The incident described above – the meeting about resource problems – illustrates a particular aspect of organizational ambivalence about groups. Whenever there are funding crises, which happen frequently in the NHS, I find there is a sudden burst of interest in groups. As in the above example, it is swiftly decided that group therapy is the most realistic way of meeting escalating demand. A group programme may then be started. But soon enough disillusionment sets in. The service is difficult to run: it takes longer than expected to set up groups; patient recruitment is difficult; there is a significant drop-out rate; outcomes may be disappointing. The group service then tends to run down, not necessarily in a deliberate way but through loss of interest and motivation. Then there is another crisis and the same thing happens again: a group programme is activated: it begins to flag; it continues but with less investment and enthusiasm; and then it runs down. This cycle can be repeated several times in the same service. I call this the 'yo-yo effect'. Groups are picked up and dropped in close succession, with very little thought about fundamental issues such as training and supervision and the need to build a framework for the group service with adequate systems which need testing over extended periods of time. Of course, there are services that do provide robust, sustainable group services that contribute greatly to clinical provision. But this is relatively unusual and more often than not there is the oscillating pattern I describe. The conclusion then reached by services may be that the groups are dispensable, too difficult to run and the outcomes too uncertain. The further conclusion is that there is something inherently problematic about group psychotherapy and that resources are better ploughed back into individual psychotherapy.

It is largely because of the above that I have in recent years devoted a significant amount of time to training IAPT practitioners in group methods. A one-year course is based at the Anna Freud Centre in London and is described more fully in Chapter 4, including my attempt to bring a group analytic perspective to the running of routine NHS group work. The course, however, to my knowledge and that of contributing colleagues, remains the only one of its kind in the UK.

A further example of the ambiguous status of group psychotherapy is found in the attitude of some of the major therapies of the day that use groups as a core component of their approach but *without acknowledging the significance of the group process*. This is particularly telling. I have in mind three widely used current approaches: *mentalization-based therapy (MBT), mindfulness-based cognitive therapy (MBCT)* and *dialectical behaviour therapy (DBT)*. All three approaches utilize groups as the primary mode of intervention but do scant justice both to group process and the therapeutic impact of the group itself. The groups are employed as settings for the application of particular therapeutic techniques, with some recognition that the group provides an interpersonal context for learning but little if any attempt to explore the group process. There are indications, in mindfulness-based cognitive therapy, at least, that the group contributes significantly to therapeutic process and outcome (Linke and Nitsun 2012), but continuing denial or reluctance to acknowledge this.

These examples illustrate the widespread tendency in health services not just to minimize the significance of the group as a therapeutic medium but to create a double standard in which the group is the core context of the therapy on the one hand but on the other is repudiated as of therapeutic value. This, in my view, is another version of the anti-group. There are several aspects to this: lack of provision for training as an essential requirement of group therapeutic practice; the denial of group psychotherapy as a *primary therapy* rather than an adjunctive therapy; the denial of the impact of the group as part of a psychotherapeutic approach; and the implication in some approaches that focusing on the group would actually disrupt or undermine the treatment effect. This has overtones of a 'groups are dangerous' mentality. These messages from alternative therapeutic approaches, problematic as they are, must be taken seriously. They reflect what I consider to be the highly contradictory culture of group work in public services. This detracts from the integrity of group theory and practice building in the clinical domain and the need for a framework within which the potential and problems of groups can be openly and fairly discussed. It reinforces a diminishing or denigratory attitude to group psychotherapy and at the same time helps to maintain the split-off idealization to which I turn my attention later in this chapter.

Splits and fragmentation in the group analytic milieu

The strength required of a psychotherapeutic approach to withstand the vicissitudes of funding and fashion – as well as the ambivalence about psychotherapy – depends to a large extent on its internal coherence as a discipline, the consistency of its theorizing and in particular the link between theory and practice. There is a need to substantiate the link between psychotherapeutic process and outcome and to be able to demonstrate effectiveness. All of this is difficult to achieve given the complexity of much psychotherapy, particularly the dynamic or analytically orientated approaches. Group analysis therefore is by no means alone amongst the psychotherapies in being subject to theoretical confusion and a variety of splits, in theory, belief, value system and so on. In itself, this is not necessarily a bad thing. It may be a sign of growth and creativity: splits and controversies can reflect development and expansion in the field. Perhaps the best-known example is the Controversial Discussions of the British Psychoanalytic Society in the 1940s that led to the establishment of three separate psychoanalytic schools of thought (Steiner 1985). This did not stop the controversies but brought coherence to a complex field and facilitated the development of psychoanalysis within an identifiable framework. On the other hand, these splits led to a preoccupation with difference, power and influence and ultimately did little to deter the subsequent swing of fashion away from psychoanalysis. If anything, it may have exacerbated the growing disbelief in psychoanalysis since the field became associated with preciousness and pomposity – the 'narcissism of small differences' – and a loss of contact with new realities and changing priorities in the psychotherapeutic field. From my time as an NHS manager of psychotherapy services, I can remember the incredulity and disdain with which non-psychological managers regarded the pettiness and prickliness – as they saw it – of psychotherapists arguing over seemingly minute theoretical and practical differences while before them the world was changing, with NHS funding and priorities moving in radically new directions. The differences between psychotherapeutic approaches therefore present a paradoxical challenge. On the one hand, they are to a degree inevitable, a sign of development and differentiation; on the other, they may create unhelpful internal divisions and weaken the field when it comes to consolidation and progress within a turbulent and competitive environment.

I wager that the group analytic field faces an even more pronounced challenge than most psychological therapies and offer two reasons for this: the considerable complexity of group theory and practice relative to other approaches; and the problem of achieving face validity, given the widespread ambivalence about groups and doubts about the value of group psychotherapy. Regarding complexity, I originally addressed this in an earlier publication (Nitsun 1996), highlighting comments at the time by writers in both the British and North American group psychotherapeutic fields (Skynner 1983; Dies 1992) about theoretical confusion and contradiction in both theory and practice. I am not convinced that there has been great progress since then: we face an accumulating body of literature that is both stimulating and encouraging but bewildering in its diversity.

When it comes to specific splits and divergences in group analysis, the most pronounced split in the UK is that between the approaches of the Tavistock Institute and the Institute of Group Analysis. This is an important, if not fundamental, split in so far as it represents the longstanding Bion–Foulkes schism, one that has had a significant impact on group theory and practice in the UK. There have been several attempts within group analysis to address this schism, including that of Dennis Brown (1985) and my own efforts (Nitsun 1996), in which I argued for a reconciliation between the more optimistic, collaboratively focused and theoretically open approach of group analysis and the more guarded, pessimistic Bion approach with its emphasis on regressive and destructive group processes. Yet, in a recent and significant publication on Tavistock group psychotherapy (Garland 2010), there was hardly a passing reference to Foulkes and group analysis. The approach in the book is strongly influenced by the Kleinian tradition, and of course Bion, but omits most other established and recognized group therapies. At the same time, much of the value system underlying Garland's approach is group analytic in essence, reflecting her own prior training as a group analyst. Reading the book, however, the impression might be that group analysis is virtually non-existent, of little consequence and has had minimal influence on group psychotherapy in the UK. (In reality, group analysis has a substantial presence in the UK; training institutes in several major cities; national and local training programmes; and group analytic therapy is by far the preferred mode of practice in both the NHS and private practice).

It is more difficult to typify the splits and divergences within the group analytic field in the UK itself, since they all radiate from a group analytic base and to a variable degree remain loyal to the Foulkesian legacy. Perhaps the most pronounced divergence is on the part of those group analysts (e.g. Dalal 1998; Stacey 2003) who adopt a more radically social perspective of group process, highlighting the impasse in Foulkes' thinking in relation to his twin allegiances to a conservative psychoanalytic model with its intra-psychic orientation and a more socially orientated approach, although this perspective has to a large extent been absorbed in core group analytic thinking. This challenges notions of individuality in much the way Foulkes did himself (1964), emphasizing the penetrating force of culture and society at all levels and demanding a clearer and more committed appreciation of social personhood. Later in the chapter I go on to question the application of this emphasis in clinical work. While adding a vital dimension, it has perhaps unwittingly problematized the clinical basis of group analytic psychotherapy. The same seems to me to apply to the increased emphasis on the social unconscious (Hopper and Weinberg 2011), again derived from Foulkes but arguing for its stronger representation in theory and practice, with little evidence so far of its application in clinical practice. I comment further on these developments below. Linked to these developments is a greater emphasis on 'applied' group analysis as it relates to cultural and organizational studies. No doubt this reflects the generativity of the group analytic approach. So, there is a sense perhaps of both the creativity of these developments and the way they attenuate the somewhat fragile fabric of group analysis, taking it into important new areas but possibly adding to theoretical complexity and confusion, particularly in my view not adding ballast to clinical practice, which for most group analysts remains their primary function and vocation.

I wish not to draw pre-emptive conclusions, since these are works in progress. I am mindful of the words of Brown and Zinkin (1994, p. 251) who argue for the value of 'partial and provisional insights' rather than a 'compendious total system', seeing a more dispersed theory as fitting much more with postmodernist culture. However, this does not address the difficulties arising for clinical practice from the lack of a sufficiently coherent and testable approach that could help to locate group analytic psychotherapy firmly in the domain of mainstream psychotherapy (although this has begun to change, in line with the work of Lorentzen, see below).

To round off this section, I wish to recapitulate a question I asked in 1996 about the epistemological underpinnings of group analytic theory. I wondered whether the splits and divergences at the time could reflect at a meta-theoretical level the inherently fragmented nature of group experience, with its propensity for anti-group developments. I speculated:

> [S]omething akin to an anti-group phenomenon would seem to operate isomorphically at different levels of discourse about the group – a negative, disruptive, or disorganizing process which infiltrates not only the group as a living process, but also the conceptual order of group psychotherapy.
>
> (Nitsun 1996, p. 6)

Continuing idealization

One way of dealing with ambivalence, doubt and uncertainty is by idealization. While idealization has a healthy function, highlighted in self-psychology as a major developmental route to relationships of substance and value (Kohut 1971), it also has defensive properties. I have previously commented about what I regard as an idealizing tendency in group analysis, including the idealization of S. H. Foulkes and the idealization of groups and group process. This view was shared by Karterud (1992), commenting on the widespread idealization in the group analytic community at the time he wrote. Psychotherapeutic movements are prone to reification, if not deification, through the narcissistic elevation of a particular theory and a particular personality or personalities associated with the approach (Kernberg 1998). We may assume that this intensifies in the face of ambivalence and doubt. Group analysis has faced the particular challenge of widespread ambivalence, if not repudiation, of groups and group psychotherapy and this may have prompted a compensatory idealizing tendency. The difficulty is that an attachment to the ideal makes it difficult to get to grips with the less than ideal and this can generate a split between the idealized and the denigrated. We know all this theoretically but it can be difficult not to get caught up in the process when faced with one's own personal and professional doubts and the natural wish to value one's own vocation and the medium through which it is achieved.

The idealization in group analysis is difficult to substantiate as it is seldom apparent in publications. Of course, those who idealize also do not see it as idealization. However, the idealization seemed to me to be expressed rather clearly in the Foulkes Lecture given by Jane Campbell in 2010. Entitled 'Islands of the Blest', this erudite and elegantly composed lecture presents a particularly positive picture of group analysis, the islands of the blest symbolizing a hypothetical community enjoying the privilege of unbounded space and time to engage and reflect in the 'true' tradition and spirit of group analysis. This is equated with a golden era in group analysis, harking back to the time of the founding fathers and the days of plenty at the original Group Analytic Practice,

88 Montagu Mansions. Campbell recognizes how much times have changed, how the fashion is much more for regulated, short-term therapies and how much this reflects cultural change at all levels of society. She mourns the loss of a more sensitive, reflective, exploratory value system. Locating the origin of group analysis in the 'crucible' of World War II, and the reparative force and social values emerging from the war, she acknowledges that this may be out of step with the far more instrumental society of today. In many ways, one can sympathize with Campbell's point of view. The world we live in is harder, quicker, more transient. But, the weakness, in my view, may be a tendency to equate all goodness, honesty and virtue with group analysis and to separate it from the rest of the world. There is much sensitive psychotherapy being conducted in other spheres, including what Campbell (2010) describes as 'the alphabet therapies' such as CBT. Within CBT, there is the development of approaches such as schema therapy, which converge with psychodynamic approaches and offer integrated ways of working which hold promise for the future (Young *et al.* 2003).

In the responses to Campbell's lecture there was both appreciation of her position and challenge to the idealization. Einhorn (2010) describes Campbell's lecture as a 'love letter to group analysis', capturing the essence of her romantic vision but asking why we need islands of the blest in the first place and pointing out that the invocation of a golden age may leave us feeling dissatisfied with the present age. Einhorn recognizes that idealization may be a defence against anxiety, especially annihilation anxiety, suggesting that group analysis is traumatized and responds as though 'our very existence' is threatened: a view I highlight in this chapter.

Thygesen (2010, p. 440), in her response to Campbell, also challenges the idealized position: 'To live on the Islands of the Blest means that the dwellers do not grow old or die but live an internal life in a world closed and separated from the rest of the world. *Is this what has happened to group analysis?*' Thygesen seeks stronger ground in critical reflection and research to substantiate the claims for therapeutic value. Lorentzen (2010) echoes Thygesen's sentiments and since then has published an important research monograph largely supporting the empirical validity of group analytic psychotherapy (Lorentzen 2014).

The above debate is a healthy aspect of contemporary group analysis – the capacity to tolerate different and conflicting viewpoints, to both appreciate and challenge the idealizing tendency. But, since idealization is so seductive, appearing and reappearing in the development of most psychotherapeutic schools, it is worth considering what conditions are conducive to its emergence. I suggest three factors:

- In line with Freud's (1921) original thinking about group psychology, groups typically throw up idealized leaders who are invested with great power. Onto the leaders – and their beliefs – are projected all the longed-for dependence of the group, the fantasies of salvation and transformation. As writers as different as Bion (1961) and Yalom and Leszcz (2005) point out, there is a universal search for the all-wise, all-powerful leader, a longing which is amplified in the group through the sheer weight of numbers and the powerful identification with the leader. Sophisticated as psychotherapists may be, and in spite of Foulkes' (1964) own criticism of authoritarian or idealized leadership, group analysts are no different from others in their unconscious longings and this to my mind is reflected in the continued idealization of Foulkes and group analysis.

- The fragility of the group as object, a construction in the minds of its members (Anzieu 1984; Nitsun 1996), invites idealized attributions in order to give it substance. This applies as much to organizations and ideologies. Many writers (e.g. Kernberg 1998) have referred to psychotherapy institutes as espousing a religious adherence to theory and leadership. Through this adherence, the institute strengthens its identity and is able to differentiate itself from other institutes and approaches. Institutional identity and elevation may entrain fantasies of immortality: we live on through the founding fathers who themselves live on through their renown and creativity. But at what cost to clinical integrity and openness to debate and change?
- The threat of reality. Given current challenges to the viability of psychotherapy, including group analysis, and the intense anxiety about survival, idealization offers a retreat and a comfort. There are numerous examples in history of threats to national and group identity that have generated idealization on a massive scale. Nazi Germany at the time of World War II is perhaps the best known, though extreme, example – serious economic difficulty and cultural humiliation in pre-war Germany creating the conditions for pathological leadership through intense national fervour and idealization of both the race and the leader (Pick 2012). The deeply destructive outcome of such developments does not equate with situations of lesser importance such as those I describe in psychotherapy institutes, but highlights how readily threats of annihilation can become intertwined with idealizing processes.

Idealization, even in lesser doses, tends to resist change. The haze of idealization obscures the glare of reality. Further, idealization tends to go hand in glove with denigration and to perpetuate splits.

The social emphasis in group analysis – a bridge too far?

In this and the next section on "the individual", I explore what I consider to be the clinically problematic implications of the social emphasis in group analysis and the way this compromises the notion of individuality. Since this is a personal view and likely to be controversial, I wish to state my position at the outset as clearly as possible.

I fully agree with the social emphasis in group analysis and see it as a major distinguishing feature, although I also believe that it is more widely acknowledged and part of contemporary psychotherapy in general than is recognized – see below. I believe, like most group analysts, that human beings are social through and through. However, I also believe that there are multiple interacting influences, such as genetics, biology, cognitive development, the behavioural learning process and fantasy that have to be taken into account and that these factors contribute to 'individuality' and the subjective nature of human experience in a way that is both the starting point and the sine qua non of the clinical endeavour. My difficulty with the social emphasis in group analysis is its tendency to exclude all other influences and to problematize the 'individual' in a way that may be at variance with the requirements of a publically accountable programme of health care that emphasizes individual outcomes and individual satisfaction. I agree at one level that the social perspective, including the social unconscious, adds depth to the understanding of the individual, but I also believe that without sufficient personalization and individualization, we may be left with over-generalized statements about the social and a neglect of what it is that makes the individual uniquely individual. Ironically, this is often the basis of people' dissatisfaction with group psychotherapy: they feel neglected as individuals, that there is insufficient space and time for them and their own problems. This may be another instance of isomorphism: in the same way I suggested that the confusing, sometimes contradictory nature of the literature on group therapy may reflect some inherent fragmentation or a dissociated anti-group influence, so theoretical compromises with the 'individual' position may mirror the perennial problem in clinical practice of individuals finding insufficient recognition as individuals in the group.

My views probably reflect my original training and career as a clinical psychologist and the positive notions of individuality and clinical outcomes that are components of this approach. Although these views may swim against the group analytic tide in some respects, I believe that I voice the concerns of other group analysts who more informally express bewilderment and uncertainty about what currently constitutes group analysis and how to articulate their roles in the most responsible and effective way.

I pick up on the long-standing problematic theory-practice link as reflected in the mid-1980's. Robin Skynner (1983), one of the leading figures in the 20th century development of group analysis, used the analogy of the emperor's new clothes to describe his confusion – and that of others – about Foulkes' theory. The question arises once more now, approximately two decades later and well into the 21st century: what has happened to group analytic theory in the intervening years and what are the implications for clinical practice? I see a complex situation, with an outpouring of writing about group analysis internationally, generating important theoretical developments and paralleled by a good deal of development and innovation in the wider application of group analysis in fields such as consultancy, supervision, organizational studies, international relations and social history. All of this seems to me valuable and encouraging. But the *clinical application of group analysis* remains problematic and lacking in coherence, a worrying situation given the rapidly changing fashions in psychotherapy, the crisis in funding in public services, and the pressure on all psychotherapists to be accountable for every aspect of their work. In my view, much of the new theoretical development in group analysis has bypassed some of the most urgent issues in the clinical application of the method – the real problems of running groups, the ambivalence people have about joining groups, the demands the approach makes on both patients and therapist, the experience of groups going wrong, the transfer to the consulting room of theoretical insights and the need for greater empirical research and outcome evaluation.

I suggest that there has been a centrifugal development of group analytic thinking that may have neglected its clinical basis. I associate this to some extent with an expanded interest in the social dimension of group analysis, an important development which is germane to group analysis, and highly generative, but in my view has contributed to a decentering and marginalization of the clinical subject. The social perspective reinforces the value of group psychotherapy by emphasizing the validity and relevance of the group as a process, in fact arguing that it is the psychotherapy of choice for many conditions (Foulkes and Anthony 1967, Stacey 2003, p. 9). The social emphasis widens the scope of understanding and affirms and elaborates the importance of context. But in other ways, in my view, it may obscure the clinical subject. A robust clinical stance requires more than anything else the detailed and recursive attention to the here and now, to the moment-to-moment interchange between therapist and patient/s, to the impact of therapeutic intervention on clinical progress, to the link between process and outcome and, in the case of group therapy, to the interlocking of individual and group processes.

The social emphasis in group analysis derives from Foulkes' well-known assertions about the great importance of the social – the individual is permeated to the core by society. It is this theoretical aspect, rather than the clinical focus, which is taken forward by writers such as Dalal (1998) and Stacey (2003) who are at great pains to point out that the social is always present in the development of the individual. An important aspect of their approach is to differentiate group analysis from psychoanalysis on the grounds that the intra-psychic perspective of psychoanalysis is limiting and inappropriate in the face of the overwhelming influence of the social. In the case of Dalal, this entails criticism of Foulkes for attempting to hold onto both his psychoanalytic roots and the social perspective. The two are deemed to be in essence incompatible and contradictory. Stacey takes this further. He argues strongly against a "both and" approach – *both* psychoanalysis *and* group analysis – and offers what he considers to be a radically social approach to group analysis. This focuses on complex social processes generated by the group, the understanding of which draws on the interaction of group members without the need for psychoanalytic explanations such as 'internal worlds' or the unconscious. The notion of the inner world comes in for particular challenge in this approach. Stacey argues that there is no such thing as an inner world other than the repetition in the mind of bodily or relational patterns that are otherwise enacted with people (2003, p. 6)

While agreeing with the social emphasis in many ways, I have serious reservations about its exclusion of an individual internal world as well as the value of such an approach as the basis for clinical practice, both individual and group. My experience, and that of other colleagues, is that a predominantly social emphasis is inadequate as a framework for practice and that it neglects crucial aspects of psychotherapeutic insight, research and experience. I have many times noticed particularly socially orientated colleagues struggling to argue the utility of the social perspective in clinical work only to resort to psychodynamic, psychoanalytic, humanistic or other clinically based theories as ways of understanding complex group problems. What Stacey presents as 'complex', in my view, turns out not to be complex at all but reductionist when presented with the frequently dense and really complicated problems we meet in the consulting room. This applies to both patients' initial presentations and the ongoing process of psychotherapy in which different levels of the same problem, as well as emerging problems, occur constantly in the ebb and flow of the group. These require careful and detailed attention, a wide knowledge base about individual and group development, an awareness of the interacting domains of genetics and history, and the capacity for flexible and recursive thinking. The social perspective is an important part of this process, adding a useful corrective to explanations that reside entirely in the intra-psychic realm, but it is *only a perspective*.

Group analysts emphasizing the social tend to discount theories that do not fit in with their perspective. Stacey, for example, is at pains to show how all psychoanalytic thinking, in its various forms and guises, including recent relational and inter-subjective theory, is flawed. He similarly refutes systems thinking. This not only excludes well-known and sometimes proven approaches but reverses the contemporary emphasis on convergence and integration in theory development (Holmes and Bateman 2002), which has marked psychotherapeutic progress in the last few decades. Theoretical openness and integration have become major features of the psychotherapeutic landscape in recent years and are regarded by many as the way forward. In fact, when Foulkes is criticized for his both-and thinking, *both* group analysis *and* psychoanalysis, we might adopt a contrary position and suggest that *Foulkes' both-and-position was an achievement rather than a failure*. From a theoretical point of view, a both-and position may be impure and inconvenient but from a contemporary clinical point of view it may be necessary, if not essential. This does not assume a blind adherence to psychoanalysis or other individual approaches but the recognition of frameworks that consider individual processes as they arise in the group and are experienced by individuals with their own subjectivity and historical narrative. This does not neglect the belief that the individual is always part of the group and that an individual process is by definition also a group process but it allows the focus to rest firmly on the individual when necessary.

I suggest that Foulkes held onto both psychoanalytic and group analytic perspectives because he was primarily a *clinician*. Foulkes was an NHS consultant psychiatrist, psychoanalyst and group analyst for several decades and would have encountered many clinical problems in a variety of contexts. As the head of a psychotherapy department at the Maudsley Hospital, he must have had considerable clinical responsibility. I suspect that he held onto psychoanalytic thinking not necessarily through lack of courage or conviction but at least partly because he found it useful, if not indispensable, in his clinical practice. This may be very different from group analysts who are not primarily clinicians or who do not face the challenge of providing large-scale psychological services for a very wide variety of patients, as I have over several decades. Apart from more congruent scientific methods, there is nothing more testing of the value and limitations of a psychotherapeutic approach than its implementation in the demanding environment of a public service such as the NHS. Some of the development of the social perspective in group analysis, as I see it, is based on theoretical assumptions that are as yet remote from the reality of the consulting room, even though they potentially may enrich it.

In my original writing on the anti-group, I took issue not only with the failure to recognize the potential for destructive developments in groups but with group analytic theory as a whole, suggesting that the loose and wide-ranging nature of the theory concealed issues and problems that were germane to the group analytic endeavour. I felt that this was epitomized in the then popular statement that group analysis is "an act of faith". This broad affirmation of the group analytic approach on quasi-religious or ideological grounds was, in my view, highly questionable, and still is. I argue that faith, especially in the clinical sphere, needs substantiation in observation and evaluation. My concern is that the social in group analysis, for all its relevance, has become the new dogma, the new faith.

The social unconscious

I have similar reservations about the clinical applications of the concept of the social unconscious. Building on Foulkes' (1964) interest in this phenomenon, the social unconscious has become the focus of explorations in a variety of mainly cultural and political spheres (Hopper and Weinberg 2011), with relatively little attention so far to psychotherapy groups. Hopper (2012, p 395) refers to the study of the social unconscious as "one of the hallmarks of contemporary group analysis" and "one of our legacies to the next generation of students and colleagues". I have also heard the social unconscious referred to as "the essence of group analysis". I myself do not know what the essence of group analysis is, or whether in fact there is *an* essence. The social unconscious presumably covers a vast terrain. But how does it differ from the "personal" or "individual" unconscious, and if it does, does this not vitiate the whole argument about social and individual processes being the same, a point so strongly emphasized in the radical versions of group analytic thinking? Further, the phenomena implicit in the social unconscious, such as the loss of information or memory about traumatic events, the impact of intergenerational transmission of unprocessed trauma and the dissociation of the publically unspeakable, are part and parcel of the substance of all literature, history and the arts generally, as well as many psychotherapeutic approaches, giving these insights a foundational status in culture rather than belonging to a specific discipline of thought, be it group analysis or any other. Even psychoanalysis, so often criticized by 'radical' group analysts for its denial of social processes, including the social unconscious, has shown increasing recognition of complex, multi-layered social influences. Two recent examples, on either side of the Atlantic, are Sklar's (2011) *Landscapes of the Dark: History, Trauma, Psychoanalysis* and Fromm's (ed. 2012) *Lost in Transmission: Studies of Trauma Across Generations*. The latter collection of papers, in particular, goes some way to addressing Freud's own important but often ignored view that 'traumatic neurosis' is crucial in understanding catastrophic experience and the link between personal trauma and the social and political histories of the 20th century (Caruth 2014).

Additionally, the unconscious, much as it is freely and generatively used in psychotherapeutic work, cannot be observed and must be inferred or interpreted, potentially making it a problematic basis for clinical work and research. Critics of the unconscious have included Erich Fromm (1980) who himself helped to generate notions of the unconscious but described it as 'a mystification'. If I personally were to struggle towards formulating an "essence" of group analysis, it would probably begin in the realm of conscious, communicative here-and-now group processes and a consideration of what makes groups tick in an operational sense. Secondarily, this might include unconscious processes, possibly including a hypothetical construct of the "social unconscious". I would start in the spirit of what is observable and on the surface and move to what is hypothetical or hidden, a trajectory I regard as appropriate to clinical data, especially in groups, where even tracking the surface is difficult. This trajectory, from surface to depth, is described in greater detail by Ogden (1992).

However, it would be wrong to state that there are no attempts to relate the social unconscious to the clinical endeavour generally and group psychotherapy specifically. The problem is that generalized statements are more common than examples and that many of the examples quoted refer paradoxically to individuals rather than groups. So, in an article that explores the utility of the concept for clinical understanding, Parker's (2014) illustrations are all of individuals, and, while describing vividly the impact of the social unconscious (although she disputes the value of the actual term) on the lives of the individuals, there is limited sense of how this is embedded in their psychological treatment as a whole – and what difference the insight makes in the longer term. Similarly, where there are group examples of the social unconscious, these tend to be illustrative rather than geared to an evaluation of what can be done technically in the forging of a more robust psychotherapeutic process. Again, my emphasis on 'what can be done' reflects my background as a clinical psychologist but is also consistent with a health care culture that prioritizes outcomes, an emphasis that I agree has become has become obsessive and limiting in various respects but that cannot be dismissed or denied in the way that some analytic psychotherapists tend to do. One of the challenges to the group process and the conduct of groups is how to represent a hypothetical social unconscious, with its longitudinal perspective and its emphasis on the hidden, the denied and dissociated – all requiring an 'in-depth' focus – in the cut and thrust of the usual group process. I agree with Hopper's (2003) suggestion of adding a dimension of 'there and then' to Malan's 'triangle of insight' and the 'here and now' (Malan 1979). In chapter 6 on the development of the group therapist, I reinforce this point, but not without recognizing the difficulty of doing so in the largely 'here and now' dynamic of the group. Groups tend to move quickly from subject to subject and generally are best left free to develop spontaneously with their own rhythm and flow. How then to embrace in-depth notions of a social unconscious, particularly if pertaining to an individual group member – which can require considerable 'vertical' time to explore – is just one of the questions that need attention from proponents of this approach. Another is how social unconscious processes bind the group as a greater whole, whether in sub-groups or the entire group, a point which is explored in applied group analytic studies of cultural process (Hopper and Weinberg 2011) but which has not, to my knowledge, been sufficiently explicated in the clinical setting.

Adding to complexity about what group analysis is at the present time is the greatly increased emphasis on cultural studies linked to the foundation matrix in nations and ethnic groups. Important work is being done here on tracking notions of the social unconscious and there are some valuable and illuminating contributions (eg, Mojovic 2011, 2014). But this is a different field of inquiry from the immediate requirements of the psychotherapy group. Of course, some of the cultural insights feed back into the clinical inquiry, since our patients and we ourselves are all products of cultural history, but the focus of the cultural investigation is within a very different framework with different issues of responsibility and consequence. Can these approaches be reconciled? Tubert-Oklander and Hernandez-Tubert (2014), writing within the South American tradition of group analysis based on the work of Pichon-Riviere, refers to the importance of the group analytic approach as concerned very broadly with "human affairs", including the study of communities and societies. He also links the group psychotherapeutic endeavour directly to this broad undertaking, arguing that the methods of inquiry and intervention are very similar. Interesting as this idea might be, I am unsure about the conflation of the clinical with the cultural and I believe greater differentiation is required if group psychotherapy is to progress more fully in its own right, given its very different context and constraints.

Critical social thinking

I wish to address a strand of critical social thinking that is not particularly group analytic but has a bearing on our practice. This is where a social perspective of psychotherapy becomes politicized. This can happen in different ways, since power relations infuse all our work and institutional relations, but I am referring specifically to a group of authors (the Midlands Psychology Group, 2011) who present an explicit challenge to what they regard as the apparently apolitical stance of most psychotherapy, including group psychotherapy. They argue that this stance is misleading, that all therapy is inherently political in the same way that life, the positions we take as people and the problems we suffer, are inherently political. Power relations influence our therapeutic value systems, beliefs and actions in the same way that everyday life is under the sway of covert or overt power dynamics. From this arises a critical challenge to customary psychotherapeutic practice that ignores social and political influences, including the power therapists hold over patients. The aims of the "critical therapist" therefore would include assistance to patients in recognizing that their problems are not due to some inherent defect or disturbance of their own but a reflection of disordered social processes of which they are for the most part victims.

The authors noted above are critical of group psychotherapy in relation to these aspects of political awareness. Pilgrim (1992, quoted by the Midlands Psychology Group, 2011, page 12) describes " the movement from individual to group therapy as presenting an (unfulfilled) opportunity for therapists and clients to connect their individual distress with that of others and ultimately with their shared social and political environments". Totton (2011, p 20) describes both positive and negative aspects of the group as the voice of a shared social consciousness. He highlights his own experience of "transformative moments" in therapy groups when individual issues reveal their collective meaning but laments the times when the "personal, infantile components" of development, including a focus on the family, are emphasized. He considers this "rather mad, or at least dissociated."

These challenging views may indeed highlight the largely conservative nature of group psychotherapy – it is true that we work within a largely conventional frame of psychosocial attributions, including an emphasis on the family. However, it could be argued that group psychotherapy holds out the hope of a more questioning and discursive approach, strengthened by the presence of several people and their different perspectives: in many ways, group psychotherapy is the most social of all the therapies. The opportunity for clients to connect their distress with that of others, which Pilgrim advocates, is well recognized in group therapy and constitutes one of the major group therapeutic factors – "universality" (Yalom 1985). This itself may facilitate a greater potential for political awareness, especially recognition of the links between personal and social distress. I made this a key point in my formulation of a group psychotherapeutic approach to contemporary sexuality (Nitsun 2006). I have found that therapy groups are often questioning of orthodox norms concerning sexual diversity. For example, whereas society at large still has large pockets of prejudice about homosexuality and bisexuality, therapy groups, because of their diverse membership, are usually less convention bound and more facilitating of sexual difference.

While agreeing that groups are capable of challenging social norms, I disagree strongly with the Midlands Psychology Group's view that psychotherapy is invalid unless it subverts social influences. The group is limited in the extent to which it can tackle fundamental social attitudes. Time is limited and most patients seek a better life within existing circumstances rather than apprehending the impact of wider social processes or having the confidence to do anything about them. It can of course be argued that this type of passivity is itself a reflection of social dominance through the 'weakness' of the oppressed. But my sense of the many hundreds, if not thousands, of patients I have seen in the NHS is that, above all, they seek understanding and support on their terms, within the framework of their experience and how they understand the world.

Some 'radical' authors seem to appreciate these constraints. They agree that the "re-authoring" of personal narratives may be very difficult given that these narratives are so integral to the power relations of society and so deeply ingrained in individuals' identity. The problem arises, in my view, when the anti-psychotherapy sociopolitical view becomes so categorical that it rules out the value of any psychotherapy at all. Writers like Smail (2001) sometimes adopt this position, one I find undermining of the attempts of many people working against the odds in beleaguered NHS conditions, doing their best to give hope to the many patients seeking comfort in embattled worlds. While radical group analytic writers do not go as far as to recommend the dismantling of psychotherapy – if anything they follow psychotherapeutic traditions – the outer limits of the social perspective reveal, in my view, the danger of the social emphasis getting so carried away with itself, that we are left with an empty psychotherapeutic canvas, one which fails to recognize the often urgent requirements of the clinical subject and fails to meet the deep and complex needs of the individuals who come to us for help.

My concern is that the injunction against thinking about individuals and inner worlds creates a subtle but powerful pressure to underplay individual perspectives in a way which undermines rather than substantiates the clinical application of group analysis. In the next section I look at this more closely.

In defense of the individual

One of the crucial aspects of group analysis, I believe, particularly in relation to the clinical subject, is its view of individuality. Foulkes argued that once the ubiquitous influence of the social is recognized, the notion of the individual is redundant. In a social interpretation of human development, the so-called individual is a reflection of myriad social connections and the concept of an individual – and individual mind – fallacious. Group analysts frequently quote Foulkes' bold statement: "the individual is an abstraction". This statement has become reified, if not deified, in group analytic culture. To my mind, it is akin to

Margaret Thatcher's famous pronouncement "there is no such thing as society". As I see it, there are such things as both society and individuals and to deny either is problematic. However one conceives of individuality and society, however interpenetrating they are, however complex the epistemologies underlying them, both are representations that inhabit the experience of millions of people and that are the commonsensical perceptions of self and world that inform what patients make of their existence. Of course, the clinician may offer a different view – which is arguably what we are there to do – but this must be sufficiently within the patient's frame of reference to be intelligible. An individual arriving for a clinical consultation would be alarmed to think of him/herself as an abstraction. In his/ her mind, he/she is a living, breathing entity, the centre of a seething universe, a profound if troubled point of reference.

While the notion that the individual is an abstraction makes sense theoretically and is useful within debates about the origins of selfhood and identity, it is problematic once transferred to the consulting room. It is another example of the unresolved tension between group analytic theory and practice. From a clinical perspective, the individual is our core concern. We are accountable *to* the individual and *for* the individual. This applies to whatever treatment is provided, although in family therapy and couple therapy, which are natural groupings, our responsibility is extended beyond the individual. While I very much agree that the therapeutic power of group psychotherapy is the group itself (Lorentzen 2014, a), this in no way precludes our responsibility for the individual. Foulkes was under no illusion about this and, for all his emphasis on the social and the group as a whole, he was clear that the individual is the ultimate concern –

> "The group is treated solely for the benefit of its individual members and its efficiency can only be gauged by the extent to which it becomes an efficient instrument for the treatment process"
>
> (Foulkes and Anthony 1967, 32–34)

Lorentzen (2014, b), in perhaps the most thorough research study to date of group analytic psychotherapy, also concludes that a greater focus on individual goals would improve group therapy outcomes.

I wish to reinforce the validity and power of the patient's own perspective in the light of what I consider to be the non-clinical emphasis on social process in group analysis. In some respects, the marginalization of the individual voice through the notion of the individual as "an abstraction" could be regarded as a political act in itself. The fact that a particular individual's voice might not hold a political view in the broad sense and is more concerned with personal suffering and the circumstances of their life does not mean it has no validity on the scale of therapeutic meaning and values. In the same way that individual preoccupations may obscure wider and larger social concerns, so a preoccupation with the wider social sphere may obscure the subjectivity of the individual, which, for all its limitations, is the point of reference to which we return in our clinical work again and again.

It is quite commonly held that emphasis on the individual and the intra-psychic is a defense against the social and a full recognition of the power of the social (Stacey 2003). But, given how difficult the clinical can be, particularly when dealing with the overwhelming and often disturbing immediacy of the psychotherapy group, how much is the emphasis on the social a defense against the personal? How much is there a retreat, or flight, into either abstract theory, or social processes, or the unconscious past, from the traumatic impact of the present? Defenses usually do not go just one way. A defense against the social is the mirror image of a defense against the personal.

I (Nitsun 2006) have previously written about what I call the "clinical imagination". I formulated the term as a way of highlighting a particular way of thinking that I regard as inherent in the clinical task. This stands in contrast to what might be called the theoretical imagination, or the social imagination, or indeed the political imagination. To summarize, I suggest the following as parameters of the clinical imagination –

- what matters is the patient not the theory
- the patient's subjectivity is key
- the patient's own sense of individuality is irrefutable
- the patient experiences him/herself as the centre of their own suffering
- what matters is what works clinically rather than what works theoretically
- what works is determined empirically and not through impression or bias
- what works clinically offers a self-correcting loop – we observe and we modify
- social factors are important but so are intra-psychic, interpersonal, biological and broader environmental processes.

I realize that in some respects I may be setting up a straw man. I am sure that most group analysts, even those who are particularly socially orientated, would agree that the 'individuality' of the patient must be respected, even if they prefer not to use the term, in so far as he/she needs to be understood in their own right, has access to appropriate care and entrusts us with his/her own personal care. But my point is echoed in sociological debates themselves arguing that a predominantly social emphasis compromises an understanding of the individual in his/her own right, within the sphere of *their* world-view: their singularity. Roseneil (2013), amongst others, notes how this potentially closes down the possibility of accounting for the lived experience of singularity, the particularity of subjectivity that is germane to the individual. If this is a problem at a sociological level, how much more is it a problem in clinical work? It is a problem that goes to the heart of psychotherapeutic practice.

Example

Returning to the issue of the social unconscious, I wish to highlight the ways in which individuals are not simply subject to the same generalized social trauma but generate their own unique responses. We could take almost any well-known, catastrophic trauma that has in some way been denied or dissociated and show how very differently people respond to the same situation. But I bring an example from my own NHS practice some years ago:

The presenting patient was a 37 year-old mixed race man, D, who had suffered from depression and substance misuse since late adolescence. He described a traumatic family background. His father was white British and his mother Indian. The marriage had taken place against the strict disapproval of his mother's parents and wider family. The family was deeply hierarchical and the mother, as a female and one of the youngest children, had been treated virtually as a slave by the rest of the family, frequently beaten and expected to carry a large burden of responsibility for daily domestic chores. She had immigrated with her family to England in the 1970's and found herself exposed to a freer culture with different conceptions of women's rights and roles. In defiance of her family, she married a white British man. For years she attempted to forge some reconciliation with her family and there were periods of some rapprochement. But, as she started having children, the difficulties exacerbated and she found herself estranged from both her family and community. She became depressed after the birth of her third child, her depression not lifting for some years and she ended up committing suicide when the patient D (the second child) was age 15. The father had taken to drink early in the marriage and had also serially abused the children. At the age of 46, five years after his wife's death, he died during a heart attack.

Soon after D's first appointment with me, his older brother (47) telephoned to ask if he and his sister (33) could come to see me. Recognizing the serious family disturbance in the case, I agreed, suggesting that we meet together with D. The meeting took place and, while there are many aspects that could be explored, including the siblings' unexpected solidarity in coming together as a group and their attempts to inform me of how they understood the situation, what I particularly want to share is the very different trajectories that the three siblings' lives had taken. The older brother A was the most successful. Identifying himself mainly as Asian, he had married a woman of the same persuasion, had two children and had a successful technology business. The younger sister R had sought a mainly white identity and had established herself as a hairdresser but experienced conflict and confusion in her sense of self and had found it difficult to sustain heterosexual relationships. She admitted to periods of depression. D, the presenting patient, had suffered most, describing an early sense of isolation that led him to drugs from a young age. His sense of a social identity was extremely confused, he had slipped between feeling black and white racially and had a painful sense of not belonging anywhere.

The social influences on this family are abundantly clear, but the point I wish to emphasize is the individual ways in which the three siblings responded to the explicit trauma of their parents' death and the barely known, half-concealed trauma their mother had suffered as an abused child and later an abused adult. While gender and birth order may have played their part in these differences, and specific family dynamics are likely to have influenced the particular roles the siblings took, there were clearly different strengths and vulnerabilities in the three siblings, different ways of dealing with identity and choice, different ways of relating to their communities. All these factors, I suggest, were probably underpinned by different genetic and constitutional proclivities, different physical make-up and – very important – different intra-psychic constellations of what it meant to grow up in such an embattled and traumatized family. I would argue that what determined the three very different pathways was not simply the social trauma, whether conscious or unconscious, but the particular internal representations each had made for and of themselves in relation to their social history. Each constellation generated a distinctly different individual that both subsumed and surpassed the social trauma.

A response to the above might be 'of course, individuals are different – as proponents of the social unconscious we are not suggesting otherwise'. I would respect this response but would continue to argue for the imprint of individuality that intersects at every point with the social in general and the social unconscious in particular. I would argue particularly for the existence of an inner world and an intra-psychic configuration that may indeed mirror aspects of the social but is informed by what makes us all social *and* individual. The task in clinical work, I suggest, is to identify this intersecting point between individual and social and not to fall back on the dogma dictated by each separately.

The impact of post-modernity

While considering the problematic potentially created by the social emphasis in group analysis, coupled with the decentration of the individual, it is instructive to consider the philosophical and epistemological basis of this way of thinking. It seems clear to me that the social perspective is as ideologically rooted and derived from as dominant a value system as the thinking that it criticizes. Hence, the social emphasis in group analysis, particularly when it places the notion of the individual under duress, is itself contextually positioned in a way that requires interrogation. The dominant philosophy to which I refer is a post-modern mentality with its emphasis on the deconstruction of the individual subject. Although the challenge of post-modernity may not be as pronounced now as it was in the late 20th Century, or not felt in the same way, it seems to me that much of the "radical" thinking in group analysis was a direct expression of these critiques, a reflection of the intellectual climate of the late twentieth century. I suggest that this requires re-evaluation in a post-postmodern context.

In order to explore this further, I draw on a helpful paper by Finlay (1997) outlining the post-modern tradition and the challenges it poses to psychoanalytic psychotherapy. Finlay notes that both the theories and practices of post-modernism pose a direct challenge to psychotherapeutic discourse, particularly therapies which base themselves on the analysis of an individual subject and which use the 'hermeneutic practice" of interpretation as an essential medium. Finlay suggests that at least three principles of postmodernism threaten the foundations of psychoanalytic psychotherapy: 1) the decentering, disintegration and death of the centred subject; 2) the historical and cultural relativization of the concept of the subject and of the human sciences; and 3) the crisis of representation.

Space does not allow a discursive analysis of these principles but I would like to highlight the notion that the subject is "dead", that it no longer exists as an entity, that it is no longer the source of discourse but "a fragmented product of dispersed discourses" (Finlay 1997). In this view, the integrity of the individual subject is not ontologically given but entirely historically and environmentally contingent. There is no absolute presence. The individual subject is thus rendered superfluous and the fields of study and knowledge that developed to understand the subject become as superfluous. As Finlay points out, this poses a major challenge to any individually centred approach, such as psychoanalysis.

The same point about the disintegration of the individual subject in the face of postmodern deconstruction exactly mirrors the situation I regard as so problematic in group practice. Group analysts who emphasize this viewpoint appear, wittingly or unwittingly, to endorse a postmodern perspective. Foulkes himself, interestingly, may be regarded as an early postmodernist in his assertion that "the individual is an abstraction", although he continued to focus on individuals in many of his published clinical reports.

In many ways I agree with the postmodern stance and welcome its challenge to many of the assumptions about individuality, including notions of inherent psychopathology and systems of categorization such as the DSM 111 that in my view over-diagnose and over-pathologize individual difference. I emphasized this point in my writing on sexuality and desire in the group where I argued for the relativization of sexual desire, preference and pathology (Nitsun 2006). The problem is when the postmodern ethos clashes with the clinical perspective in psychotherapy, if not all of health care. The whole notion of outcome evaluation relies on notions of individuality, including individual progress, individual sensibility and individual health. No clinical approach, in my view, can afford to lose sight of the individual. A psychotherapeutic approach that eschews notions of individuality runs the risk of losing its ground and undermining its own foundations.

The challenge is not to jettison the wisdom of postmodernism. The crucial lesson concerns the importance of social / historical context and in my view this is indisputable. However, the question is how we reconcile the individual subject with a deeper contextual inquiry. Not to take account of context would, in my view, be irresponsible, but to alter the clinical perspective in a way that marginalizes the individual in favour of the social, is, in my view, equally irresponsible.

Ways forward

Throughout this chapter, I have emphasized the need to strengthen the theory-practice link in group analysis and to position group psychotherapy more strongly in an ambivalent if not hostile environment. In this last section I make some suggestions, not in any grand, comprehensive way but by offering some ideas, within the framework I espouse that recognizes both the social and the individual.

Research

I have deliberately excluded research as a focus in this chapter as it is largely outside my remit but I agree fully with the general view that research in the group analytic field has in some ways just begun, with the positive consequence that there is a great potential. This is where the weakness in the theory-practice link could be addressed more fully, exploring theoretical implications for practice and how they are born out in the process of research. Part of the problem is the rigid expectation of what constitutes acceptable empirical data, the field until recently dominated by the randomized controlled trial as the "gold standard" of research (Grossman and MacKenzie, 2005). Group psychotherapy has been particularly disadvantaged here, given its complex character as a treatment modality serving several people in the same setting, creating more confounding variables than is usual in psychotherapy research. There are encouraging signs of change in the research culture that may be of benefit here, however, offering new opportunities in the understanding of the treatment effects of group process and the development of theory linked to clinical research. That the time is ripe for this sort of development is richly supported in a valuable article by Greene (2012) on new research perspectives in group psychotherapy. Greene notes a spirit of challenge to the hegemony of the RCT. A groundswell of opinion highlights the limitations of data yielded by RCT's, not only the questionable significance of data generated on such a broad scale but the lack of relevance to core clinical issues concerning change and the individual variations in clinical outcome. A "new generation of research", according to Greene, moves towards a closer examination of what happens in the consulting room, using direct experience to clarify some of the major issues that preoccupy clinicians, either as an end in itself or as a pathway through to RCT's that are more linked to clinical reality and therefore possibly more generalizable and useful on a broader stage. In London, two networks of group analytic practitioners have recently come together to attempt some basic evaluation of our group psychotherapy data – the Fitzrovia Group Analytic Practice (where I work privately) and the Group Analytic Network, London are joining forces to establish a framework for clinical audit that will hopefully continue and strengthen in the future. Early results are promising.

Professional links

Another idea concerns greater openness to other disciplines. Group analysts working in the NHS have opportunities to meet a wide-range of mental health professionals and psychological therapists of different persuasions. I suggest there is the potential here to develop more active and productive links. This would not only counter the tendency of analytically orientated therapists to isolate themselves, or to be seen by others to be doing so, but would have the value of collaboration and cross-fertilization. In chapter 4 on group analysis and CBT, I describe my own efforts to cross the divide between group analysis and more mainstream psychological approaches, including devising a training course on group methods for IAPT psychologists. This has been a useful way of both encouraging the wider application of group work in the NHS and of spreading the influence of group analysis in areas in which it is unknown and unrecognized. In this way, a group analytic approach becomes accepted not through theoretical argument or persuasion but by demonstrating its value in areas that are a major priority in the NHS environment. While I speak of the NHS, I am sure that there are equivalent possibilities in other settings. A parallel development has been the creation in recent years of new training courses at the Institute of Group Analysis in London that are aimed at group psychotherapists in general, people working in public services seeking generic skills in group work rather than long-term specialist analytic training. This approach tends to arouse fears of diffusion in diehard practitioners: the cherished practices of old might be weakened and undermined. I personally believe that these fears are counter-balanced by the advantages of actively forging links with other disciplines and therapeutic approaches and thereby achieving a wider sphere of credibility and influence.

Practical tools

Two areas of potential development focus more directly on strengthening the clinical application of group analysis. One is assessment for group psychotherapy and its implications for selection. *Assessment for group*, in my view, remains one of the most problematic aspects of our work. There is still a dearth of writing and research on this crucial aspect and on how assessment mirrors people's actual participation in groups. *Preparation for group* membership, in my view, is also under-developed. All too often, especially in the hurly-burly of the NHS with its time pressures, patients are placed in groups with minimal preparation. The experience of an unstructured group, with all its ambiguities and uncertainties, can then be extremely anxiety provoking and I suspect that the significant drop-out rate in NHS groups is at least in part a consequence of inadequate preparation. Further, it is not only patients who need to be prepared. As mentioned by Sharpe (1995), we have a responsibility to the organizational context in so far as the patient entering a group affects others in the treatment network and it behooves us to communicate clearly to other staff what group psychotherapy involves and how the patient's problems will be addressed.

It is necessary to recognize the anti-group in patients as well as staff in the treatment team. It seems to me a folly to assume sufficient motivation that translates into regular and committed group attendance. Fears and suspicions about groups, in my experience, are readily evoked when a patient joins a group and it may be a mistake to ignore this in the hope that it will go away. I have previously proposed the notion of a *group template*: we each have a set of constructs and beliefs about groups based on our historical experience of groups, starting in the family group (Nitsun 1996). This template remains operative through life, influencing the person's relationship to groups, usually in a self-perpetuating way, so that fantasies and anxieties about groups are reinforced through actual experience in groups. This includes anti-group representations and their roots in a hypothetical social unconscious. I suggest that recognition of patients' *group template* as linked to their *group history* may facilitate pre-group assessment as well as enabling a more constructive entry into group therapy.

A final suggestion for the way forward reflects my afore-going emphasis on the individual. While the literature on group analysis proposes a variety of group developmental models, what is missing is a sense of *individual development from a group perspective*. In other words, how do we view an individual's developmental history from the point of view of the group? What does it mean to grow up as an individual who of necessity belongs to a primary group such as the family, as well as the range of groups he/she will encounter in their life trajectory? Having a more detailed sense of this developmental journey would equip us with 1) a better understanding of the link between individual and group developmental processes, 2) a deeper appreciation of the variety of problems and pathologies that might emerge in the individual-group configuration, akin to Friedman's (2007) relational disorders, 3) a firmer knowledge base on which to assess an individual's suitability for group treatment, (and the group's suitability for the patient), 4) an increased potential to predict that individual's behaviour in the psychotherapy group and 5) a greater ability to appreciate how that person's group template will influence the dynamic of a particular psychotherapy group. In a sense, I suggest standing the usual developmental vantage point on its head: looking at the individual through the lens of the group, group history and group relationships, rather than the other way round, but maintaining the individual as the prime focus. I suggest that a model based on the above would be a valuable tool in strengthening the clinical application of group psychotherapy.

Summary

To summarize, this chapter began with reflections on the vulnerable state of psychotherapy in the NHS and the particular challenges facing group analytic psychotherapy. The question of survival looms large: will group therapy withstand the increasing funding crises and the cultural shift away from both analytically orientated and long-term approaches? I am attempting to reclaim some of the lost or nearly-lost ground that group analysis has sustained in the clinical sphere. To some extent group analysis may be the victim of its own success, given the expansion of theory and its applications in diverse directions. But the core clinical subject, in my view, may have been lost to view. I have referred to this as the *decentering of the clinical subject* and attempted to formulate a *clinical imagination* that would give priority to the individual. In parallel there have been difficulties in the area of research, at least partly because groups are such complex subject matter for research. But there are promising signs of change. I make some additional suggestions for the way forward, including a greater openness to working with other disciplines and fields of clinical inquiry, so as to counter the tendency towards isolationism in analytic psychotherapies. I also raise the question of formulating a theory of individual development based on a group perspective that might provide a better framework for assessment for group therapy and a stronger predictive basis for participants' entry into group treatment. Finally, I reflect on the anti-group processes inherent in the push-pull development of group analytic psychotherapy and how this is entrained in the problematic dialectic of idealization and denigration of the group.

References

Anzieu, D (1984) *The Group and the Unconscious*. London: Routledge and Kegan Paul.

Bion, W. F. (1961) *Experiences in Groups*. London: Tavistock.

Blackmore, C., Tantam, M., Parry, G. and Chambers, E. (2012) Report on a systematic review of the efficacy and clinical effectiveness of group analysis and analytic/dynamic group psychotherapy, *Group Analysis*, 45, 46–69.

Bowden, M. (2002) Anti-group attitudes at assessment for psychotherapy, *Psychoanalytic Psychotherapy*, 16, 246–58.

Brown, D. (1985) Bion and Foulkes: basic assumptions and beyond, in Pines, M. (ed.) *Bion and Group Psychotherapy*. London: Routledge and Kegan Paul.

Brown, D. and Zinkin, L. (eds) (1994) *The Psyche and the Social World: Developments in Group-Analytic Theory*. London: Routledge.

Campbell, J. (2010) The islands of the blest, *Group Analysis*, 43, 413–32.

Dalal, F. (1998) Taking the Group Seriously. London: Karnac.

Dies, R. R. (1992) Models of group psychotherapy: sifting through confusion, *International Journal of Group Psychotherapy*, 42, 1–17.

Einhorn, S. (2010) Response to a love letter: May 2010, *Group Analysis*, 43, 433–9.

Finlay, M. (1997) Post-modernizing psychoanalysis/psychoanalyzing post-modernity, Paper presented at After Post-modernism Conference 1997, McGill University/The Focusing Institute.

Foulkes, S. H. (1964) *Therapeutic Group Analysis*. London: Allen and Unwin.

Foulkes, S. H. and Anthony, E. J. (1967 [1957]) *Group Psychotherapy: The Psychoanalytic Approach*. Middlesex: Pelican Books.

Freud, S. (1921) *Group Psychology and the Analysis of the Ego*, SE 18, London: Hogarth Press, 1953–74.

Friedman, R. (2007) Supervising group analysis: a relations disorder perspective, *Group Analysis*, 40, 250–68.

Fromm, E. (1980) *Beyond the Chains of Freedom: My Encounter with Marx and Freud*. London: Sphere Books.

Gans, J. S. (2010) *Difficult Topics in Group Psychotherapy*. London: Karnac.

Garland, C. (2010) *The Groups Book: Psychoanalytic Group Therapy: Principles and Practices*. London: Karnac.

Greene, L. R. (2012, 9 July) Group therapist as social scientist, with special reference to the psychodynamically oriented psychotherapist, *American Psychologist*. Advance online publication; doi: 10.1037/a0029147.

Grossman, J. and MacKenzie, F. J. (2005) The randomized controlled trial: gold standard, or merely standard? *Perspectives in Biology and Medicine*, 48, 516–34.

Holmes, J. and Bateman, A. (eds) (2002) *Integration in Psychotherapy: Models and Methods*. New York: Oxford University Press.

Hopper, E. (2012) Book reviews: *The Uninvited Guest from the Unremembered Past* (Coles, 2011) and *We Remember: Child Survivors of the Holocaust Speak* (Child Survivors Association of Great Britain, 2011), *Group Analysis*, 45, 394–5.

Hopper, E. and Weinberg, H. (2011) *The Social Unconscious in Persons, Groups and Societies, vol. 1*. London: Karnac.

Karterud, S. W. (1992) Reflections on group-analytic research, *Group Analysis*, 125, 353–64.

Kernberg, O. F. (1998) Institutional problems of psychoanalytic education, in *Ideology, Conflict and Leadership in Groups and Organizations*. New Haven: Yale University Press.

Kohut, H. (1971) *The Analysis of Self*. New York: International Universities Press.

Lawes, A. E. (2000) The generality of hypothetico-deductive reasoning – making scientific thinking explicit, *American Biology Teacher*, 62, 482–95.

Linke, S. and Nitsun, M. (2012) Group therapeutic factors in mindfulness-based therapy, Paper submitted for publication.

Lorentzen, S. (2010) Some ideas on how group analysis can survive: response to lecture by Jane Campbell, *Group Analysis*, 43, 450–64.

Lorentzen, S. (2014) *Group Analytic Psychotherapy: Working with Affective, Anxiety and Personality Disorders*. London: Routledge.

Lorentzen, S., Ruud T., Fjeldstad, A. and Hoglend, P. (2014) Comparison of short-term and long-term dynamic group psychotherapy: a randomized clinical trial, *British Journal of Psychiatry*, 203, 280–87.

Midlands Psychology Group (2011) Psychotherapy and politics: uncomfortable bedfellows? *Group Analytic Contexts*, 54, 9–16.

Mojovic, M. (2011) Manifestations of psychic retreats in social systems, in Hopper, E. and Weinberg, H. (eds) (2011) *The Social Unconscious in Persons, Groups, and Societies*. London: Karnac.

Mojovic, M., Despotovic, T. and Sataric, J. (2014) 'Conception trauma' of group analysis in Serbia, *Group Analysis*, 47, 113–27.

Nitsun, M. (1996) *The Anti-group: Destructive Forces in the Group and their Therapeutic Potential.* London: Routledge.

Nitsun, M., Stapleton, J. H. and Bender, M. P. (1974) Movement and drama therapy with long-stay schizophrenics, *British Journal of Medical Psychology*, 47, 101–19.

Parker, V. (2014) An exploration of the concept of the social unconscious and its application to clinical understanding, *Group Analysis*, 47, 30–41.

Pick, D. (2012) *The Pursuit of the Nazi Mind.* Oxford: Oxford University Press.

Pilgrim, D. (1992) Psychotherapy and political evasions. In Dryden, W. and Feltham, C. (eds) *Psychotherapy and its Discontents.* London: Sage.

Roseneil, S. (2013) Beyond 'the relationship between the individual and society': broadening and deepening relational thinking in group analysis, *Group Analysis*, 46(2), 196–210.

Ryan, M., Nitsun, M., Gilbert, l. and Mason, H. (2005) A prospective study of the effectiveness of group and individual psychotherapy for women CSA survivors, *Psychology and Psychotherapy: Theory, Research and Practice*, 78, 465–80.

Sharpe, M. (1995) Training of supervisors, in Sharpe, M. (ed.) *The Third Eye: Supervision of Analytic Groups.* London: Routledge.

Singer, J. L. (1980) The scientific basis of psychotherapeutic practice: a question of values and ethics, *Psychotherapy: Theory, Research and Practice*, 17, 372–83.

Skynner, R. (1983) Group analysis and family therapy, in Pines, M. (ed.) *The Evolution of Group Analysis.* London: Routledge.

Smail, D. (2001) *The Nature of Unhappiness.* London: Robinson.

Stacey, R. D. (2003) *Complexity and Group Processes.* Hove: Brunner-Routledge.

Steiner, R. (1985) Some thoughts about tradition and change arising from an examination of the British Psychoanalytic Society's controversial discussions (1943–1944), *International Journal of Psychoanalysis*, 12, 27–71.

Thygesen, B. (2010) The islands of the blest or Fahrenheit 451. Response to lecture by Jane Campbell, *Group Analysis*, 43, 440–9.

Totton, N. (2011) Psychotherapy and politics: is there an alternative? *Group-Analytic Contexts*, 54, 17–21.

Tubert-Oklander, J. and Hernandez-Tubert, R. (2014) The social unconscious and the large group part 1: the British and the Latin American positions, *Group Analysis*, 47, 99–112.

Yalom, I. B. and Leszcz, M. (2005) *Theory and Practice of Group Psychotherapy.* New York: Basic Books.

Young, J. E., Klosko, J. S. and Weishar, M. E. (2003) *Schema Therapy: A Practitioner's Guide.* New York: The Guilford Press.

Chapter 4

Group analysis and cognitive-behavioural therapy (CBT)

In this chapter I go out on a limb to look at two psychotherapeutic approaches that are regarded as virtually opposite. To some degree, I also deviate from the case I made in the previous chapter for greater theoretical coherence within group psychotherapy by considering the relevance for group analysis of a very different therapeutic philosophy. My focus though is not so much, or not only, on theoretical integration as it is on the political and practical implications of psychotherapeutic distance versus psychotherapeutic convergence. There is a largely egocentric view in much clinical practice. Most if not all psychotherapeutic disciplines have a solipsistic view of what constitutes meaningful psychotherapy. They are bound by their own belief systems and institutional practices and their investment in the survival of their own cultures and professional practices. But by so doing, I suggest that they risk estrangement from the broader field of psychological therapies and paradoxically weaken their own position. I wish to challenge this aspect of group analysis and do so by describing the very different approach of CBT – and the advantages of looking at it from a non-prejudiced perspective.

Introduction

This chapter considers two very different psychotherapeutic approaches, group analytic psychotherapy and cognitive behaviour therapy (CBT), within the same clinical frame. By bringing together two such different disciplines, my intention is to open a debate about psychotherapeutic discourse, questioning the way in which different therapies are relegated to separate universes and what this does to the overall field of practice. By contrasting the value systems, assumptions and methods that inform the two approaches I seek to interrogate the often rigid categories that inform our work. This is at a time of both pressure and fragmentation in the psychological therapies when there is a need for mutual understanding and rapprochement. On the surface, group analysis and CBT would appear to be the unlikeliest of bedfellows, coming from very different traditions. Juxtaposing them within the same frame highlights some major differences. At the same time, there are unexpected connections between the two, particularly when it comes to what actually happens in psychotherapy, as opposed to the ideology and rhetoric sometimes associated with 'purity' and 'professionalism' in the psychotherapies. In the overall spirit of convergence and integration that marks much of psychotherapeutic development in the last few decades, I aim to consider possible areas of overlap and linkage between CBT and group analysis that challenge notions of therapeutic exclusivity and difference. This may be a fruitless exercise in the eyes of some who wish to adhere to strict institutionalized notions of psychotherapeutic identity and difference but I suggest that it is important to approach the subject with an open mind and to consider what might emerge positively from the comparison.

Two characteristics mark the ascendance of CBT in the last few decades. The first is the worldwide spread of CBT as the evidence-based 'treatment of choice', offering seemingly effective short-term treatment for a wide range of psychological problems. This is particularly the case in western countries, where the development of CBT has coincided with a greatly increased demand for psychological therapy, severe pressure on public funding and a cultural leaning towards brief solution-focused therapies. The second characteristic is the controversy surrounding the implementation of CBT on a large scale, its proponents strongly matched by its critics and detractors. This ranges from the mild to the vehement, a great deal of resentment being directed at those funding and promoting CBT services, those arguing its merits and those practising it: indeed the entire culture and epistemology surrounding the theory and practice of CBT. The field is racked by polarization around these issues, an emergent 'them' and 'us' or 'pro-CBT' and 'anti-CBT' dichotomy that fuels arguments and debates (House and Lowenthal 2008).

Group analysis, as I see it, may have joined in on the 'anti-CBT' front. Where group analysts refer to CBT, in both public discourse and publications, it can be in pejorative terms. In public lectures I have attended in London in recent years, the presenters expressed some degree of disdain for CBT. These views were shared with audiences of hundreds of people and, if unchallenged, may be regarded as representing the majority view in group analysis. But, while the theme of CBT hegemony was subsidiary to the main lecture theme in these cases, the public rejection of CBT values and principles reflects a position that is emblematic of most present-day analytic, non-CBT psychotherapies and that merits exploration in its own right. The anti-CBT lobby probably signifies the understandable anxiety about survival that is common to psychodynamic psychotherapies at the present time and that is readily linked to CBT as the perceived opposition, siphoning funding, professional support and public goodwill away from analytic psychotherapy. But how this concern is addressed and what implications it has for inter-disciplinary relations is another matter – and not a subsidiary one.

Group analysts in any case may wish to question the nature of professional rivalry and dichotomy, generating a culture that promotes rigid allegiances and allows for little if any divergence. These are often based on stereotypes and misconceptions that are seldom open to question, creating cultures of intolerance and opposition. As I see it, the overall psychotherapy field, particularly the analytic approaches, has not been served well by these splits. Funders and managers of services are quick to pick up the splits and not unusually, in my experience, make adverse judgements of the whole field. Analytic psychotherapists in the NHS have been commonly seen as insular, out of touch, obsessed with minor differences and putting psychotherapeutic hegemony ahead of real concerns about funding, legitimacy and accessibility of service: in particular, being deaf to what clients value, want and benefit from. Inability – or unwillingness – on the part of psychoanalytic psychotherapists to engage with these issues, rather than sheer ignorance and irrational aggression on managers' parts – I suggest – is in some measure responsible for the recent attacks on psychotherapy in the NHS and the traumatic loss of funding. I must be careful not to generalize though: I am probably reflecting an extreme rather than typical situation but unfortunately it is the extreme that makes the strongest impression and is most easily remembered.

I come to this task via many years of experience as a clinical psychologist in the NHS where I have straddled the fields of psychology and psychotherapy and for approximately three decades was the head of a large NHS psychological service which represented therapists from all the major persuasions, including psychoanalytic, group analytic, systemic and cognitive-behavioural therapies. My own professional role in the last decade has been more as a specialist myself, becoming consultant psychologist in group psychotherapy in a London NHS trust. My group analytic training has had a strong influence on my work. However, in both incarnations of my NHS career I have had considerable contact with CBT practitioners and have had to consider the merits of CBT in the context of high demand for psychological help in large, underprivileged and under-resourced communities. More recently, I developed a particular interest in *Group Cognitive-Behaviour Therapy (GCBT)*, which is a much newer field than individual CBT, and shows promise as an effective addition to services (Bieling *et al.* 2006). This culminated in my convening the Diploma in CBT and Innovative Group Approaches at the Anna Freud Centre, London, which is now in its third year. The success of the course has not only enlarged my contact with CBT as a discipline but has also confirmed my interest in this as an area of possible convergence, reinforcing my belief that the psychotherapies have much to learn from each other. I could see that group analysis had something to offer group CBT but also that aspects of CBT were not as foreign to group analysis as might be supposed. The course has also given me an opportunity to explore newer and exploratory group approaches in the 'innovative' aspects of the curriculum. This draws together a number of people in the UK who are innovating group methods in a range of community settings, sometimes but not always within a CBT framework.

This chapter has several aims:

- an outline of the main criticisms of CBT;
- an understanding of CBT for non-CBT practitioners;
- addressing some of the commonly held prejudices and misconceptions about CBT;
- comparing the different epistemological bases of group analysis and CBT;

- suggesting areas of similarity between the two disciplines;
- assessing the implications for clinical practice of a more inclusive view of both CBT and group analysis.

Criticisms of CBT

Before embarking on an account of what CBT actually is, it may be useful to outline some of the main criticisms of CBT. This will help to orientate the analysis and discussion that follows, highlighting the particular concerns and anxieties generated by CBT in the wider psychotherapeutic milieu. I suggest that some criticism may be justified but that equally that some of it derives from lack of familiarity with the field and the stereotypes and misunderstandings that then arise, especially where there are powerful vested interests one way or the other: either pro-CBT or anti-CBT. Since CBT is perceived as a threat in the anxious atmosphere concerning the future of dynamic psychotherapies, it is understandable that there is some persistence of negative attitudes towards CBT. But let us consider what these attitudes are. I highlight the following criticisms, to a large degree confirmed in a comprehensive and thoughtful work by House and Lowenthal (2008), aptly titled *Against and For CBT*:

1   CBT is a totalizing approach that has marginalized other psychotherapies and undermined healthy diversity in the psychotherapeutic field (Samuels 2008).
2   It is a mechanistic, superficial therapy that totally lacks depth: 'a quick fix for the soul' (Leader 2008).
3   The evidence base it proclaims is spurious, reflecting an over-valuation of randomized controlled trials and a neglect of other research evidence and clinical data (House and Lowenthal 2008).
4   It is a solipsistic approach that disregards other psychological therapies.
5   It is highly directive, formulaic approach that takes no account of the patient's views.
6   It fails to address concerns about power in the therapeutic relationship, cultivating client compliance rather than autonomy. It is in need of 'an ethical stance so as avoid domination and abuse' (Proctor 2008).
7   It has become an agent of social control and its success reflects a cynical form of 'social engineering' (Guilfoyle 2008).
8   The therapeutic relationship is ignored and there is a particular avoidance of therapist subjectivity (Samuels 2008).
9   There is silence about major existential and psychotherapeutic concerns, such as meaning and purpose (Samuels 2008).
10   It is a purely technique-based therapy that requires little training and experience.

What is CBT?

CBT can be summarized as a form of talking therapy that focuses on the individual's assumptions, beliefs and thought processes and the way these maintain disturbing emotions, dysfunctional behaviour and problematic relationships. Through systematic reappraisal of the patterns that link thoughts to feelings and behaviour, the therapy aims to develop more constructive psychological functioning. The therapy is usually structured and mainly short-term, the number of sessions averaging ten. It provides directive input but emphasizes the patient's own construction of reality and depends on a collaborative relationship between therapist and patient. The patient is encouraged to participate actively in the therapy, often in the form of behavioural and social experiments as well as monitoring of thoughts, feelings and mood. Although it tends to be disorder specific, and has evolved treatments that are tailored to specific disturbances, the CBT model of psychopathology is based on learning and reinforcement rather than assumptions about normality and deviance. As such, it may be amongst the least pathologizing of therapeutic approaches. There is a strong emphasis on outcome evaluation and the patient's subjective sense of change and improvement is given high credence. Originally conceived for particular problems, especially anxiety and depression, CBT has increasingly been applied to a wide range of conditions, in fact probably the entire gamut of psychological difficulties ranging from problems of self-esteem to borderline and psychotic disorders, from learning difficulties to sexual problems, and from mild communication problems to hallucinations and delusions. It is used in individual, group, couple and family formats (Datillio 2010; Epstein and Baucomb 2002) and has well-developed applications to problems across the life-cycle, from infants and children to older adults (Stallard 2005; Rogers 2010).

CBT is distinguished from most other psychological therapies by having a strong evidence base. This has led to it being regarded as the treatment of choice in many clinical settings, particularly public services where there are significant funding and resource constraints and where there is close scrutiny of the use of funds. But the evidence-based aspect of CBT has been the subject of much controversy, commentators frequently questioning the basis of the research and the assumptions about research evidence (House and Lowenthal 2008). CBT has to some extent addressed these criticisms. This has led to notions of *practice-based evidence* (Barkham *et al.* 2010) alongside *evidence-based practice* and an increased use of qualitative alongside quantitative data within CBT. The approach has also, over the years, become more flexible and inclusive, incorporating ideas associated with approaches as divergent as gestalt therapy and interpersonal psychotherapy (Harwood *et al.* 2010)

Historical perspectives – the origins and development of CBT

CBT was started in the USA in the mid-1970s by Aaron Beck, a psychoanalyst who had become disaffected by traditional psychoanalytic theory and practice, particularly concerning the length of the treatment and the sometimes less than impressive outcomes (Beck *et al.* 1979). Beck brought together the two previously separate streams of behavioural and cognitive psychology, offering a paradigm that combined the previous emphasis on learned behaviour with the insights of cognitive psychology. The integrated cognitive-behavioural approach quickly became influential and popular, not only providing a short-term practical approach to psychological problems but lending itself more readily to empirical research than most other forms of therapy. With an accumulating evidence base, CBT began to capture some of the ground previously held by more psychodynamic and humanistic therapies, eventually becoming the dominant psychological therapy in services across the world. In the UK, where there was an active CBT presence from its earliest days, with major contributions to the evolution of CBT, the approach found a particularly welcoming home in the NHS with its mounting funding pressures and escalating demands for treatment. This was reinforced by the establishment of the NICE (National Institute of Clinical Excellence) guidelines for evidence-based practice, highlighting approaches that had generated convincing research evidence of efficacy and effectiveness and differentiating these from approaches that did not (although within the narrow framework of randomized controlled trials: the subject of much criticism).

The spread of CBT in the UK in the last decade or two was strongly boosted by the Layard Report of 2008, in which Richard Layard, a senior health minister at the time, underscored the value of evidence-based psychological treatments as a basis for developing widespread services at the primary care level of the NHS. The report advocated the funding of these services on an unprecedented scale and made a significant impact on the Labour government of the time. In due course, the plan generated funding worth millions of pounds and a national network of services was set up under the title 'Improving Access to Psychological Therapies' (IAPT).

Much of the resentment about CBT was provoked by this initiative. Layard had angered many with his seemingly naïve vision of CBT as a 'happiness' therapy, bringing emotional well-being to the population at large. Even more so, his optimistic equation of CBT therapy with a dramatic reduction in psychological suffering, such that depressed people en masse would return to work and save the government enormous sums of money in benefit funds, became the target of sharp criticism of CBT as an agent of social engineering and state control (Guilfoyle 2008). This move coincided with the gradual discrediting of mainstream NHS psychotherapy services, particularly psychoanalytic psychotherapy, and the increasing loss of funding to these services. Whether or not there was a direct link between these changes, CBT and its formalization within IAPT services became identified as the 'enemy'. The pity about this association is that Layard in some respects was more positively socially minded than he is credited with, challenging the culture of consumerism and isolationism as toxic by-products of western society (Pilgrim 2008). Further, at a time when other psychotherapy services were suffering appreciable losses, the Layard initiative succeeded in attracting far more significant funding that had ever been assigned to psychotherapy of any sort, generating huge budgets to fund psychological services across the UK. Whatever questions there are about the model of treatment, this initiative considerably enhanced recognition and treatment of common psychological difficulties in the community. When we consider the statistics of thousands of people seen in IAPT services nationwide in the years 2008–13, we have to acknowledge the value in broad terms to the population of the UK, whatever our doubts about CBT. Further, although there is still a strongly prescriptive approach in some IAPT services, with an emphasis on fidelity to the model and an insistence on evaluation and quantification, this is a reflection of the times and not just CBT. Further still, as previously mentioned, the IAPT model is opening up to other non-CBT approaches that offer a reasonable evidence base. Hence, interpersonal psychotherapy (Weissman *et al.* 2000), dynamic interpersonal therapy (Lemma *et al.* 2011) and integrative couple therapy (Epstein and Baucomb 2002), to mention just a few, have all been incorporated in the IAPT framework in the last few years. Finally, and of particular relevance here, group approaches have increasingly been developed in IAPT, as reflected in the Anna Freud course I convene – which I describe in more detail below.

Beyond the constraints of the IAPT model, CBT has itself become an increasingly diverse approach. Much of the CBT that is practised is still routine short-term, largely manualized therapy but the approach has evolved in interesting directions, including schema therapy, which takes full account of the patient's past, of internal models of relationships along attachment lines and uses a transference–counter-transference frame in conceptualizing the client–clinician relationship (Young *et al.* 2003). CBT has also embraced mindfulness, one of the most popular approaches in recent decades, in the form of mindfulness-based cognitive therapy (MBCT), and it has spawned acceptance and commitment therapy (ACT). These new additions are commonly referred to as the 'third wave' in CBT development, the first having been behaviour therapy and the second the conjunction of cognitive and behaviour therapy (Hayes 2004). This addresses one of the criticisms of CBT noted above, that it is static, solipsistic and closed to new contexts and new approaches. In fact, it is a fast moving, rapidly diversifying approach. There has been some criticism of this very fact as well, that CBT is colonizing other psychotherapies in a way that further diminishes the wider field. But this view, although there is some truth in it, reflects the aforementioned generalized anxiety about psychotherapy survival in the non-CBT milieu and this can create exaggerated perceptions of exactly what CBT is up to.

Personal impressions

Before looking 'objectively' at the underlying principles of CBT, I wish to share some subjective impressions of the approach as I have known it over a period of about 30 years. As previously noted, I have employed and managed CBT therapists in my role as NHS head of service, supervised the group work of CBT therapists, worked clinically in close association with CBT therapists and have developed a group-based course for CBT practitioners.

I have never doubted the value of CBT in clinical services. With dramatically increasing referral rates for psychological help in the 1980s, the addition of a practical, short-term therapy to the framework of services was in my view a boon. It also suited the NHS setting. Most people referred knew very little about psychotherapy, wanted relatively quick input and some practical guidance rather than an in-depth, long-term commitment. CBT fitted the bill. Further, CBT has *face validity* (Gliner and Morgan 2009): it is accessible, understandable and common-sensical, which is often reassuring to people who have little psychological sophistication and might be intimidated by the subtler, unstructured and more interpretive analytic psychotherapies. Overall, the results also seemed to me congruent. I do not draw on statistics here, since the evidence is so wide, spanning several treatment contexts, but my impression is that the clinical outcomes are generally favourable and satisfy the overall requirements of evidence-based practice. Most recipients report satisfaction with their treatment and feel that they have benefited. That some do not benefit and others deteriorate some time after their CBT therapy has ended is hardly surprising, given that no one psychological therapy can claim universal and lasting success, and undoubtedly what is good for some patients is not necessarily so for others. I therefore do not hold truck with analytic colleagues, individual or group, who regard the failed CBT patients who come their way for further assessment or treatment as proof of the inadequate nature of CBT as a totality. Inevitably, psychotherapists will be referred CBT failures rather than successes and this is an unfair basis on which to judge the overall efficacy of a psychological therapy. In my experience, although with some reservations, the effectiveness of CBT as presented in the documented evidence is largely reflected in clinical practice. That CBT sometimes fails and that it is limited in scope does not detract from its value.

I wish to add something about CBT *practitioners.* Having stated support in general for the approach, I want to comment on the therapists. Far from the picture of mechanical beings methodically carrying out their prescribed and manualized treatments, I have found most CBT therapists to be as sensitive and respectful of their clients as most other therapists. It is true that there is generally a diminished emphasis on the therapeutic relationship in CBT, but I perceive most practitioners conscious of the need to develop a therapeutic alliance and to work hard at it. Although there is usually limited time to delve into patients' pasts in great detail or depth, most CBT practitioners take at least adequate histories and show an appreciation of the impact of patients' early development and life experience on their present concerns. They similarly show an awareness of current social context and are by no means blind to the political influences on patients' lives. In fact, I have possibly found CBT therapists to be the least judgemental of all my psychotherapy colleagues. I generally find them modest rather than arrogant and see them as more open to other approaches, including group analysis, than is commonly assumed and is sometimes the case for non-CBT practitioners.

This does not mean that I have no criticisms of CBT. It is true that it can be superficial; that it is sometimes practised in ad hoc, facile ways; that its understanding of human behaviour is simplistic; that it often tends not to take sufficient account of past history and more complex relational issues; and, in particular, that it restricts the range of themes available for enquiry and exploration in a given treatment. But this is within the limits of the approach, constrained to a large degree by NHS funding and performance standards that impose considerable time pressures on practice. In fact, some of my criticisms are related more to the systems within which CBT operates, such as IAPT, than to the approach itself. As elaborated in Chapter 2, I am critical myself of the bureaucratic, target-driven, industrialized culture of the NHS. So, I agree to some extent with critics of IAPT who regard it as dominated by an economic agenda, with an exaggerated emphasis on speed and volume of delivery, rather than on quality, and on a reduction of practice to too narrow a conception of therapeutic exigency. That CBT lends itself to this sort of influence may be a problem but it is largely the fault of the system that embraces and exploits the approach rather than an inherent flaw in CBT itself. Viewed from a demographic perspective, the widespread practice of CBT also reflects the extremely high level of demand for psychological help in current society and the question of how this can be delivered in as effective and economical way as possible. That CBT is able to contribute to this agenda may be to its credit rather than its discredit.

The main principles of CBT

Having described the basics of CBT, outlined the main criticisms of the approach and shared some of my impressions as a clinician, I return here to some core aspects of CBT. In this section I set out some of the principles that guide CBT. These are well-known and accepted within the CBT milieu but largely unfamiliar outside this framework. By describing these principles, I hope to address some of the criticisms I have previously highlighted.

I draw on the outline provided by Bieling and colleagues (2006):

Collaborative empiricism

This refers to the working relationship between therapist and client and emphasizes that the therapy is a joint undertaking. 'Collaborative' emphasizes a spirit of constructively working together and 'empiricism' the engagement in an active process of exploration that yields information about what is helpful to the client, what can be built on as the therapy progresses and which contingencies either facilitate or hinder progress. While the therapist offers guidance within a structured and goal-orientated framework, much emphasis is placed on what actually happens in the client's experience and what sense therapist and client can make together of this experience.

The criticism that CBT renders the client a passive recipient of therapy is to my mind mistaken and is countered by the principle of collaborative empiricism. The client is usually regarded as an active participant whose views on the therapy are elicited. The therapist is not simply a controlling, didactic presence but one who generally takes a facilitating, supportive role, inviting the participation of the client in a shared venture. Of course, the exact nature of the process will vary from one therapy to another and in some contexts the therapist's more 'directive' or psycho-educational role may be more prominent than in others. But the idea that CBT is always a rigid, mechanical exercise, a form of brainwashing, is erroneous and misleading. Mansell (2008), a CBT commentator, laments the 'authoritarian archetype of CBT' and regards the approach as actively helping clients 'to become aware of their conscious experience of meaning-making'. The emphasis on meaning-making accords with much contemporary psychotherapy, including mentalization (Fonagy and Bateman 2008), and contradicts the perception of CBT as a vacuous exercise encouraging conformity and control.

In *group* cognitive behavioural psychotherapy, the notion of collaborative empiricism takes on added significance. Since there are several patients in the group, the involvement of all in a joint venture is crucial. As the group itself is regarded as the therapeutic medium, collaborative empiricism becomes all the more important in GCBT and offers greater interpersonal potential than individual CBT in the same way that group psychotherapy generally provides a more interactive environment than individual psychotherapy. The notion of collaborative empiricism is close to the spirit of all group psychotherapy, whether group analytic, interpersonal or CBT.

Socratic dialogue

Critics of CBT may be surprised to find that Socratic dialogue, indeed dialogue of any sort, is part and parcel of CBT! In CBT terms, Socratic dialogue refers to the construction of all therapeutic enquiry as an enquiry based on first principles: nothing, no meaning or assumptions or attributions, can be assumed without open enquiry. The CBT therapist, contrary to stereotype, is not envisaged as an expert who weighs in with all the answers but an informed guide who seeks to engage the patient in a spirit of mutual enquiry. This approach is transferred to the group in GCBT, the enquiry aiming to elicit the wisdom, experience and views of all group members. Of course, the group CBT process is structured: there are sections devoted to the therapist teaching or giving information, to homework setting, feedback about the week, reviews of progress and so on, but this is punctuated by a process of enquiry which regularly goes back to basics and seeks to create meaning out of the welter of problems brought to the group.

The notion of Socratic dialogue goes some way to addressing the particular stereotypes of CBT as a dialogue-free zone and an exercise that is exempt from resonance and reciprocity (Brown 2006). The 'dehumanized' attribution of CBT stands corrected here. Mansell (2008) appropriately emphasizes 'the spirit of inquiry and curiosity that is prevalent in so much cognitive-behavioral theory'. It behoves critics of CBT to take account of this aspect of CBT as not very different from the value system of their own preferred therapies.

Guided discovery

Guided discovery follows along the lines of both collaborative empiricism and Socratic dialogue by encouraging an attitude of curiosity about experience, complementing the more directive aspect of CBT. Clients are encouraged to consider their attempts to construe the therapeutic endeavour as a journey of discovery, bringing insights and discoveries back to the therapeutic table for processing and helping to facilitate further progress. The principle of guided discovery, in my view, is a reflection of an exploratory, even imaginative aspect of CBT that is seldom credited.

Controlled experimentation

CBT differs from analytic and other psychotherapies by instigating a change process based on behavioural and other experiments. This experimentation is guided by the therapist within safe parameters and a feedback system that evaluates progress. The experiments may start in the consulting room itself, with the therapist as witness, and progress to life outside the consulting room, but usually in a carefully programmed way that does not expose the client to too much risk of failure. This approach is usually embodied in the CBT homework programme which forms a pivotal point in many CBT treatments and which is the stimulus for ongoing review or progress. These experiments, whether in vivo in the group or part of the homework task, are an important aspect of *group CBT*. This aspect differs from the majority of non-CBT approaches that do not prescribe actual experimentation or homework although, as I will consider later, this may happen in more informal or spontaneous ways in more traditional group psychotherapy.

Relapse prevention

Given the relative brevity of the treatment process, and the common tendency people have to relapse, CBT practitioners put great store by relapse prevention (Bieling *et al.* 2006). In both individual and group CBT, the last session or few sessions may be devoted to relapse prevention, formulating strategies for maximizing and maintaining the changes made and stabilizing progress. Non-CBT therapists, when dealing with endings, also have an eye to the future and clarifying which factors may support or hinder the client's progress. But CBT does this in a more methodical way, with explicit strategies aimed at relapse prevention. Follow-up sessions are part of this process.

How does group analysis come into this?

The preceding discussion has focused mainly on CBT, with some reference to psychotherapy in general and group analysis in particular. But it is necessary now to draw group analysis into sharper focus.

Returning to the position stated earlier in this chapter, group analysis and CBT are, on the face of it, very different psychotherapeutic approaches. But while some of these differences are incontrovertible, others are open to question. In the next section, I attempt to clarify some of fundamental differences between the approaches. I then go on to look at areas of convergence or situations in the clinical sphere where group analysis and CBT can support and reinforce rather than compete and disqualify each other.

Differences between group analysis and CBT

Origins: group analysis derives from a coming together of several disciplines – psychoanalysis, gestalt psychology and social psychology, more recently influenced by inter-subjective and relational approaches. CBT emanates from a behavioural psychology tradition, later extended by the addition of cognitive therapy.

Therapeutic form: group analysis is entirely group based although there are applications to individual therapy (Nitsun 2001); CBT began with individual therapy and has only recently been extended to groups (Bieling *et al.* 2006).

Philosophical approach: group analysis holds a strongly social perspective, drawing on a foundational notion of human connectedness; CBT is more individually focused with a major focus on the client's internal thinking and belief systems, although this has been modified to some extent in group CBT.

Method: group analysis encourages an open, exploratory dialogue based on Foulkes' notion of 'free group discussion' (Schlapobersky 2002) and is mainly a long-term approach; CBT is structured, time-limited and goal-orientated. Its valuing of Socratic dialogue and collaboration is less well-recognized.

Scientific: group analysis has only recently begun to embark on formal process and outcome research; CBT is grounded in scientific considerations such as the hypothetico-deductive method that generate the reciprocal interplay of theory, research and practice.

Effectiveness: group analysis, in line with the above, has a meagre evidence base: CBT operates within a system of ongoing evaluation and is arguably strongly evidence-based.

Familiarity: group analysis, although influential as a way of thinking in the UK and abroad, has limited presence as a psychological therapy: CBT is widely known and represented in clinical services across the world.

The main point about the differentiation above is to contrast group analysis with a psychological therapy that is rooted in a very different tradition and to consider what this difference might mean in practice. In my view, the most striking differences are: 1) CBT's grounding in the link between theory, research and practice, reflecting a rigour that group analysis could benefit from; 2) the power of an evidence base, whatever reservations there may be about the nature of research evidence; and 3) the focus on the individual as the point of clinical significance and responsibility. In Chapter 3, I outline my concerns about the obfuscation of the individual in group analysis through the over-arching perspective of the group: 'the decentring of the individual', as I call it. In that chapter I argue that, while this might make theoretical sense, the failure to elaborate the individual in clinical terms disadvantages the clinical agenda of group analysis, making it difficult to justify the approach as an equal amongst others in a culture of evidence-based practice. The group endeavour does not alter the fact that the point of clinical accountability in our therapeutic work remains the individual.

Similarities and convergences between the two approaches

While there are of course marked differences between CBT and group analysis, there are also surprising and unexpected similarities. There is firstly the discovery that CBT espouses notions of collaborative empiricism and Socratic dialogue. Although the framework within which this is manifested is very different from group analysis, recognition of the value of dialogue and collaboration, as noted above in the section on CBT principles, is largely contrary to what is commonly associated with CBT. Group analysis, on the other hand, has a long tradition of interest in dialogue, supported by many writers as a fundamental principle of group analytic psychotherapy (Foulkes 1964; Brown 2006; Schlapobersky 2002). I (Nitsun 1996, 2006) have challenged the possibility of an over-emphasis on the verbal aspect of dialogue in group analysis on the grounds that human communication is more complex than that which is expressed through words. However, I fully recognize the overall value of dialogue and the linked processes of mirroring, resonance and reciprocity in the practice of group psychotherapy. Equally, I am reassured by the importance accredited it in CBT.

In my own work with CBT practitioners, particularly in the development and supervision of CBT groups, I have drawn strongly on the communicative tradition of group analysis and introduced linked group analytic principles into a CBT framework. Given that CBT espouses the processes of collaborative empiricism and Socratic dialogue in the explication of the therapeutic task, I have sought to add to this the interpersonal and inter-subjective aspects of dialogue and attempted to add relational depth to communication processes in group CBT. This appears in various instances to have had a socializing effect on the groups I have supervised and to have strengthened the collaborative function amongst group facilitators and group members. In this way, I believe, it is possible to bring together aspects of CBT and group analysis in a creative way.

Example 1: How group analytic thinking can inform and strengthen a CBT approach

This example is drawn from the course on group work for IAPT practitioners I convene with colleagues at the Anna Freud Centre. The course arose in response to the recognition that IAPT practitioners are increasingly required to run groups, of a mainly CBT or psycho-educational kind, virtually without training of any sort in group work. The year-long course is designed to give students an overview of evidence-based CBT groups, an appreciation of alternative group approaches, including innovative community-based interventions for difficult-to-reach populations (which is also within the IAPT remit), and an introduction to group process awareness. I teach the latter part of the course, from a largely group-analytic perspective, and collaborate with CBT and innovative-group teachers in jointly setting up and facilitating experiential exercises, as well as group supervision. The following is an example:

> I am supervising the group process of a twelve-session CBT group for depression. The two group facilitators have brought the third session of the group for supervision. According to the group protocol, the facilitators are required to cover set didactic material each week, systematically imparting the CBT approach to depression. They use a manual that is quite stringent in its requirements, assuming that a specific part of the syllabus is faithfully covered each week. The facilitators are finding this difficult as they sense group members want space in which to talk more freely about their problems. The dilemma is that this impedes progress on the psycho-educational front. However, when the facilitators attempt to adhere to the manual, group members appear to become restive and resistant. A male group member, Don, also becomes very dominant at times, angrily sharing details about his difficult relationship with his wife. This further adds to the tension in the group. The two facilitators feel overwhelmed and unsure of how to manage the group process.

In my supervisory approach, I formulate a view of the group process, with particular attention to group-stage developmental processes and the maintenance of the group therapeutic frame. Based on my own understanding of what is happening, I suggest the following:

* The group is at an early stage of development in which anxiety is probably high and inclusion–exclusion a major dynamic. The group material suggests

that participants are struggling to belong, that the facilitators may have paid insufficient attention to this process and that their adherence to the didactic input is to a degree estranging the group. What can they do to address this? How can they maximize a sense of inclusion for the group as a whole while at the same addressing the CBT task?

- Facilitators need to attend to the figure-ground configuration in the group (an important group analytic principle). This usually requires switching focus from individual to group and back again. In the present situation, they need to contextualize Don's individual outpourings in the group as a whole, actively bringing in the group at times when he dominates rather than feeling they have to control Don.

- Since this is a group for depressed patients, the fact that members want more opportunity to talk is a favourable sign, even if this does not fit with the main aims of the group. Participants might otherwise be so weighed down by feelings of guilt, shame and despair that they cannot talk at all. Their making it difficult for the facilitators to progress the teaching is paradoxically a sign of life, a glimmer of hope. If this constitutes a challenge to the facilitators, it could be seen as a healthy challenge.

- Don's angry dominance in the group, difficult as it is to deal with, may similarly convey the anger behind the depression, not just in his case but in the others as well. His protest could therefore be seen in positive terms as an attempt to express something for the whole group. If the facilitators recognize this, how can they respond in a way that utilizes Don's contributions to the advantage of the others? Will the CBT protocol allow them to share with the group the insight that depression can be seen as internalized and self-directed anger?

- As much as group members need to express themselves openly, there is a task boundary that must be recognized. This is a short-term CBT group rather than long-term psychotherapy and some accommodation needs to be found on the part of both facilitators and group members. If this becomes an all-talking group with members overturning the group protocol and the facilitators yielding to the challenge, this might not just confuse the boundaries of the task but create a lack of safety. If things then go wrong and the group becomes rudderless and chaotic, members may end up feeling disappointed, blaming the facilitators or feeling responsible themselves for the mess. This could then play into patients' depressive anxieties, perhaps repeating an earlier trauma that engendered a sense of damage and disappointment.

From the above, it can be seen that CBT group therapists are not generally trained in understanding group process, while also lacking an awareness of the way group tensions connected with the index problem, in this case the hostility underlying depression, can infiltrate the group process. This requires an understanding of parallel process, enactments and repetitions, and thoughtfulness about how to deal with these phenomena while safeguarding the task and purpose of the group. In discussions like this, I usually introduce the group analytic concept of dynamic administration as a prime consideration for conducting groups (Foulkes 1964). This emphasizes the importance of protecting the frame of the group as the foundation of effective group work. This requires some tolerance of the paradox of running groups of this kind, where there is both a structural task to be implemented and a spontaneous social process. The challenge is how to reconcile these potentially conflicting trends. Even reflecting on this may be a helpful supervisory intervention. As noted above, I do not normally tell supervisees what to do but raise questions and consider alternatives that may be possible within the frame of the CBT group.

My interventions along these lines are usually welcomed and assist CBT group facilitators in managing situations that may be outside the CBT frame of reference. Contrary to what critics might predict, CBT practitioners, in my experience, highly value analytically informed supervision of this sort. Through this we have been able to develop a relationship of mutual respect and the course my colleagues and I run appears to be having a considerable influence on practice, particularly the development of group-based services in IAPT.

A student's reaction

I include comments from a student on the last cohort who completed the course:

Reflections on Making Groups Work in IAPT Training
15th May–25th July 2014
What I learned on the course that equips me for future practice

"I particularly valued the sessions on group process. It was something we had all struggled to manage at times, and recognised as becoming forgotten in the wake of content-heavy sessions. Seeing the group itself as an entity and a therapeutic tool was incredibly helpful in valuing group therapy as an intervention. I hope to be able to convey this to colleagues and clients also. I think we have all been guilty of viewing group interventions as less valuable and enjoyable than individual therapy, whereas I have learned to appreciate that receiving CBT in a group setting can be therapeutic in itself. Many process issues were intuitive and affirming, but incredibly valuable in being labelled and made explicit. It felt to me like the first time I read about common thinking errors. These factors are crucial to improving my own practice and cascading learning to my colleagues"

Example 2: How CBT thinking can assist and strengthen group analytic psychotherapy

Looking at the intervention in the reverse – how CBT could inform group analysis – I have begun to see in the interactional process of group psychotherapy the possibility that members intuitively provide a function that is similar to the CBT process. While the purpose of analytic groups is not a pragmatic goal-orientated one, it is very common that participants support each other's personal strivings and plans in active and collaborative ways. Most individuals joining psychotherapy groups come with life problems with which they seek assistance in the group. Other members often function as informal therapists who help to encourage, monitor progress, give feedback and revise goals. Although this happens informally in psychotherapy groups, much of it could be described in CBT terms as forms of guided discovery, collaborative empiricism and controlled experimentation. Group members actively help each other to look at options, explore alternatives, try out different behaviours, consider outcomes, revise plans and so on, *in a similar though less structured way than in CBT therapy.* This is not reflected in the theory of group psychotherapy, yet it happens in some form in most therapy groups. It is a product of spontaneous interaction in the group, an aspect that can be difficult to capture when describing group process and hence is not particularly well-documented in group psychotherapy protocols. From a CBT perspective, however, it may be seen as a crucial component of the therapeutic process.

The following example is based on a group in private practice. In this weekly group, Jeff shares the ups and downs of his romantic life. He is dating a woman Kelly on whom he is very keen but she appears to have a boyfriend in tow. It is the first time that he has felt so much for anyone but he is perplexed and does not know how to deal with Kelly's competing relationship. He has brought the problem to the group several weeks in a row. His relationship with Kelly appears to be strengthening but the group picks up his frustration and distress at the continuing element of ambiguity. Over the weeks the group considers with Jeff his various options: he could withdraw from the relationship; he could wait and see what happens; he could tell Kelly about his feelings and see how she responds; he could confront Kelly directly about the boyfriend and deal with whatever the outcome is. In the course of these discussions, Jeff is asked to say what he would really like, what it would feel like if Kelly commits herself to him. Is he ready? Does he want a long-term relationship? Does he want to get married, have children? Not only does the group engage with Jeff on these issues but their interest and acceptance help him to express his feelings and understand his motives. When Jeff affirms his strong interest and desire for Kelly, the group encourages him to tackle the problem head on, to clarify with Kelly whether her other relationship is of consequence and what her feelings are about Jeff. Jeff now challenges Kelly to good effect: she describes her other relationship as tailing off and affirms her interest in Jeff, asking him to bear with her while she more actively disentangles herself from the other man. In subsequent weeks, the group enquires about the emerging process.

This vignette illustrates an aspect of the group process that is not generally recognized or described in the literature and that gains clarity through a CBT lens: the powerful practical support group members give each other. It suggests that processes of confrontation and challenge, feedback and monitoring are important parts of the therapeutic process that are likely to occur in groups, irrespective of the therapist's and group's orientation, given people's natural inclination to identify with each other's difficulties and to offer support and encouragement. This accords with several of the group therapeutic factors delineated by Yalom and Leszcz (2005) such as altruism, socialization, interpersonal learning and group cohesion but adds the possibility of an as yet unnamed dimension which could be described as 'social learning' or perhaps 'behavioural learning'. This is similar to interpersonal learning but has a more practical dimension. It also has a cognitive aspect in so far as the group spends some time enquiring what Jeff's thoughts and beliefs are about Kelly: what he wants from her, where he sees the relationship going, why he holds back in significant ways. While these processes may be integral to group therapy, it is useful to see them in CBT terms, suggesting that a so far largely unidentified group therapeutic factor may be at work: a process of group collaboration and proposed experimentation that progressively supports and guides individuals through the resolution of their problems. In this sense, the work of a psychotherapy group, on the face of it very different, is similar in some respects to that of a CBT group.

It is of interest that in this example the approach taken by the group is exploratory in a practical sense rather than uncovering hidden and unconscious aspects of Jeff's problem. It is likely that the 'hidden' aspects are by now sufficiently recognized in the group not to have to repeat them. This would have freed the group to take a more actively encouraging, behaviourally orientated approach to Jeff's difficulties.

To sum up the group process as I could see it through a CBT lens:

- The group spontaneously engages in a process of guided discovery about Jeff's relationship with Kelly.
- It creates a supportive framework which helps Jeff to validate his interest in Kelly and invalidate some of his negative assumptions about her.
- It encourages him to actively try out certain behaviours with her, taking risks which he might previously have avoided, in the spirit of collaborative empiricism and controlled experimentation.
- The positive effect of his risk-taking reinforces a sense of personal and group efficacy, reinforcing hope about the possibility of therapeutic change.
- The approach is largely outside the therapist's theoretical frame and mode of intervention but empowers the group in a way that is consistent with a group analytic value system.

Discussion

Working across the divide between group analysis and cognitive-behavioural therapy, I am very aware of the limited extent to which each discipline usually embraces the other. CBT practitioners have the constraints of a highly specific model that requires fidelity to its principles and findings, all the more so in an evidence-based culture that tends to demand conformity to established practice. Yet, possibly because the group field is new for many CBT therapists, and is a relatively underdeveloped field that throws up many difficult situations and questions, there is a surprising degree of receptivity and curiosity about what a group analytic group-process perspective has to offer. If anything, the constraints may have more to do with practical considerations, such as the pressure of completing a structured ten-week group for depression, for example, which makes it difficult to give time to group analytic considerations and to try out more divergent methods. I am also aware that these observations are based on a fairly unique situation: a training course on group methods for CBT therapists in which participants have chosen to pursue this particular approach and in which the group analytic perspective is offered as an integral aspect of the training. CBT therapists in other situations may be less giving in their interest and generosity.

But, if anything, I find more resistance the other way round – group analysts taking account of CBT principles. Analytic psychotherapists are by nature cautious and conservative. Some of this is understandable: an aspect perhaps of professional integrity. But the group psychotherapeutic field is in some ways underdeveloped and in need of fresh conceptualization as well as firmer clinical grounding – and so may benefit from curiosity and openness to other approaches. I hesitate because elsewhere in this book I make a point about theoretical incoherence in group analysis, implying the need for greater clarity and internal coherence (Chapter 3). However, I offer a divergent perspective here as a way of challenging our common assumptions. Although there are pertinent and useful models of group psychotherapy supported by well-known group therapeutic factors, there remains a sense that we often do not know what is happening in groups and how to understand what makes them therapeutic. The CBT perspective suggested is an alternative approach, highlighting the group's function as a form of collaborative empiricism, generating a comprehensive dialogue around the problem at hand and encouraging patients' active attempts at dealing with the problem.

There are no doubt very good reasons why psychotherapists mostly adopt and work within a unitary mode of psychotherapy: training, professional considerations, the striving for competence and the sheer challenge of working effectively within a single therapeutic modality, let alone several modalities. But is this approach viable in a changing world in which our assumptions are constantly challenged? Are we too bound by loyalty to our chosen orientation, an attitude that is inculcated in most training organizations and that reinforces assumptions about professional identity and integrity? These attitudes all too easily become ossified, creating splits in the overall field that lead to stereotyping and polarization. If I have a jaundiced view of this, as noted above, it derives from my experience as a head of service in the NHS in which I was party to discussions about therapeutic difference that created considerable frustration not just amongst psychotherapists themselves but amongst non-therapists, including managers and funders of services. When questions loomed about funding, the allocation of resources and the direction of services, psychotherapists in the same service were often unable to agree on a way forward. They were more likely to become entrenched in their positions than show the generosity and goodwill required to sit down together and thrash out a plan for survival. This made it all too easy for managers to 'divide and rule': to find drastic solutions that meant in some cases the demise of whole departments and in others a significant loss of resources.

But the pressures of funding should not in themselves enforce untimely changes in traditions that have their own value and integrity. I am also not suggesting a sudden discombobulating and reinvention of therapeutic frames. It is more a case of the psychotherapies showing a greater interest and respect for each other – and an awareness of the opportunities that arise in a dynamic environment in which therapists can talk to and help each other. There is a considerable need for process supervision of CBT of the kind I have described, especially of group CBT, where the literature and training take little account of process factors and where group analysts can make a valuable contribution. This is a useful avenue for further development at a time when group analytic practitioners are uncertain about their roles in the NHS and other public services and how they can bridge the gap with the other therapies. I would highlight the potential value for group analysts of a greater receptivity to CBT and how the approach can support and amplify some of what we already do. This does not mean that group analysts should retrain as cognitive-behavioural therapists but that a CBT perspective may help to make sense of what we do and possibly direct our attention in different ways to the group therapeutic process.

I hope that the examples I gave earlier convey, however tentatively, the value of looking at these divergent approaches from a complementary perspective. It is for reasons such as these that I am keen to encourage thinking 'outside the box', however tenuous the comparisons I draw in this chapter. Both CBT and group analysis, in their different ways, have some distance to go in the struggle to adapt to the rapidly changing environment of healthcare and psychotherapy. CBT, for all its evidence-based credentials, is still undergoing development and having to deal with far greater expectations of what it can realistically achieve in over-stretched services. But it is heartening to see the conclusions emanating from the CBT literature, which in some ways are remarkably open and affirming of a mature psychotherapeutic value system – rather than reflecting the narrow philosophy with which CBT is usually associated. Mansell (2008), a senior CBT practitioner and theorist, offers a good example of such an open-minded and discursive view of psychotherapeutic culture. While defending the integrity of CBT, Mansell highlights the requirements of *any effective and acceptable psychotherapy'*. His views may surprise non-CBT readers. I quote in full Mansell's view of the requirements of contemporary therapy. These are the words of a committed CBT therapist describing the requirements of an ethically sound psychotherapy. The therapy:

> "– needs to consider the person in their social context and their immediate interpersonal interactions because of the close relationship with inner mental processes:
> – must be based on more than the standardized evidence base, because it needs to match the needs of the clients to whom it is targeted when put into practice in a particular context;
> – is likely to be at odds with a purely medical model of mental 'illness', and so needs to develop ways to accommodate to, or transform, its health-service context;
> – needs consistently to monitor the process of control, sense of purpose, and the balance of power during therapy so that clients can gain a perspective of control in their lives; and
> – needs a coherent theoretical model to guide its core principles that evolves in a dynamic way in response to new evidence or new ways of thinking about that evidence."

(Mansell 2008, pp. 30–1)

I have quoted Mansell's statement in detail because of its pertinence and because *it could equally have been made by a group analyst!* The emphasis on social context, interpersonal interaction, sense of therapeutic meaning, awareness of the therapist–patient power difference and the need for a dynamic response to change (cherished group analytic beliefs) are all there. It illustrates my point that the value systems and aims of the different psychotherapies may not be in as much conflict with each other as is commonly assumed. The perpetuation of splits may be unnecessary and disadvantageous. There is potential in considering what draws us together rather than what draw us apart.

In some ways, I suspect, I have attempted the apocryphal as far as some readers may be concerned: bringing group analysis and CBT to view under the same umbrella. To some it may seem futile to look at links and overlaps between two such different approaches. But I am hopeful that I have at least prodded the conscience of some and pricked the curiosity of others, that there is enough in what I say to create disquiet about what are usually perceived as incontrovertible differences. I am not suggesting any easy integration of the two approaches or some form of seamless morphing one into the other. Rather, I am presenting ideas that might help us to think 'outside the box'. I have presented the principles of CBT in such a way that hopefully the approach will seem more meaningful to non-CBT practitioners. I have also given examples of how the two approaches can inform and complement each other. This opens the possibility of joint work and mutually supportive relationships. Further, I have highlighted what I consider to be the dangers in maintaining psychotherapeutic exclusivity and an adherence to the 'pure gold' of a chosen discipline. This creates stereotypes and generates a split, fragmented psychotherapy culture, which has particular disadvantages in the ever-changing contexts of healthcare and psychological therapies. In the end, survival may depend on reducing the narcissism of differences and fostering sufficient openness and humility to embrace difference.

References

Barkham, M., Hardy, G. and Mellor-Clark, J. (2010) *Developing and Delivering Practice-based Evidence: A Guide for Psychological Therapies.* Chichester: John Wiley.

Beck, A. T., Rush, A. J., Shaw, B. F. and Emery, G. (1979) *Cognitive Therapy of Depression.* New York: The Guilford Press.

Bieling, P. J., McCabe, R. E. and Antony, M. M. (2006) *Cognitive Behavioral Therapy in Groups.* New York: The Guilford Press.

Brown, D. (2006) *Resonance and Reciprocity: Selected Papers by Dennis Brown.* Hove: Routledge.

Datillio, F. M. (2010) *Cognitive Behavioral Therapy with Couples and Families: A Comprehensive Guide for Clinicians.* New York: Guilford Press.

Epstein, N. B. and Baucomb, H. (2002) *Enhanced Cognitive-behavioral Therapy for Couples: A Contextual Approach.* Washington, DC: American Psychological Association.

Fonagy, P. and Bateman, A. (2008) The development of borderline personality disorder – a mentalizing model, *Journal of Personality Disorders*, 22, 4–21.

Foulkes, S. H. (1964) *Therapeutic Group Analysis.* London: Karnac.

Gliner, J. A. and Morgan, G. A. (2009) *Research Methods in Applied Settings: An Integrated Approach to Design and Analysis.* New York: Routledge.

Guilfoyle, M. (2008) CBT's integration into societal networks of power, in House, R. and Lowenthal, D. (eds) (2008) *Against and For CBT.* Ross-on-Wye: PCCS Books.

Harwood, T. M., Beutler, L. E. and Charvat, M. (2010) Cognitive-behavioral therapy and psychotherapy integration, in Dobson, K. S. (2010) *Handbook of Cognitive-behavioral Therapies.* New York: The Guilford Press.

Hayes, S. C. (2004) Acceptance and commitment therapy, relational frame theory, and the Third Wave of behavioral and cognitive therapies, *Behaviour Therapy*, 35, 639–65.

House, R. and Lowenthal, D. (eds) (2008) *Against and For CBT.* Ross-on-Wye: PCCS Books.

Leader, D. (2008) A quick fix for the soul, *The Guardian*, 8 September.

Lemma, A., Target, M. and Fonagy, P. (2011) *Brief Dynamic Interpersonal Psychotherapy.* Oxford: Oxford University Press.

Mansell, W. (2008) What is CBT really, and how can we enhance the impact of effective psychotherapies such as CBT? In House, R. and Lowenthal, D. (eds) (2008) *Against and For CBT.* Ross-on-Wye: PCCS Books.

Nitsun, M. (1996) *The Anti-Group.* London: Routledge.

Nitsun, M. (2001) Towards a group-analytic approach to individual psychotherapy, *Group Analysis*, 34, 473–83.

Nitsun, M. (2006) *The Group as an Object of Desire.* London: Routledge.

Pilgrim, D. (2008) Reading 'happiness': CBT and the Layard thesis, in House, R. and Lowenthal, D. (eds.) *Against and For CBT*. Ross-on-Wye: PCCS Books.

Proctor, G. (2008) CBT: The obscuring of power in the name of science, in House, R. and Lowenthal, D. (eds) *Against and For CBT*. Ross-on-Wye: PCCS Books.

Rogers, A. (2010) CBT for older people, in Grant, A., Townend, M., Mulhern, R. and Short, N. (eds) *CBT in Mental Health Care*. London: Sage.

Samuels, A. (2008) Foreword, in House, R. and Lowenthal, D. (eds) (2008) *Against and For CBT*. Ross-on-Wye: PCCS Books.

Schlapobersky, J. (2002) The language of the group: monologue, dialogue and discourse in group analysis, in Brown, D. and Zinkin, L. (eds) *The Psyche and the Social World*, London: Jessica Kingsley.

Stallard, P. (2005) *A Clinician's Guide to Think Good-Feel Good: Using CBT with Children and Young People*. Chichester: John Wiley and Sons.

Weissman, M. M., Markowitz, J. C. and Klerman, G. L. (2000) Comprehensive Guide to Interpersonal Psychotherapy. New York: Basic Books.

Yalom, I. B. and Leszcz, M. (2005) *Theory and Practice of Group Psychotherapy*. New York: Basic Books.

Young, J. E., Klosko, J. S. and Weishaar, M. E. (2003) *Schema Therapy: A Practitioner's Guide*. New York: The Guilford Press.

Chapter 5

The group as refuge

Group psychotherapy in inner London

Much of the work of group analysts in the British National Health Service consists of regular, usually weekly, group psychotherapy in out-patient or day-patient settings. There is a long tradition of this sort and group analytic psychotherapy remains one of the few long-term psychological treatments still available in the increasingly cash-strapped and evidence-based culture of the NHS. But, in my experience, the groups meet with considerable difficulty, faced with a multitude of complex and severe problems, problems that have often resisted other forms of psychotherapeutic help. This is compounded in urban settings where the high levels of ethnic diversity, social disorganization and economic disadvantage contribute further complexity. The groups can demonstrate markedly anti-group characteristics, sometimes leaving conductors feeling troubled and anxious about what they offer. In this paper, I describe a group service I have run for fourteen years in inner-city London. I highlight the intensity of problems that beset the psychotherapy groups, how they reflect disparities in the local community, and I raise questions about the applicability of the group analytic method in these settings. It seems to me crucial that we recognize and understand these difficulties in order to evolve methods that are robust enough to withstand the weight of psychological disturbance in our groups and the increasing challenge to all psychotherapy to demonstrate its usefulness. The difficulties encountered have left me to construe *refuge* as a key function and to evolve the notion of the *group as refuge*. This is concerned more with fundamental levels of survival and belonging and less with analysis. Group analysis provides a strong frame within which to understand the psychosocial challenges I am describing, as well as the process aspects of the groups, but, I believe, in settings of this sort, requires modification as a therapeutic intervention.

Introduction

This chapter turns attention to the contemporary world of the inner city seen through the prism of an NHS group analytic psychotherapy service. The urban landscape and its diverse, fragmented community symbolize the demographic changes, social upheaval and changing patterns of mental illness that are characteristic of the twenty-first century. In the last few decades, the populations of British cities have become far more diverse, social isolation more pronounced and mental heath problems more widespread than in the preceding century. Much of this has been exacerbated by the economic recession and downturn of the years 2008 onwards but this only highlights a picture that had been building for decades. At the same time, the picture is by no means uniform. There are marked contrasts between rich and poor in parts of the city. The area in which I run a group service is typical of some central London areas in its clashing demographics. On the one hand, in Archway (where my service is based), the community is largely disadvantaged and of a lower socio-economic bracket, a community which reflects enormous diversity and marked levels of social, psychiatric and psychological morbidity. On the other hand, just a mile or two down the road, is fashionable Islington. This is one of the most expensive parts of London, home to politicians, professionals and successful artists, whose levels of social and economic need are very different. Although there are marked differences in character, the two populations are at the same time interspersed, so that in Archway there are well-heeled inhabitants and in Islington there are extremely disadvantaged sections of the population. These close juxtapositions highlight all the more the differences between the two populations; as if opposite social worlds exist side by side.

The community

A city with two faces

The group service I run is based in a tall, imposing building in Archway, not quite a tower block but with the distinctive character of 1960s construction. The building itself is well-maintained, with stunning panoramic views of London from the fifth floor where the psychotherapy department is located, forming a contrast to the urban sprawl below, much of it run down and dilapidated, some of it up and coming, an uneasy mix of commercial and residential. There are rambling council estates, shops, pubs, cafes and restaurants. The traffic is dense and never ceasing, with spaghetti junctions on which cars, fleets of buses, underground and overground trains constantly and noisily converge. Above all there is the passing parade of the local inhabitants in their extraordinary variety as they trudge the pavements, wait for buses going in all directions or descend into the underground to get their trains. London has become one of the most diversely populated cities in the world and this is very much a feature of the population in this part of London.

The building in which I work is in the heart of Archway. The local population, which generates most of the referrals to the group service, reflects many of the demographic changes that started in the twentieth century and continue until the present time. Whereas this area, and others like it in London, once housed integrated local communities, the face of the community has progressively been transformed by immigration and population drift. The area still has some, though increasingly few, long-standing communities, generally the working-class families which for generations have lived here and usually inhabit the council estates. These are mainly of English and Irish descent. There is a large contingent of Africans and Afro-Carribeans who immigrated over decades starting in the 1950s. There are European immigrant families, Greek, Turkish, Portuguese, Spanish, Italian, that go back some generations. More recently, there are the immigrants from Eastern Europe – Poles, Russians, Lithuanians and Latvians, as well as people from the Balkan states, Bosnia, Serbia, Croatia. There are Asians from different countries and different denominations – Indians, Pakistanis, Chinese. Some of the above are refugees who together with asylum seekers form a significant minority in the population. On the periphery of this complex population is another large, shifting, itinerant population, people passing through London, staying for brief periods of time, generally young adults from smaller English cities, students, labourers, sex-workers, the homeless. Not surprisingly there is a very high degree of social fragmentation and dysfunction. The once cohesive community has broken down. There is marked social isolation and loneliness in the midst of the multitude, substance abuse on a wide scale, prostitution, violence and crime. Unemployment is rife. There are pockets of poverty.

But, as noted above, Archway is just one aspect of this London conurbation. Just a short bus ride away is rich, trendy Islington, with all the trappings of success – smart houses, garden squares, sleek cars, expensive restaurants, fashionably dressed residents. And, yet, as noted, there are also dilapidated building estates, homelessness and substance misuse in the midst of this otherwise affluent area. One moment you are in upmarket Upper Street: turn the corner and there are bleak, sprawling council estates, signs of urban waste and decay, hooded teenagers sitting menacingly on street corners.

My description probably tallies with the situation in many large cities across the world, cities which have seen continuing change in their populations over recent decades: urban growth and rebuilding occurring under the pressure of mounting populations and greater ethnic and cultural diversity. This is largely a product of globalization, of shrinking boundaries and the merging of populations who once lived far apart, suddenly thrown together in new and unfamiliar settings, desperate to make a better life than they have previously known but often finding overwhelming obstacles and feeling stranded in the metropolis. What is different in the UK from most other countries is the dominance of the National Health Service, a service to which every British resident and most non-residents have access and which often serves as a fragile, unwitting container of the multiple and complex problems of communities in crisis. Hence, the inner London community I describe, with its pressures and changes, and the health service with all its own vicissitudes and crises, co-exist in a complex ecology in which anxiety about survival is often the linking theme.

How do people from this community come to group therapy and what do they bring to the group? How is the endemic social disorganization and dysfunction reflected in the group and to what extent is it possible to form an alternative symbolic community with group members? Some prevailing group themes include pressing questions about safety, survival, shelter, sanity, belonging, exclusion and isolation. How possible is it to find hope in this fractured world? How does one deal with the humiliation of a low or non-existent income in a city as richly resourced as London, particularly when the discrepancies are as glaringly obvious as in this part of the city? Frustration and anger are very close to the surface and the problem of facing one's own and others' rage raises the question of how despair and destructive wishes are contained within an environment that itself feels on the edge of implosion and disintegration. There are parallels with the health service itself. The NHS is so subject to drastic raids on funding, service closures and arbitrary but devastating reorganizations that it suffers breakdown and rupture at the same time that it attempts to treat breakdown and illness (see Chapter 2). The therapy groups reflect all these problems, highlighting the predicament of all those entangled in the web of care, including the group therapists themselves.

Referrals for groups – voices from the city

There have been important and far-reaching demographic changes in the populations served by group psychotherapy since Foulkes' time. In the space of the approximately 70 years since he started running groups in Exeter, not only have populations in most UK cities grown, with far greater ethnic and social diversity, but the patterns of mental illness and psychological disorder have widened and altered in significant ways. It is important to recognize this at the outset, since group analysis, in my experience, is sometimes practised in a way that suggests that the patient population is unchanging and that the original clinical methods are there in perpetuity.

Statistics suggest that there is now a greater rate of psychiatric morbidity than ever before and that this is exacerbated in inner-city environments (Paykel *et al.* 2000). Whereas in Foulkes' time most problems were diagnosed within the binary of psychosis and neurosis, there is now a complex range of conditions, including psychosis, borderline conditions, personality disorder, emotional dysregulation, narcissistic disorders, the autistic spectrum, depression of varying degrees of severity, anxiety in many forms and different varieties of phobic and obsessional disorders. These conditions not unusually co-exist with drug- and alcohol-related problems and 'dual diagnosis' or even 'triple diagnosis' is common. Although the group psychotherapy service I run has exclusions such as active psychosis and severe borderline disorder, most of the patients referred suffer from one or more of the above conditions. Additionally, they have complex and longstanding psychological problems, including marked relationship difficulties, a history of broken relationships or absence of any significant relationships. Family histories reveal marked fragmentation and dysfunction. Trauma and abuse are endemic. Disorders of self are common.

By far the majority of referrals come from the Archway area, possibly because this is the area in which the service is based and there is more immediate access for Archway residents. Most of these referrals are from the more diverse and disadvantaged social groups. Fewer referrals come from the affluent areas, particularly the rich part of Islington, possibly because these residents are much more likely to be referred for private psychotherapy. The fact that the preponderance of referrals is from the lower income bracket means that there is also a greater admixture of ethnic diversity and higher levels of social isolation and disorganization, with the contrasting sense of a very different, more cushioned class secluded in their comfortable homes. In fact, most of our patients' presenting problems are as much, if not more, social than they are psychiatric, creating an overall impression of a fractured and embattled community with people struggling for self-preservation in the heart of London.

The large number of migrants and immigrants bring their particular problems. I differentiate between the two groups as follows: migrants are mainly British-born individuals who have moved from another part of the United Kingdom to London; immigrants have come to London from another country. On the face of it, immigration is the more disruptive and traumatic experience, especially where there is forced immigration, flight or the search for asylum (Grinberg and Grinberg 1989). However, migration within the UK itself can be a deeply problematic experience linked to family breakdown and abuse. The following is an example:

James (41) had lived in London for nineteen years, having left the northern English industrial town where he was born and raised. A single man, he was unemployed and socially isolated. He was referred for depression but significant communication and interpersonal problems raised the question of an underlying Asperger's syndrome. He was further disadvantaged by a particularly strong, indecipherable northern English accent that led to people avoiding him. He described a brutal family history. He was one of seven children raised by an alcoholic and violent father, his mother having left when James was eight. He had a highly anti-social adolescence, engaging in criminal behaviour that led to many years in remedial institutions and foster homes. When he came to London, he decided to make a fresh start but found it impossible to get work or make friends. He reported spending many hours on public transport for no reason other than having something to do and somewhere to go, travelling across the city by day and night. He had lived like this for years, totally marginalized, with no sense of purpose or meaning.

Immigrants from abroad often have even more dramatic histories of rupture and dislocation. Whereas some immigrants are successful at adapting to the new country and society, overcoming their sense of loss and uncertainty through active adjustment to their new environment (Grinberg and Grinberg 1989), those who come our way are usually in a different category – the dislocated and the dispossessed. Chronically unable to establish a sense of belonging and identity, they have fallen into a social and existential chasm, connected to neither their country of origin nor the new country. First-generation UK residents who are the offspring of immigrants in the previous generation often carry the burdens of loss, displacement and confusion, struggling to support parents who have never adjusted to the 'new' world, sometimes unable to speak English after years of living in the UK. Others are cut off from their families in hostile recrimination or despair, unwittingly repeating the rupture of immigration in their present lives. Two examples illustrate these features:

Farah (59) is a Pakistani woman who left Pakistan as a child, having witnessed her father being shot by police and her mother assaulted and raped. She escaped to the UK with two siblings, trying to maintain a fragile connection but feeling increasingly alienated. A professional woman, she was able to find intermittent work from which she drew a modest living and a modicum of self-respect. But this was insufficient to withstand the shadows of trauma and abandonment and she suffered periods of intense depression. In recent years, she had remade contact with relatives in Pakistan and started returning to Lahore, only to find herself suspended between cultures, appreciating the familiarity of home but no longer fitting in, temporarily relieved when returning to London but soon feeling like an outsider once again. Her attempts at emotional intimacy with men invariably floundered, undermined by deep culturally-based conflicts about the role of women.

Gil (38) is a first-generation British resident, the only son of Portuguese parents who ended up in London with few resources, little orientation to a new culture and embroiled in a disastrous marriage which fell apart soon after they immigrated. The father disappeared from the scene early on, leaving Gil in an intensely ambivalent relationship with an embittered, reclusive mother who resented her son's opportunities and kept him in a guilt-inducing, close-binding relationship. He succeeded in establishing neither an occupational nor social identity, drifting between groups, finding some enjoyment and comradeship in weight-lifting but becoming increasingly tense in his interpersonal contacts, easily feeling ridiculed and excluded. He gave the impression that beneath his self-deprecating exterior, he was filled with rage and could explode at any moment. In part his social withdrawal was to avoid conflict and confrontation, in case violence erupted. He presented for treatment in a demoralized state, convinced that nothing could help him, that he was destined to remain a failure and that the best he could hope for was to survive in a hostile world.

These examples could be repeated many times over, with myriad variations on the themes of loss, trauma and alienation. In some ways, the migrants' and immigrants' stories epitomize the tragic predicaments of people in our local community, mirrored when they enter NHS services, which can feel like entering another country. By the time they are referred for group therapy, patients have often been through the mill of psychiatric assessment and treatment, little of which has had any positive or lasting effect. Referral for group therapy is often the end of the line. Sometimes, there is a glimmer of understanding amongst referrers that these are social problems as much as psychiatric disorders and group treatment is seen as potentially providing them with the support and sense of belonging they lack in their lives. In principle, this may be true and a valid reason for referral. In practice, however, the weight of 'social suffering' (Hoggett 2008) and the compounding impact of financial and emotional chaos, is so great that the chances of helping these people in a psychotherapy group are tantalizingly present but realistically limited.

What of the rich inhabitants of the smart pockets of affluence in this part of London? The reality is that these people are not immune from the toll of emotional disturbance, family breakdown and social dysfunction. Money is not necessarily a hedge against the problems of life. But people from this community who need psychotherapeutic help usually gravitate towards private practice. Generally, they have the means and the knowledge that equips them to do so – and of course their chances of successful treatment are greater, since they have wider choice, they do not have to languish on waiting lists, they can decide for how long they need help (very different from NHS psychotherapy) and they may have the emotional vocabulary that might make them more accessible psychotherapeutically. The point, though, is not so much how the better endowed members of the community fare in psychotherapy. It is more what they represent politically and culturally in the context of those, such as James, Farah and Gil, who are a large minority, the disadvantaged and dispossessed. If it is difficult enough to be poor, unemployed and socially dysfunctional in inner-city London, how much more so when exposed to the privilege, wealth and well-being of people living virtually on your doorstep? These observations highlight the painful discrepancies between the haves and the have-nots, the rooted and the uprooted or un-rooted, all within a few square miles of London. This introduces notions of inequality and injustice and points to the inevitable manifestations of envy and estrangement that add a sting to the already difficult plight of the poor and the marginalized in inner-city society.

Am I safe? – surviving in the city

In as diverse, disadvantaged – and sometimes dangerous – a community as described, one of the prevailing anxieties concerns survival. Many of the groups I have supervised in this setting have included at least one person directly affected by murder or other serious physical attack, while some of the groups have included a perpetrator of violence. In one group, a member's teenage nephew was murdered by a youth gang during her time in the group. She arrived at the group one day in a state of shock, shared the news and left hurriedly to be with the family. Another man was preoccupied with vengeance for the murder of his brother in a gang shooting some years earlier, his default position being that he would one day hunt down and destroy each and every member of the gang. These events bring the threat of violence and death close to the group, creating unsettling and lurking fears of violence. Although this is not the part of London with the highest crime rate and incidence of violence, there is a great deal of it about, particularly in the lower-income groups, with considerable domestic violence, drug- and alcohol-related violence and gang violence.

Sometimes an air of ambiguity surrounds the event: who was perpetrator and who was victim, and how did it happen? In one case Nico, a member of a weekly group, had killed his brother with a kitchen knife some years earlier in a violent argument. His explanation was that this was an accident that occurred in the panic of self-defence. His brother had lunged towards him, grabbing his throat. Desperate, Nico threatened him with the knife but the brother lunged further forward and accidentally impaled himself on the knife. Nico was acquitted of both murder and manslaughter but some doubt existed about what had actually happened. Even the conductor described looking at Nico, the patient, and wondering whether he had told the whole story. In another group, Allison, a mother of two, described how her life disintegrated following an accident in which she killed a child in a car accident. The child had darted out of nowhere in front of the car. There was good reason to believe that she was innocent but was this really the case? Could she have stopped in time? Did her depression that day render her prone to causing an accident? Did her exhaustion with life, including her own family, play a part in the accident?

Fears of destructiveness are compounded by the presence of serious emotional disturbance. Although our psychotherapy groups exclude actively psychotic patients, some members have serious psychiatric histories, including schizophrenia and bi-polar disorder. These patients are usually not violent themselves but have anxieties about violence and fears of being regarded as violent, largely because of the popular misconception that all schizophrenics are dangerous. While knowing at one level that this is untrue, they may doubt themselves and are very aware of others' prejudices about the 'crazy'.

A young man, previously diagnosed as schizophrenic, in one of the groups became extremely anxious when he had to fill in an application form for a driving licence. He froze at the question of whether he had a mental illness, his main fear being that he would be refused a licence if he revealed the truth. Although there were some grounds for concern, his anxiety was exacerbated by a fear that he could not fully trust himself and hence be trusted by others. In the midst of this episode, he had a dream in which he was being hunted for the murder of an innocent man. The challenge of filling in the application form had triggered acute doubts about whether he was safe and would be regarded by others as safe. In cases like this, the level of anxiety about personal responsibility is high. Patients' fears of destructiveness may undermine their right to agency and self-assertion.

The question 'Am I safe?' can take different forms: 'Am I safe with myself?'; 'Is someone else safe with me?'; 'Am I safe with another person?' These anxieties are inscribed in group narratives in which the fear of annihilation is seldom far from consciousness. This means that members' trust in themselves, each other and the group is often fragile and hard to sustain. Talking about oneself in a group carries not only the usual vulnerability about self-exposure but also the added fear of provoking aggression and potentially triggering violence. A different fear concerns revealing something secret from the community where gangs can be powerful and vengeful, and having to pay the price of one's disloyalty. Cryptic references to activities in the community sometimes bear the stamp of the unmentionable. The group then can feel enshrouded in doubt and anxiety about what is safe to divulge and what might be too dangerous.

The fear of destructiveness, one's own and that of others, makes it difficult to tolerate difference and disagreement:

In one group, Graham, a man with a history of aggression was confronted about his responsibility for a marital problem. He became increasingly incensed with the person challenging him, saying it was time for him (Graham) to do something like leaving the group and beating up someone in the supermarket. The group tried to reason with him but nothing could pacify him and he left, never to return. He was probably anxious to avoid a physical fight breaking out in the group, but the prospect of his doing so outside the group was alarming. Although the group recovered its momentum, the event left the group with a sense of anxious responsibility and concern about further enactments.

In a later section I deal more fully with the anti-group manifestations of groups such as this. But it will be clear from the above that these groups generally have considerable difficulty becoming – and staying – a group and that there are frequent assaults on the group frame. In my description of the determinants of the anti-group (Nitsun 1996, 2005), I highlight *fear of annihilation* as an underlying theme. There are different aspects to this: the anxiety patients themselves bring to the group, given their fragile sense of self and fears of harm; what they bring from their embattled communities; and what dangers the group situation itself evokes.

These fears are often present in advance, when group therapy is first offered to patients, and account partly for the resistance many people have to group therapy. They can also account for sudden drop-outs. I have argued that the underlying anxieties of joining and being in a group are underestimated both in the literature and in practice (Nitsun 1988a, 1988b). The groups I describe in my service are a reminder that the necessary cohesion we strive for in groups can be hard won.

Survival fears are further exacerbated by actual illness and death in the course of a long-term psychotherapy group. If a group runs for several years, which is common in group analytic psychotherapy, it is likely that illness and mortality will strike at some point. I know of numerous patients who have either started a group with a moderately serious illness or become ill in the course of the group and I have also heard of the death of group members. Serious physical illness and death confirm fears of human vulnerability and mortality.

Sometimes illness and death go unnoticed in the fragmented community outside the group. Because of social withdrawal and isolation, an individual may languish unnoticed in illness and incapacity. Sometimes people die without anyone knowing. Days, weeks, months later a body is found.

A poignant example occurred in the later phase of a long-term group. Sharon was a vulnerable, isolated woman who had suffered with a serious abdominal condition much of her life. While in the group, she had intermittent recurrences of the illness. Having seemed a lot better and committed to the group, she then fell ill again. She had missed two sessions and there was no call from her. The conductor wrote to her but received no reply. One morning before the group started, he accessed his computerized health records to undertake some routine administration. When he opened Sharon's file, the message hit him like a thunderbolt. It said simply: 'Patient found dead in her flat.' When he searched further, it appeared that Sharon's condition had rapidly deteriorated and, severely dehydrated, she died. Devastated, the conductor shared the information with the group. Shock ran through the group. As the reality of what happened sunk in, it evoked a deep sense of humility and compassion. Ironically, in the muddled community from which Sharon came, the therapy group was probably the one group that recognized and mourned her death. Psychotherapy groups, for all their limitations, are small enough and caring enough for illness and death not to go unnoticed and to bring out the element of humanity that is sometimes lost in the dense, indifferent crowd inhabiting the inner city.

Disempowerment and dependence

Unemployment, poor education, lack of opportunity and the debilitating effect of illness all contribute to an embattled sense of the future and the loss of a personal vision, other than surviving day to day in the midst of loneliness and the small and large indignities of everyday life. This is compounded by financial shortage. The lack of a consistent income and reliance on meagre benefits creates many restrictions. The freedom simply to leave home, to pay for transport and to afford basic household supplies, let alone enjoying entertainment or indulging in the occasional luxury, are all curtailed. Life is often confined to four walls and there is a sense of shrunken horizons in the midst of one of the world's greatest and most plentiful cities.

Shame and humiliation are common responses to chronic deprivation. The contrast between rich and poor that I mentioned earlier adds to the humiliation. Various studies demonstrate a greater incidence of mental illness in populations in which there is a wider socio-economic disparity between groups (Paykel *et al.* 2000). Further, in London at present there is ongoing controversy about dependency on the state, fuelled by the coalition government's active drive to curtail benefits and get people back to work (Syal 2013). Much of this is focused on the intervention of Atos (a firm contracted to conduct work capability assessments). Patients are required to complete a complex and demanding form and then submit to a gruelling interview process designed to establish eligibility for benefits – or not. The outcome is often disadvantageous: individuals could be summarily stripped of existing benefits and face a dramatic reduction in income support, housing and other benefits.

The Atos interviews for some months preoccupied patients attending a weekly psychotherapy group. It was clear that the process had generated renewed fears of destitution. Interestingly, this group became much more cohesive in response to the threat posed by Atos. Most of the patients in the group were in the same boat: having summarily to undergo the assessment process and facing this on their own. But the group became very supportive. Patients were able to offer each other advice. Some had already been through the process and could give tips on how to deal with it. The support, though, was not just practical. People identified closely with each other, getting to know more about each other's predicaments and caring about the outcomes of the process. It was as if the common enemy – the state – had brought them closer, counteracting their own anti-group tendency. The extent to which the group could offer support was striking, highlighting a specific group function – to support patients' efforts on the margins of social control. The benefits assessment process, although widely regarded as unfair and crude, nevertheless had some positive spin-offs. Some patients felt able to consider their strengths anew, to make concerted efforts to find work and to deal with practical problems such as housing.

While the therapy group can help to empower members in certain ways, in other respects it is powerless to do anything other than mirror feelings of helplessness and inadequacy. Part of this is the experience of being a patient in as large an organization as the NHS. Of course there are no easy solutions in organizations that are dealing with so many thousands of people. But, from the patient's perspective, this only further reinforces the sense of insignificance, of being a tiny cog in an enormous wheel. Again, this quite often paradoxically creates cohesion in psychotherapy groups, through the shared sense of disempowerment and the frustration this generates. It can be difficult for therapists to judge how much this reflects real frustrations in NHS treatment and how much it reflects underlying issues about disempowerment, not unusually stemming from stifling experiences of marginalization and humiliation in family and social groups.

The mirroring processes described are true not only of patients but also NHS staff, including psychotherapists. There is more or less constant anxiety about resources in the NHS. This is worse in some services than others: some health trusts are better resourced for psychotherapy. But generally, an atmosphere of financial pressure and insecurity prevails, in the shadow of threatened or actual cuts. Additionally, with the growing emphasis on performance management, targets and payment by results, long-term psychotherapy methods, with their low turnover of patients and inconsistent outcomes, are increasingly vulnerable. Therapists responsible for these services often feel anxious about their jobs, their futures and for how long they will be able to continue working with their groups. The plight of patients, their sense of deprivation and disempowerment, is mirrored in the problems of staff struggling to keep afloat in their institutions.

Group and social refusal

It is important to recognize that although I have described elements of helplessness and dependence as part of the emotional constellation of the patients, their response to group psychotherapy is not just one of passive indifference. They are often angry, resistant, rebellious and attacking, sometimes of the entire NHS system and of the group specifically. This is similar to the refusal of people in the category of 'the homeless, the dangerous and the disordered', described by Scanlon and Aldlam (2011). These authors explore this group's great ambivalence about engaging with services and the complex and frustrating relationship they establish with the helping agencies who attempt to draw them into statutory and non-statutory services. Our patients are not as inaccessible and consistently rejecting of help as the people Scanlon and Adlam describe – nor quite as desperate – but a vein of refusal is not uncommon in responses to treatment. A similar response may come from immigrant populations who have difficulty adjusting to their new environment and accepting the treatment on offer.

Marta began talking about how much she disliked London as a city. She had lived here for several years, having emigrated from Spain, but had never grown used to it. She found it dirty, inhospitable and oppressive. Jim, a Londoner, was offended by this and an argument quickly sprung up between the two. Jim had himself been a reluctant group member, attending erratically and complaining that the group was of no help to him, but in this argument he became angrily defensive of London, the NHS and the 'wonderful' treatment provided. When Marta refused to budge on her position, Jim grew angrier and scoffed at the conductor for bringing in such ungrateful people. Eventually, in a fit of pique, he left the group and did not return that session. In this enactment, Marta's rejection of the city had provoked a critical reaction from Jim who could then project all his resistance and refusal onto her. Both were struggling with different forms of refusal, mirroring each other but unable to distinguish what belonged to whom.

There are many contradictions in the way patients relate to the whole notion of care. The NHS is overwhelmed by human need and psychotherapy services are usually stretched to the limit, but the problem is not simply one of inadequate resources. It is how to accommodate the complex and ambivalent needs that patients bring to treatment, including their wish not to be patients and not to be treated. This is sometimes expressed directly in therapy and sometimes symbolically:

Lucy told the group how she had found a lost kitten in the street. It was tiny and hungry. Not a cat lover herself, she nevertheless took pity on the kitten and brought it home, putting it in a cardboard box with a blanket. The group was touched by the story. In subsequent weeks, they enquired about the kitten and Lucy described the mixed feelings she had about it. She had quite grown to like it, but it was messing in the house and she was unsure of whether to keep it. Jill suddenly became critical of Lucy saying that she was heartless, that her attitude to the kitten reflected something hard and unfeeling in her. Others in the group were dismayed by Jill's criticisms and supported Lucy's right to decide what she wanted to do with the kitten. The debate became entangled with further disagreements in the group, members feeling unfairly criticized by each other, leading to intense conflict. The conductor commented on how the tenderness group members had initially shown towards the kitten had been submerged in the anger and cross-accusations. The conductor also interpreted that she might need to be entrusted with the small, hungry, messy side of the group members (like the kitten) and look after it for them. Lucy, seeing this, too, as a criticism, became angry and said she wished she had never mentioned the 'damn cat' in the group. Here, the fate of the kitten in the box appeared to symbolize the considerable ambivalence group members felt about allowing themselves to be cared for, to be 'accommodated' (as in the box) emotionally. The fractious group concealed the wish to trust and depend, to be contained, blaming each other for being rejecting and uncaring and thwarting the conductor's attempts to support the group.

A different form of refusal is reflected in the difficulty members have in accepting group boundaries and norms. Although resistance to boundaries is a common problem in groups, I have found this to be more pronounced in NHS psychotherapy groups, sometimes making it very difficult to establish a stable group frame. The basic requirements of group participation, such as regular attendance, punctuality and sending messages about non-attendance, are often flouted. Group members casually and frequently miss sessions, sending no messages and arriving at the group at very different times. Reminders that a minimal degree of adherence is necessary for the development of the group are seemingly heard but not heeded. This form of anti-group behaviour is usually an enactment of some underlying and uncommunicated difficulty, some anxiety about a threat posed by the group, but the non-adherence may also reflect a fundamental refusal of the treatment frame.

A particularly problematic attack on the group frame concerns meetings and relationships outside the group. The rejection of this specific rule – that extra-group meetings are out of bounds – is usually enacted in meetings of the whole or part of the group in cafes and car parks, even in members' homes. The group therapist's challenges to this behaviour are usually met with resistance. There is an insistence on personal and social rights. As suggested by Hyde (1991), this rebellion may conceal frustrated longings for the idealized conductor or reflect a counter-dependent move concealing fears of dependence. However, it may also reflect an underlying sense of emotional and social deprivation. Members may meet separately to supplement the meagre supplies of the group: the one and a half hours a week that paradoxically the group so often has difficulty accepting may yet feel like a drop in the ocean given the degree of isolation that many people experience – and the depth of their emotional need.

These extra-group meetings are in my experience very difficult to deal with. The combination of rebellion and the protestations about 'our right' to meet – including the possibility that the meetings at one level *may* serve a valid social purpose – makes it very difficult for conductors to stand their ground. A related difficulty concerns two people meeting outside the group, sometimes as friends, sometimes for sexual or romantic purposes. Of course, this problem is not confined to NHS groups and is challenging in whichever group setting it occurs. However, I think it happens with greater frequency in NHS groups and reflects similarly mixed motives – rebellion, and at the same time, an expression of unsatisfied and sometimes desperate longings for a relationship. I have written about this in greater detail in a previous publication (Nitsun 2006), suggesting that this sort of acting-out must be looked at in the context of the group as a whole since the 'transgressive' couple's enactment may contain an important message about the group, whether the group is addressing a fundamental need – or not – and whether the group conceals rather than reveals members' desires and attractions. The relationship-outside-the-group can reflect a particularly stubborn refusal by not just the couple but by the group as a whole, since I have known groups to collude with the enactment, aware all along that it is happening but keeping it well-hidden from the conductor – until the news suddenly erupts. This is a form of 'Oedipal' enactment, the whole group colluding with the 'guilty' couple in the attack on the parental group, particularly the conductor.

I have previously highlighted the hatred of authority as under-emphasized in group analytic literature and practice (Nitsun 2009). There are usually good reasons for this hatred, connected with the abuse of authority by parents and other figures of authority in the patient's development. This is compounded in the UK by dependence on authority (the state, the health service and so on), often experienced as arbitrary and oppressive in much the way I described above. The combination of refusal, rebellion and hatred of authority in groups may be powerful obstacles in groups (Billow 2010).

The anti-group and the development of the group

Much of what I have described reflects an anti-group position that is common to many of our patients. Aetiologically, this is not surprising, given their adverse family and group histories. Few patients have had the positive experience of a containing, nurturing group: many have experienced isolation in groups, fragmented groups, abuse in groups. As described in Chapter 3, this forms a group template, an underlying predisposition to perceive and experience groups negatively, according to learned expectations (Nitsun 1996, 2006). The psychotherapy group is bound to recapitulate these experiences – though hopefully with the potential for 'corrective recapitulation' (Yalom and Leszcz 2005). In this section I describe the developmental process whereby the group may make the journey from an anti-group to a more functional and constructive therapeutic group.

All the hallmarks of the anti-group and the factors construed as 'anti-group determinants' are present (Nitsun 1996, 2005) in these groups. These include the fear of annihilation I mentioned earlier, reflected in the question, 'Am I safe?' Further determinants are fears of exposure and narcissistic injury, psychological trauma, the frustrated longing for an idealized relationship, the alienation of desire, attacks on linking, projective identification and failures of communication. The latter three determinants are especially important as they relate to the communication process in the group. While Foulkes (1964) emphasized communication as the essence of psychotherapy, he emphasized mainly verbal communication and the gradual transformation into words of the inchoate and the 'autistic'. While this is an important aim, it cannot simply be assumed to happen. As I have described in several publications (Nitsun 1991, 1996, 2006), communication in groups can be fraught with misunderstanding, misattunement and what I refer to as 'contaminating communication' in which an individual or group feels in some way sullied or infected by the communication. This can happen through projective identification as well as attacks on linking (Bion 1959), which obliterate psychological meaning and create an incoherent group atmosphere. The psychotherapy group can be more akin to a 'gang' in the way that Rosenfeld (1971) described a highly defensive, mafia-like internal organization that attacks the hand that feeds it. Although I have placed much emphasis on the social environment of the inner city, its pressures and divisions, as influencing the problems we see in our groups, I also believe that this is not the whole story. Group processes are formed through complex conscious and unconscious intra-psychic and interpersonal processes that have to be understood on their own terms and not only as reflections of external phenomena.

A group psychotherapist is more likely to see the anti-group in its 'pure' form in NHS services of this kind than in other settings, particularly private practice where people are more positively motivated to join a group: they choose to join a group and their social and group history is also generally more benign. In the NHS, there is high degree of group refusal at the outset, patients often electing not to join a group. As Bowden (2002) reported on the basis of a study of NHS patients' treatment preferences, many patients tend to decline group therapy, seeing it as unsafe and unconvincing as a therapeutic option. NHS psychotherapy groups take a long time to gel, given the difficulties in recruitment and the many slips between patients being put on the waiting list and their joining a group: there may be fall-out at several stages. The start of the group as a whole, the first few months, is usually fraught. The lack of trust and survival fears I described in my paper on the early development of the group (Nitsun 1988) are particularly marked. The potential of the group to fragment is a constant concern. As in any anti-group process, the effect is contagious. People dropping out of the group suddenly, angrily, or without explanation, has a demoralizing effect on the group. Yet, there is often a curious reluctance to challenge members' poor attendance or wish to leave the group. Rather, the remaining few in a diminishing group question whether they should stay. New members joining arrive to find a depleted group, wondering whether this is a place they want to be. Some come and go quickly and a debilitating chain reaction is set in motion. Underlying this is a question that may preoccupy the group conductor: will this group survive?

Mark, a group analyst in training, described his anxious reaction to a downward spiral in his group's development. The group had started on a surprisingly high note. Group members seemed to appreciate the opportunity to be in a group and there was a sense of early group cohesion – and a tendency to deny ambivalence about the group. The discussions were lively and seemingly productive. However, once aggression in the group became manifest, ostensibly in the form of conflicting views on religion, tensions quickly grew and became increasingly personal and problematic. When one member in high dudgeon decided to leave the group, attendance generally started faltering and reached a point where, out of a previous six members, only one, two or three were attending any given session. The conductor worked hard to salvage the group but felt increasingly despondent. He described waiting for the group to start one day and no one turning up. He experienced an acute fear of abandonment, a vision of being left entirely alone. The group survived but the conductor periodically experienced a fear of abandonment.

The process here is akin to my description of the latent and manifest anti-group (Nitsun 1996). Here, the group initially appears cohesive but has a quality of strain, conformity or a group false-self (Fried 1979): a 'too good group'. When something goes wrong in the group, the edifice cracks and a latent anti-group breaks out. In this particular group, the conductor was left holding powerful projections of fear and abandonment.

How is a group transformed from a group in crisis, such as in the above example, to a grounded and functional therapeutic entity? How does it approach what I have referred to as the converse of the anti-group: the group as an object of desire (Nitsun 2006)? Fortunately, in most groups, the constructive momentum of the group outweighs the destructive and, gradually, the group begins to solidify. This happens inconsistently, periods of cohesion alternating with un-cohesion in an unpredictable process. But, usually, a core of committed members begins to emerge. This may entail several abortive group memberships, patients coming and going, but a smaller, more settled group gradually materializes. The survival of the group in the face of loss and fragmentation is itself a strengthening factor and through this experience the group comes to take responsibility for itself, to value its identity and integrity as a group (Nitsun 1996, 2006). For members who stay the course, this may be the first time they have participated in a group that has endured, to which they can belong and on which they can depend.

As I usually argue, the anti-group may have the paradoxical value of confronting members with their own destructive and self-destructive tendencies. Once this is open to scrutiny, and there is some understanding of these tendencies, the process usually shifts towards greater reflectiveness and a greater sense of personal responsibility. The work of the middle and later stages of the group is usually concerned with understanding self and other, a slow collaborative process of making sense of relationships and taking the risk of greater intimacy and deeper attachment. In this strengthened group culture, it is possible to begin to address differences more openly and to appreciate others for their otherness.

Other examples of the kind of progress in a group I am describing reflect the day-to-day reality of people living in this part of London. Often this concerns members' immediate living circumstances and, for example, how they deal with the daily impingements of life on a council estate, the trials of long-term unemployment and the constant and painful negotiation of self-respect in a society that provides little respect for individuals. The development of compassion for self and other is an important aspect. The following is an example of a change that took place approximately eighteen months into an ongoing group:

> Trevor, age 42, lived in a small flat on a housing estate. He had ongoing difficulty with neighbours, frequently getting into minor disputes that escalated out of proportion and blaming others for the problem. This reflected his overall anti-social, anti-group tendency. He was particularly discomfited and enraged by a black woman living next door who was given to fits of crying and shouting and he described how often he felt like rushing into her flat and silencing her with a punch in the head. The group was initially wary of Trevor, keeping him at arms' length, but gradually let him in, recognizing the anxieties that made him so anti-social, and at the same time challenging some of his prejudices. He gradually grew somewhat more tolerant of others. One day he revealed to the group a softening of his attitude towards his black neighbour. He had heard a story about her that touched him: she had lost a child through a wasting illness some years ago and had never been the same since. Trevor began to understand the woman as a person and presented to the group a somewhat humbler, compassionate side when he reported this. The group encouraged this side. He continued to have difficult social relationships but became more aware of his part in these difficulties.

Here, the group had a humanizing function, so important in the inner city where the embattled conditions can undermine concern for others.

To round off this section on the anti-group, I will highlight the distinction between the 'pathological anti-group' and the 'developmental anti-group' (Nitsun 1996). The distinction is meant to be flexible and not rigid, but having the distinction may help to assess the severity of the problem. The developmental anti-group describes a common situation in which doubt and criticism of the group, including hostile attacks and a tendency towards fragmentation, appear as part of the process of the group's development. Here, members are testing the boundaries and resilience of the group. From this often emerges the strength and durability of the group.

I describe this as a dialectical process in which the constructive and potentially destructive processes are mutually generating (Nitsun 1996, 2005). The pathological anti-group occurs when the dialectic breaks down and the group sinks into impasse or fragments and its continuity is under threat. The difference between the two types of anti-group has technical implications. Whereas the developmental anti-group may require little more than facilitation, recognition and understanding, the pathological anti-group requires active intervention on the part of the conductor. Depending on the situation, the conductor may need to address boundary infringements, reset group rules and address hostile conflicts, as well as reviewing the group composition, if the impasse cannot be shifted.

The group conductor

The groups run in a typical inner-London NHS service are usually perplexing, sometimes dispiriting, but ultimately a rewarding experience for group conductors. The lurking possibility that the group might not survive is the greatest challenge, triggering considerable anxiety and doubt in the conductor about his or her competence. One reason I have emphasized the very real difficulties in these groups is to normalize the anxiety of the therapist. I made this point when originally formulating the notion of the anti-group (Nitsun 1991), noting that group psychotherapists tend to assume responsibility for difficulties in their groups when the process itself may be inherently problematic. I have seen many conductors struggle with fears of group disintegration and a sense of their own failure. The emotional impact can be profound: consider the reaction of the therapist in the example in which he felt overwhelmed by fears of abandonment as he waited anxiously for group members to arrive. The encounter with the anti-group is inevitable in groups of this kind and tends to generate the conductor's own anti-group (see Chapter 7), evoking feelings of hatred and exasperation with the group – perhaps the group equivalent of 'hate in the counter-transference' (Winnicott 1949).

Group therapists in NHS settings often have to manage feelings of disappointment, if not disillusionment, in the group process. In my experience, they tend to start anxiously but optimistically, welcoming the challenge of working with a group of such diversity, hoping that the group will help people to come together in a spirit of understanding. Possibly this is an invitation to heroism on the part of the therapist – an opportunity to make a real contribution, to work towards integration and transformation. This is in spite of warnings that these are difficult groups to run. There is usually surprise at how long it takes to set up the group, how problematic the recruitment process is and how impingements of various sorts impede early group formation. Then there may be alarm when the difficulties continue and sometimes worsen. As the group gradually comes together, however, sometimes unexpectedly after a period of fall-out, there is relief and a degree of renewed optimism. Usually, by the end of the group, the conductor's faith in the group is largely restored.

The conductor has to deal with ways in which he/she is both different and similar to patients. Almost any conductor is in a privileged position compared to NHS patients and this can be a source of discomfort, if not guilt. The therapist is clearly in the category of 'haves' relative to patients as 'have-nots'. But, at another level, the therapist is a person with his or her own problems. In my experience, therapists who choose to work in groups have their own concerns about belonging and have had to deal with their own developmental injuries. 'We are all asylum seekers', says Morgan (2011), reflecting on the problems of working with the most displaced and desperate people in our care. Analytic psychotherapy groups, especially in these settings, tend to evoke strong identifications with patients, both consciously and unconsciously, potentially blurring the line between conductors and group members, and there is an ongoing task for group conductors in managing the sometimes fragile boundary between self and other.

Titmus (1974) talks about the 'gift relationship'. In his work on social policy and welfare practice, he emphasizes the central importance of relationships of reciprocity and mutuality in working with the less privileged. This form of relationship cannot be assumed, however: it has to be worked at and usually comes about ambivalently and painfully. Part of the learning is the challenge to one's expert position and the need to accept a position of not knowing and not getting it right. This includes recognition of one's own hatred and sadism and, in NHS group work, as highlighted above, resentment about the burden of responsibility one carries for the group. As I see therapists struggling over time with their difficult groups, I also see the development of a mutual vulnerability in their relationship with patients. Group psychotherapists perhaps more than most encounter the dimension of universality through the many stories that inhabit their groups: this includes themselves and their own stories.

Learning in these groups includes consideration of the therapist's representation of authority. Although the democratization of the group remains an ideal, and is heavily inscribed in the value system of group analysis (Foulkes 1964), the challenge is how to take authority when needed. I have previously written about an element of denial of authority in group analysis (Nitsun 2009), which I see as a reflection of the idealization of both Foulkes' legacy and the group process itself. I believe this can result in what Gustafson (1979, cited in Hoggett 2008) described as 'pseudomutuality'. This form of mutuality is predicated on a denial of difference between patient and practitioner and a denial of the understanding and knowledge, however tentative, that the therapist possesses. There are times in any group, but particularly these troubled groups, when the threat of individual and social breakdown materializes, for example in a patient disintegrating into psychosis or making a serious suicide attempt or enacting violence. There is then an urgent appeal to the authority of the therapist. The therapist needs to make decisions, to act, to manage the crisis. He/she cannot leave it to the group. Group therapists working in these situations face the challenge of accepting their limitations and vulnerability at one level but owning their own authority at another. The solution is neither the suspension of authority nor the inappropriate exertion of authority but the modulation of authority in line with the requirements and demands of the group. There are ways of representing authority in a fair, open and transparent manner, when group members can be included in the decision without handing the decision to them in toto. In itself, this may be a salutary lesson for group members used to feeling crushed by authority or wanting to crush authority through their hatred and envy. Hoggett's (2008) notion of 'democratic authority' gets close to what is possible and appropriate in the group setting. In my Foulkes Lecture (2009), I highlighted the value of *wrestling* with authority. I argued that group members may acquire their own authority more readily by engaging with authority and finding their strength in the process than by being faced with an ambiguous situation in which authority is blurred.

Finally, having focused on the difficulties group conductors experience in this setting, it is important not to minimize the pleasure and satisfaction that can be derived from the groups. When a group comes together after periods of frustration and fragmentation, as it gains in closeness and depth, the experience can be very rewarding. Some of the examples above reflect this. Conductors not unusually describe feeling very moved by the hard-won gains patients make and the sensitive and sometimes profound humanity that emerges in the group.

Reflections on group analytic technique

Group psychotherapy remains one of the few psychological treatments available to NHS patients and is especially relevant in situations such as I have described – largely disadvantaged communities in inner cities with a high rate of diversity and social fragmentation. As Sluzki (2012) suggests, the urgent need to rebuild social networks in contemporary communities may be met by a wider application of group therapy. However, it is important not to overlook the problems of implementing such services. Although I ended the previous part of this chapter on a relatively optimistic note, giving examples of significant progress in groups, it is necessary to highlight that these were hard-won gains, often against a background of pronounced group anxiety and fall-out. In this section I consider aspects of the group analytic approach that may require modification, which options there are for change, and a possible re-envisaging of the group under the term 'the group as refuge'.

As noted earlier, the populations we now serve are very different from those in Foulkes' day. Foulkes and Anthony (1965) described group referrals as 'largely psycho-neurotic' and although they occasionally mention a psychotic patient in a group, we are now dealing with far greater diversity and intensity in both mental health problems and cultural background. Foulkes and Anthony also made a point about the need for a minimum level of verbal ability in group patients and, more so, refer to the 'common ground' in patients that can be 'taken for granted'. This includes 'talking the same language against the same background of national feeling' as well as 'other shared conditions such as ... religion, social background, intelligence, education, profession, marital status' (1965, p. 65). This list of what

Foulkes and Anthony felt able to assume in their groups highlights dramatically how mental health populations have changed in the intervening years. Their selection criteria, if applied in present circumstances, could seldom be met.

Given the mix of languages our patients speak, English not being their first language and often a poor second, as well as the low level of literacy generally in the population, the requirement of 'the same language' is largely unachievable, let alone other criteria such as commonalities in religion, ethnicity, social background, education and profession. Part of the challenge of the groups is to evolve a shared language of understanding without expecting more of patients than they can manage or exposing them to damaging feelings of difference and inadequacy. Communication problems are further aggravated by patients' difficulties in mentalizing their own and others' responses, especially in borderline-type disorders, creating failures of attunement and understanding that can impede and undermine linguistic propensities and hence the therapeutic task itself.

These linguistic and cognitive difficulties highlight the non-directive, unstructured aspect of group analytic psychotherapy and the relatively passive role of the conductor. Groups of this sort have a level of ambiguity that tends to arouse rather than reduce anxiety and, in my view, may not be particularly facilitating of the kinds of patients I describe. Apart from dealing with the challenges of their own lives which brought them to the group, patients face the daunting challenge of entering a group of strangers, in a relatively unstructured and undirected setting, with all the anxiety that pronounced difference evokes, as well as all the ingrained mistrust and suspicion that their past experience has bequeathed. My impression is that the traditionally low-key, non-directive and sometimes unresponsive attitude of the group analyst, combined with the ambiguous and confusing group task and the strong emphasis on verbal communication and articulacy, may not be appropriate or helpful. The research findings of Karterud (2011) are relevant here. Karterud undertook a controlled study on the treatment of borderline disorder, comparing the impact of group analytic therapy with that of group mentalization-based therapy. He found that mentalization, a structured approach using explicit interactional methods aimed at strengthening interpersonal understanding (Fonagy and Bateman 2008), was more effective. Our NHS patient population could not be classified as exclusively borderline but there are sometimes specifically borderline patients and others who have distinct borderline features. Whatever the diagnosis, the question is whether the group analytic method could be strengthened by modifications along the lines of mentalization groups. A more active, more directly engaged role on the part of the conductor, in my view, would be beneficial. An approach like mentalization, which focuses on direct communication between people and correcting errors of understanding, may facilitate the development of verbal communication skills that in turn could help to strengthen relationships and commitment to the group. At the same time it could impart skills of living that are useful in the cut and thrust of everyday life. The mentalization approach in any case is highly compatible with group analysis, approximating 'ego training in action' (Foulkes 1964) and the inter-subjective mode of group analysis (Brown 1994; Schulte 2000). Combining an approach of this kind with group analysis may strengthen both.

> A brief example of a situation where mentalization might have been used effectively is the group described earlier in which Jim could not tolerate the difference of opinion he had with Marta and left, threatening violence. Language differences contributed to the tension. The group conductor in this case was fairly passive, waiting to see how the group interacted. Instead, he could have taken a more active mentalization stance. This might have helped Jim to explore his reactions in the group more openly; helped Marta (an Italian) to explain herself more fully in the English language; addressed the impact of language differences on the group; and involved the whole group more directly in an attempt to understand the disagreement.

I suggest that it is useful to reconsider the overall nature of therapy in the group and how this influences group functioning. My sense is that 'deep' therapy aimed at exploring unconscious processes or encouraging therapeutic regression is not particularly what patients in this setting understand or want. In my own group experience with this population, and that described by colleagues and supervisees, I have been struck that the most meaningful sessions are sometimes those in which something relatively simple happens. Patients come in from their harassed lives, often literally from the cold, coping with significant isolation and loneliness and crippling economic stresses, and find in the hour and a half of the group much-needed respite. The group provides temporary shelter. Patients appreciate being in a warm, comfortable setting, they chat about their difficult days and their immediate stresses. They seem to like being there and do not seem to need anything else, at least for the moment. They may go on to talk about problematic relationships, present and past, sharing life narratives with each other and so on, but this too is conversational and not necessarily open to intense scrutiny by the therapist or anyone else. My sense is that at these times the group functions as a *refuge* – a refuge from the madness of the outside world and a refuge from their inner distress and perplexity. When this happens, it is best, I believe, to let the group be. These are times when the group comes together, when people can begin to trust each other. *The group as refuge* seems to me a valuable achievement and different from what we usually expect from analytic therapy groups. I believe that once this is achieved, it is also more possible to work psychotherapeutically at the level of insight and change.

In conclusion, NHS psychotherapy groups in inner-city areas present a considerable challenge, while remaining an important part of service provision for complex mental health problems in this troubled and changing environment. The approach described here in some ways resembles what Foulkes (1948) described as 'open air psychiatry'. By this he meant not literally working in the open air but working within the community, with a sense of the impact of social processes within the community. NHS psychotherapy groups are often a microcosm of the societies in which they take place, reflecting the cultural diversity, social division and widespread mental health disturbance that mark the urban environment of the twenty-first century. The breadth and depth of these issues create a complex therapeutic task that can put severe strains on the conductor. The anti-group is seldom far from the picture, with a high degree of either explicit or implicit group refusal or enactment. These difficulties, in my view, invite consideration of whether group analytic therapy in its familiar form is the most helpful approach. The chapter suggests a re-envisaging of the therapy group as a *group as refuge*, with suggestions for a more active, engaged stance on the part of the conductor and the utilization of more structured interventions, such as mentalization. This does not rule out much that is valuable in group analysis, including the in-depth appreciation of both individual and social factors, the understanding of group processes and working towards greater group integrity.

References

Billow, R. M. (2010) *Resistance, Rebellion and Refusal in Groups*. London: Karnac.

Bion, W. F. (1959) Attacks on linking, *International Journal of Psychoanalysis*, 40, 308.

Bowden, M. (2002) Anti-group attitudes at assessment for psychotherapy, *Psychoanalytic Psychotherapy*, 16, 246–58.

Brown, D. (1994) Self development through subjective interaction, in Brown, D. and Zinkin, L. (eds) *The Psyche and the Social World: Developments in Group-Analytic Theory*. London: Routledge.

Fonagy, P. and Bateman, A. (2008) The development of borderline personality disorder, *Journal of Personality Disorders*, 22, 4–21.

Foulkes, S. H. (1948) *Introduction to Group Analytic Psychotherapy*. London: Heinemann.

Foulkes, S. H. (1964 [1986]) *Therapeutic Group Analysis*. London: Karnac.

Foulkes, S. H. and Anthony, J. A. (1965) *Group Psychotherapy: The Psychoanalytic Approach*. London: Penguin.

Fried, K. W. (1979) Within and without: the examination of a ubiquitous resistance in group therapy, in Wolberg, L. and Aronson, M. (eds) *Group Therapy*. New York: Stratton.

Grinberg, L. and Grinberg, R. (1989) *Psychoanalytic Perspectives on Migration and Exile*. New Haven: Yale University Press.

Gustafson, J. (1979) The pseudomutual small group or institution, in Lawrence, G. (ed.) *Exploring Individual and Organizational Boundaries*. Chichester: John Wiley.

Hoggett, P. (2008) Relational thinking and welfare practice, in Clarke, S., Hahn, H. and Hoggett, P. (eds) *Object Relations and Social Relations*. London: Karnac.

Hyde, K. R. (1991) Idealization and omnipotence within the group matrix, *Group Analysis*, 24, 279–97.

Karterud, S. (2011) Constructing and Mentalizing the Matrix, *Group Analysis*, 44, 11–17.

Morgan, D. (2011) Asylum: one step beyond, *New Associations*, issue 7, Autumn.

Nitsun, M. (1988) Early development: linking the individual and the group, *Group Analysis*, 22, 249–60.

Nitsun, M. (1991) The anti-group: destructive forces in the group and their therapeutic potential, *Group Analysis*, 24, 7–20.

Nitsun, M. (1996) *The Anti-group: Destructive Forces in the Group and their Creative Potential.* London: Routledge.

Nitsun, M. (1998a) The organizational mirror: a group-analytic approach to organizational consultancy, part 1 – theory, *Group Analysis*, 31, 245–67.

Nitsun, M. (1998b) The organizational mirror: a group-analytic approach to organizational consultancy: part 2 – application, *Group Analysis*, 31, 505–18.

Nitsun, M. (2005) Destructive forces, in Motherwell, L. and Shay, J. (eds) *Complex Dilemmas in Group Psychotherapy.* New York: Brunner-Routledge.

Nitsun, M. (2006) *The Group as an Object of Desire: Exploring Sexuality in Group Therapy.* London: Routledge.

Nitsun, M. (2009) Authority and revolt: the challenges to group leadership, *Group Analysis*, 42, 325–48.

Paykel, E. S., Abbott, R., Jenkins, R., Brugha, T. S. and Melzer, H. (2000) Urban-rural mental health differences in Great Britain: findings from the national morbidity survey, *Psychological Medicine*, 301, 269–80.

Rosenfeld, H. (1971) A clinical approach to the psychoanalytic theory of the life and death instincts: an investigation into the aggressive aspects of narcissism, *International Journal of Psychoanalysis*, 52, 169–77.

Scanlon, S. and Adlam, J. (2011) Defacing the currency: a group analytic appreciation of homelessness, dangerousness, disorder and other inarticulate speech of the heart, *Group Analysis*, 44, 131–48.

Schulte, P. (2000) Holding in mind: intersubjectivity, subject relations and the group, *Group Analysis*, 33, 531–44.

Sluzki, C. (2012) The group therapist as social network enhancer: a new area of inquiry, *Forum: Journal of the international Association for Group Psychotherapy and Group Process*, 5, 39–53.

Syal, R. (2013) DWP to blame for fitness-to-work tests fiasco, *The Guardian*, 8 February.

Titmus, R. (1971) *The Gift Relationship.* London: Pantheon.

Winnicott, D. W. (1949 [1992]) Hate in the counter-transference, in *Through Paediatrics to Psychoanalysis.* London: Karnac/Institute of Psychoanalysis.

Yalom, I. B. and Leszcz, M. (2005) *Theory and Practice of Group Psychotherapy.* New York: Basic Books.

Part III

Developmental perspectives

Chapter 6

Being a group therapist

A journey through life

We increasingly recognize the profound effect therapists have on their work – and the effect their work has on them – but the group psychotherapist in his/her personal and professional capacity has seldom been studied in depth. The person of the therapist will influence almost every aspect of psychotherapeutic practice – from choice of therapeutic approach to clinical strengths and vulnerabilities. To understand the specifics of this process would appear to be a priority. In order to fill what I see as a significant gap in the literature, I set out to explore the group therapist in three dimensions – past, present and future – aiming to build up a picture of the developmental journey that makes a group therapist what he or she is. In addition to coverage of the relevant literature, I offer some specific hypotheses and illustrate some of my notions with biographical and autobiographical material. Not surprisingly, the group psychotherapist's own relationship to groups, including his/her group history, emerges as a predominating theme.

Introduction

Why do some psychotherapists choose to work in groups and others not – and why do some choose group as their primary therapeutic mode, sometimes in preference to individual therapy? These questions, which seem fundamental to our professional identity and field of endeavor, have seldom been addressed in the literature on group therapy. This stands in contrast to the large number of publications on training and development as an individual psychotherapist or a psychotherapist in general (which is usually assumed to be an individual therapist). While not addressing group practice explicitly, many of the questions and insights generated in the wider literature are relevant to group psychotherapists. Sussman (2007), for example, refers to psychotherapy as a 'curious calling' and sets out to explore both the conscious and unconscious reasons for becoming a psychotherapist. Weinberg (1998) similarly enquires about the decision to become an individual psychotherapist – why did we cross that road? – and explores the personal, social and professional reasons for choosing to become a psychotherapist. But this still leaves unanswered the question of why some psychotherapists choose *group* as the primary goal of their training and practice. In this paper, I set out to address the gap in our knowledge about this aspect of our development. There are some overarching questions:

- Why did we take the path that led to our working as group psychotherapists?
- What predisposes us to choosing the field of group practice?
- What distinguishes us, if anything, from other psychotherapists?

A further question presents itself early on in this chapter: why has there been so little attention to the reasons therapists choose to work in groups? What does it say about the field of group psychotherapy? This question may have no clear or single answer but I pose it anyway, allowing the question to hover in the background of this exploration of an important but underemphasized subject.

In this chapter, I consider specifically the motivation to train and work as a group psychotherapist. I explore the group therapist's own personal history, with a particular focus on group experience through life, including the influence of the therapist's own family group. I consider which aspects have led to the decision to train and work in the field. While interested in individual narratives, I seek also to discover trends and patterns that suggest commonalities within the wider profession. Further, I explore what impact the group therapist's reasons for seeking this field have on his/her functioning as a group facilitator and in addition how past and present identifications influence perception of a future role. While pursuing historical influences, I have a particular interest in the practitioner's actual work: how life development influences the therapist as he/she navigates his/her way through the uncertain and often unpredictable terrain of the psychotherapy group.

It is increasingly recognized that psychotherapy in all its forms represents a co-construction of the therapist and patient in interaction and group therapy is no exception. But, in spite of the fact that the group comprises members other than the therapist who all have a therapeutic function for each other, and together influence the group process, the group therapist remains in a central and influential role (Nitsun 2009; Billow 2011; Lorentzen 2014). This, in my view, applies whatever the group psychotherapeutic model, be it group analytic, interpersonal, systemic or other, even though each model espouses a different leadership model. The choice of which model to pursue and how to implement the leadership role is itself personally and subjectively determined and a vehicle that brings into play the characteristics and qualities of the therapist in terms of values, attitudes and biases. If anything, because of the complexity of the group process, given the presence of several people with their own personalities and agendas, the leadership challenge to the group conductor is more pronounced than in any other form of therapy. The importance of group therapist variables is of course recognized professionally and is often discussed in group supervision as well as workshops and training events. But, in my view, our collective wisdom on 'who the group conductor is' is insufficiently documented in the literature.

Insights from psychotherapy in general

There is a substantial literature on the motivation and making of psychotherapists in general. It is useful to begin here.

Positive reasons for doing psychotherapy

Since much of this chapter focuses on the hidden and symbolic motivations of the group therapist, some of which reflect personal difficulties and defensive constellations, it is necessary not to lose sight of the positive, healthy reasons for choosing this area of work. The following themes are highlighted in a paper by O'Leary (2011). These refer to psychotherapy in general but they are easily applied to the group therapist. In the next section, I summarize O'Leary's points but add some caveats about the group psychotherapist:

- *A powerful interest in story-telling.* If this is true of the choice of individual therapy as a profession, how much more does it apply to groups with their multiple narratives? Edelson and Berg (1999) give stories and story-telling a major focus in their re-imagining of the group.
- *Fascination with language and verbal communication: an interest in metaphor and symbolism.* The therapeutic group is a stage on which many languages are spoken and group material is often laden with metaphor and symbolism. Schlapobersky (1994) refers to the language of the group as a central motif.
- *Psychological mindedness.* The therapist's interest in what makes people tick, coupled with the capacity for empathic understanding, is fundamental. The interest in self-and-other relationships is intrinsic to the practice of group therapy (Harwood *et al.* 2012).
- *'A robust appetite for creative interaction and support among peers ... critical to becoming a good therapist'* (O'Leary 2011, p. 42). This point emphasizes a group dimension of affiliation and belonging, which is highly congruent with group psychotherapeutic values.
- *Resilience – critical to confidence and the creative use of self, whether gained through living or in the course of therapy* (O' Leary 2011). Whether resilience itself is a motivational factor, I suggest, is questionable. We probably gain resilience in the passing of time and through the progress of our work rather than it existing a priori as a motive for becoming a therapist. But being a group therapist certainly requires resilience, especially in the face of a hostile anti-group!

The wounded healer

Much of the literature to a large degree assumes the positive, healthy reasons for people seeking to become therapists and instead concentrates on the problematic aspects, highlighting the flawed and fallible nature of the therapist's personality. This can be summed up by the notion of 'the wounded healer', an archetypal explanation of the vulnerable, even damaged aspects of the helper in caring professions ranging from medicine to nursing and psychotherapy (Groesbeck 1975). A number of papers and books explore the individual's choice of psychotherapy as a profession arising from a sense of vulnerability, from some degree of emotional damage, the motivation to do this work reflecting both the desire to help others and to help oneself (Klein *et al.* 2011). Qualitative studies and some quantitative studies (Bager-Charleson 2010) describe difficult and painful aspects in the childhood development of future psychotherapists: family dysfunction; under-protective or over-protective parenting; poor parental models; triangulation of the child in the parental relationship; and a high incidence of anxiety, depression and self-esteem problems in the family in general and the child in particular. Alice Miller's writing on 'the drama of the gifted child' (Miller 1997), although not specifically focused on psychotherapists, sums up the emotional climate in which a particular sort of child grows up: the individual who from early on is a drawn into a protective relationship with the parent/s. The usual parental function is reversed and located in the child, who then becomes estranged from his/her own emotional needs and fails to receive the attention and help needed to support his/her own emotional development.

The shadows of benevolence

O'Leary (2011) asks whether 'the wound' of the wounded healer is central to the ability to practise effectively as a psychotherapist or inimical to it. What are the shadows of the benevolence and altruism that may be integral to the therapeutic function? There may be a narcissistic need for power, admiration, influence and a tendency to create dependence in others. There may be a need for the other as patient, the container of stress and suffering, while the therapist assumes the position of the wise helper. These manoeuvres enable the therapist to remain in a seemingly invulnerable position, able to maintain a high degree of anonymity and an appearance of control, even if it does not always feel that way in the heat of the therapeutic encounter – or away from the consulting room. The danger of projection onto the patient of the needy, vulnerable self is that it estranges the therapist from his/her own needs. For some therapists there is a tendency to live vicariously through the patient, relying on the patient for a 'life'. People may become therapists because they have difficulty reaching others emotionally in their own lives and maintaining close relationships. In the therapeutic role, they have opportunities for a level of contact and intimacy that may be difficult to achieve in their own relationships, at the same time protected by their role and the safe distance they can maintain.

The power of unconscious aims is underscored by Sussman (2007). He focuses on the therapist's unconscious conflicts as a motivator to enter the profession. Sussman at the same time emphasizes that the person of the therapist constitutes his or her primary tool and has an ongoing influence on his work: hence the importance of the personal analysis and more generally having a framework within which the psychotherapist's development can be understood. O'Leary (2011) argues that understanding the person of the therapist is not just of academic interest or professional self-indulgence: rather, he sees it as a necessary part of responsible practice and professional credibility; a focused, thorough study of why people become psychotherapists, and how these reasons impact on their work, would strengthen credibility and stimulate both theory and practice (O'Leary 2011).

All these themes apply as much to group therapists as to individual or other therapists. The same combination of strengths and vulnerable areas, the same shadows of benevolence and the same sorts of interpersonal anxiety must apply. But how do group psychotherapists differ?

Group analytic voices

Having stated that very little has been written about the subject, it is important to recognize the few writers who have sought to comment on the person of the group conductor and the influence of their background and history. Interestingly, these voices appear to come largely from the group analytic field, as far as I can see, reflecting the emphasis on the conductor as a group member but also a focus of projection, embracing transference and counter-transference developments that by definition emphasize the conductor. Group analysts tend to believe that group analysis always includes the conductor: *group analysis is analysis of the group by the group, including the group analyst.*

S. H. Foulkes (1964), the founder of group analysis, made a strong statement about the significance of the conductor. The group therapist's personality, in his view, is *the most important factor* in influencing the outcome of the group: it is an 'overwhelming influence' (Foulkes 1964, p. 161). Foulkes went on to suggest that the group therapist *creates the group as an unconscious reflection of himself.* These are bold and far-reaching statements, particularly given Foulkes' heightened emphasis on the group as a whole and the impact of overall group process: yet, here he is elevating the influence of the therapist above all else. Foulkes went on to say that through projective identification, the conductor personifies members of the group as split-off parts of himself, for example, the scapegoat and the conductor's favourite. Hence, even the emergence of particular roles and identities in the group is seen as an expression of the conductor. Foulkes further suggested that these developments might reflect unresolved tensions/aspects of the therapist that require further analysis. Foulkes takes an unequivocal stand on the influence of the conductor's personality but does not in his publications delve further into the group conductor's personal history.

In subsequent decades group analysts hardly pursued these views. Perhaps the importance of the conductor-as-person was assumed and appeared to require no further published comment. But, in recent years, group analysts have begun to confront this theme and to ask related questions. Einhorn (2013) raises the question of why people seek training as group analysts and brings herself directly into the picture. She reflects on her choice of a therapeutic field, analytic group psychotherapy, which is currently under threat on ideological and clinical grounds and involved in a struggle for professional survival. The issue of survival, including the survival of the group itself, is key in Einhorn's considerations in the same way that it weaves in and out of this book. But Einhorn describes the value of the reflective space in group analysis as a major reason for her choosing this work, alongside the width of its scope in addressing social as well as personal concerns. She is open about her personal motivations and offers the following explanation for becoming a group analyst:

> I became a Group Analyst at a more unconscious level to repair internalized, destructive feelings as a legacy from parents who did not understand what it was to be a child. These destructive, internalized feelings had also been transmitted from historical experiences that had not been processed emotionally. The secrets that could only be felt created fear but I wanted to understand and try to be informed.
>
> (Einhorn, 2013, p. 11)

This very open statement, emphasizing the influence of family history, especially parents, and the power of the unprocessed aspects of the past, reinforces my earlier observations and anticipates a fuller exploration of the subject of the group analyst's personal history that comes later in this chapter.

Outside of British group analysis, there has recently been a clear statement highlighting the importance of the group leader. Billow (2011), very similarly to Foulkes, but writing in the relational psychoanalytic tradition, places great importance on the influence of the group conductor. He also does not explore the therapist's history beyond his/her persona in the therapy group but makes two committed comments:

> Every intervention the therapist makes (including silence) is filtered through his or her subjectivity, of which the therapist has imperfect knowledge.
>
> (Billow 2011, p. 299)

> The members' shifting perceptions of who the therapist is impacts everything that takes place in the group.
>
> (Billow 2011, p. 299)

Billow's comments highlight the inter-subjective nature of the group therapist's influence. The therapist's interventions are the expression of his/her own subjectivity while at the same time members are continually attuned to the therapist as a person.

The few voices quoted above, unusual but valuable in making such explicit reference to the importance of the group conductor, are compelling in the way they describe the very creation of the group, its moment-to-moment progress and its assignation of roles as a reflection of the therapist's actual and subjective presence. We also have indications of the impact of the therapist's past development, the striving to understand previously unprocessed family communications and the wish to repair an internal sense of damage.

Interim findings and suggestions

Based on preceding observations, and anticipating a further exploration, I suggest the following:

- Like other psychotherapists, group therapists come to this work with a mixture of altruistic and self-centred motives reflecting their own developmental concerns. Notions of therapist vulnerability and 'the wounded healer' apply as much to group psychotherapists as to any other therapists.
- Group psychotherapists choose this field because of unresolved aspects of their own group experience that they wish to explore and process in a psychotherapeutic context. This might include: 1) the wish to repair the original family group; 2) the wish to reconfigure the internal group; and 3) the wish to belong and find a cultural home.
- The unconscious influences of the group therapist may be far-reaching, including the creation of the group and the creation of group roles reflecting the therapist's unconscious.
- In spite of their own likely personal difficulties in groups, group psychotherapists have a specific attraction to groups as a therapeutic medium and believe in the healing potential of groups. They choose this work for reasons associated with a social perspective, including the importance of belonging and community. The strength of the social motive, in combination with the particular wish to resolve the family narrative, as well as a belief in the therapeutic potential of groups, is distinctive to the group psychotherapist.

The past

The group therapist's history

A detailed study of the development of group psychotherapists is beyond the scope of this chapter. Instead I attempt to construct a framework within which we may consider some of the main parameters of development that influence the choice of group work as a profession. Later, I give an autobiographical example that illustrates some of these ideas.

The group template

The question is how best to establish a framework for exploring the impact of the therapist's group development on his or her choice of work. I suggest that it is useful to draw on the concept of a *group template* (Nitsun 1996). To summarize, the group template is a synthesis of the main impressions and attributions of groups that an individual builds in the course of development over time. It originates in the primary family group and is reinforced in subsequent group experience, such as play groups, school groups, peer groups, work groups and so on. I am not suggesting any rigid form of template but an overall sense of what it is like *to-be-in-a-group* and how it might be to join a group. This for some people is mainly positive: groups are good, supportive, inclusive, helpful. For others, it is mainly negative: groups are difficult, to be avoided, anxiety-provoking, exposing, alienating. The group template is not only a product of past experience, I suggest, but a predictor of future experience. It influences individuals' expectations of groups in an ongoing way, so that people relate to groups in ways that are consistent with expectations. So, the group template can become a self-fulfilling prophecy, reinforcing underlying assumptions and conclusions ('I knew I would like/dislike the group'). I (Nitsun 1996) have also described these experiences in terms of a *group object relation.* This is a more complex construct, drawing on object relations theory, but it points to the same phenomenon as the group template: a personal schema concerning group experience that influences and is influenced by ongoing group relationships.

The main question here concerns the group therapist's own group template: what experience and expectations of groups he/she brings to training and practice. This is likely to be complex: enough positive experience to believe in groups and become a group therapist and enough negative experience to stimulate the need for repair. Positive aspects may stem from experiences of safety, collaboration and personal recognition in groups over a significant period of time, together with a sufficient sense of constructive rivalry and conflict resolution, all facilitated by the presence of appropriate and helpful leadership in the form of parents, teachers and others in authority. Negative aspects derive from a lack of containment in the group, a sense of danger and implosion, fragmentation rather than cohesion, destructive envy and rivalry, and the absence of constructive or containing leadership. The latter are all components of the anti-group and I believe that at least some of the motivation to train as a group therapist derives from both conscious and unconscious representations of the anti-group. What balance exists between these poles of course varies from individual to individual but I suggest that for someone seeking a career in the group field there will be both a positive leaning towards groups and a painful group inheritance that seeks understanding and repair. This leads onto a fuller consideration of the therapist's psychological inheritance.

The shadows of heritage

Of the various existing models of 'psychological inheritance', one that I find particularly useful is that of Durban (2011). This is a model not of groups or families per se but a general schema that embraces notions of trauma and unconscious, unprocessed experience and its impact on development. Durban emphasizes early modes of handling psychogenetic heritage and the shadows these cast on psychological adjustment. Drawing on theories of trauma and its influence on development, he posits three different ways of dealing with the shadow:

- *Living with a shadow* is the normal condition where our heritage is an inseparable counterpart of our movement through life: like a silent, unobtrusive background adding depth and volume to each and every experience. We are in touch with trauma but not possessed by it.
- *Living under a shadow* implies the unconscious phantasy of being oppressed, possessed, haunted and persecuted by the dark cloud of the shadow. Our existence is infused with trauma. This is resonant of Fraiberg's 'ghosts in the nursery' (Fraiberg et al. 1975).
- *Being the shadow* describes early developmental catastrophes that profoundly penetrate the proto-self or what Damasio (1999) calls 'core-consciousness'. The shadows are deeply absorbed in a way that makes existence contiguous with the shadow. Here pathological, self-destructive modes interfere drastically with the evolution of the psyche and sense of self.

I would add to this model some further ways of dealing with the shadow:

- *Denying* the shadow, in which there is a strong attempt at avoidance, requiring a form of denial that conceals a painful history.
- *Splitting* the shadow, in which the bad, deleterious aspects of the shadow are split off from good representations, so that the person lives in a sharply divided world.
- *Projecting* the shadow – putting the unwanted aspects of past experience, family history and self-representation into others, whether individuals or groups. This is an aspect of splitting the shadow.

I think it is also worth considering a healthy way of dealing with the shadow: *reconciling* the shadow. This is akin to *living with* the shadow but indicates a more active relationship to the shadow, with a higher degree of acceptance and resolution, probably achieved pro-actively through an effort of will and the creative processing of trauma and loss. Forgiveness may be an important component. Frost and Alonso (1993), in their brief treatise on becoming a group therapist, refer to the need for 'some level of forgiveness towards the family of origin, including resolution of sibling rivalry and management of dependency and aggression'. Forgiveness and reparation would seem to be crucial components of reconciling with the shadow and strengthening the group psychotherapist's purpose.

I suggest that group experience, especially family group experience, can be understood within the framework of the shadow of trauma, as outlined by Durban, since there is probably hardly a family that has not experienced trauma. The advantage of Durban's model is that it differentiates levels and types of adjustment to the trauma, making it a useful framework for considering individuals' level of trauma integration and hence the implications for psychotherapy, as either patients or practitioners, or both. What light specifically does it throw on group therapists' motivations? The main questions concern:

- the way we have assimilated our own social history, including trauma, and how we deal with the unresolved aspects of our history;
- whether there is sufficient awareness and forgiveness to have reconciled with the shadow of psychological heritage;
- the extent to which we as therapists transfer the shadow of our own heritage to the psychotherapy group.

It is useful within this framework to consider *the purpose and value of group psychotherapy as a form of therapy*. I suggest that belonging to a group provides a greater sense of continuity with the universal order of social and cultural history. This comes about through members sharing a wider range of historical narratives than can be accessed in other therapies. The group serves to both amplify and defuse the particular shadows of group members. Being in a group can help to integrate past, present and future into a meaningful whole, generating the connective tissue through space and time that makes the difference between a chaotic past filled with threatening shadows and a coherent sense of self across time. When people share stories of the past, the 'there and then', this is an important function of the group – not necessarily a defence or resistance.

An illustration

In keeping with the biographical spirit of this chapter and the emphasis on the group therapist's lifetime development, I wish to share some aspects of my own development and its relevance to my identity and work as a group analytic psychotherapist. I do this in a series of pictures of myself at different stages of development.

Picture 1: 1950

I am seven, a small child walking down the dusty road of a small provincial town, De Doorns, in the rural western Cape of South Africa. My family is one of the few English-speaking families in the town and one of only three Jewish families.

There is an undercurrent of anti-Semitism in the town. The town is also divided racially since these are the early days of apartheid. The black population lives in a shanty town on the other side of the railway line from the white, predominantly Afrikaans population.

I feel rather lost and lonely. As the youngest of three children, I am quite often pushed away by my older brother and sister. I have friends in and around the town but when, on a day like today, I don't see them, I miss company. My parents are very preoccupied with running their business, a large department store in the centre of the town. They both came to South Africa in the earlier twentieth century as refugees from the pogroms in Eastern Europe. They have worked very hard to make a go of their business and raise a family in this remote, rather inhospitable environment. Shadows of the past hang over them. My mother came from an impoverished life on the fringes of Siberia, having lost siblings through hunger. My father left half his family in Lithuania when he emigrated to South Africa. The remaining family was all murdered in the Nazi invasion of Lithuania. My mother sometimes refers sadly to her losses but my father does not speak at all about his until many years later, when as psychology student I enquire about his family history. He then says it is too painful to even think about but manages to confide in me some of what happened. This is all he knows: the story is incomplete.

Picture 2: 1962

I am nineteen, studying psychology, sociology, English and history of art at the University of the Witwatersrand in Johannesburg, where my family moved some ten years ago. I am struggling, not academically but with finding myself in my late teenage years, having had a difficult adolescence in a very conventional, repressive Jewish community and feeling anxious about the more fluid social world of the university. I am unsure of my sexual orientation and this makes it difficult to locate myself socially and sustain friendships. A few years later I am training as a clinical psychologist at the same university. As part of my training at the local psychiatric hospital, I have to attend a 'staff sensitivity group'. The group is run by a highly active leader who seems to side with some people and marginalizes others. I dislike the group intensely and, against the advice of my supervisor, I leave. This causes a flurry in the staff community – my action is seen as defiant and people both resent and envy me for leaving. I left because I felt I could hardly survive in the group, the splitting and hostility was so intense, and I felt so lost and threatened.

Picture 3: 1990

I am 47 and am living in London. I emigrated here 22 years ago seeking further training as a psychotherapist, wanting to explore my interest in art and mostly wanting to get away from the stifling atmosphere of South Africa still in the thick of apartheid. I have by now done well professionally, have a stable partnership, have a strong network of friends – and have recently completed training as a group analyst. Although my sense of belonging to groups has strengthened and I enjoy positive experiences in professional and social groups, I am mindful of the great struggle I had to reach this point. I remain conscious of my own ambivalence about groups as a therapeutic medium, as well as the pervasive resistance to groups I find amongst patients and staff in the clinical settings in which I work. I decide to write a theoretical paper for my group analytic training on the theme of 'The Anti-group', which leads to further publications on this theme.

Picture 4: 2013

I am 69 and writing this book, a follow-up to the 1996 publication on the anti-group. The concept of the anti-group has been an abiding interest in my work as a group analyst. The anti-group is linked to experiences of loss, disappointment and despair, amplified in the group setting. However, I am more convinced than ever of the constructive implications of the concept: by recognizing and dealing with the anti-group, we are more likely to find a way to the creativity of the group. My interest in the more joyful, playful and sexual aspects of group psychotherapy is the subject of my second book, *The Group as an Object of Desire: Exploring Sexuality in Group Psychotherapy*. Yet, I vacillate between an optimistic view of the therapy group and a pessimistic view.

Linking the above biographical sketch to my proposed thesis about motivation to train as a group psychotherapist, I can make some connections. I very much grew up in the shadow of my ancestral past with immigrant parents trying to forge an existence for themselves and their family in a community in which they were isolated and marginalized. The lack of processing of a major trauma, the Holocaust, and its effect on my father, as well as my mother's depression about early loss and the separation from her primary family, created a family group in which there were considerable fears of conflict and abandonment. Anger could not be expressed with any degree of safety. I imagine there were deep fears of destructiveness, as if the traumas of old could be repeated all over again. Growing up during apartheid South Africa must have mirrored these fears. There was a profound sense of social oppression and schism. There were great tensions about difference and inequality; the erosion of opportunity through race and colour; a denigrated sense of self and other that had shameful and humiliating aspects. There was also a growing sense of impending danger – 'the bloody revolution' that white South Africans for decades feared was on their doorstep. My own group template, I believe, was of an unsafe, threatened group in which the risk of loss, shame and humiliation was ever present. My psychogenetic heritage was perhaps pitched somewhere between living *with* the shadow and living *under* the shadow. *Reconciling with* the shadow was yet to come, though never complete.

My original choice of clinical psychology as a core profession is not surprising when viewed as an attempt to understand not just others but myself in the midst of an implosive social and political environment, as well as a threatened family group. On the positive side I had loving parents and rivalrous but playful siblings. There were moments of great joy and laughter when the family could relax and let go. If aggression could not be countenanced, there was nevertheless affection. My parents also had very positive qualities: my father driving and determined and my mother, with a mere smattering of education, the 'doctor' of the family who was an astute diagnostician and dietary expert. So, when I eventually came to seek training as a group analyst, I was doing so in the shadow of historical group and social difficulties but also with some belief in the restorative power of the group and its transformational potential.

The present

The group therapist's influence on the group

In this section I pursue the question of how the group practitioner, with his/her particular shadows of heritage, influences the group process. I return to the past but my greater interest here is on how this all translates into the present. I largely agree with Foulkes' (1964) assertion that the conductor's personality is the most important factor in influencing the outcome of the group, a view more recently echoed by Billow (2011) who refers to the power of the therapist's subjectivity and group members' shifting perception of 'who the therapist is' as impacting everything that happens in the group. But the nature of psychotherapeutic groups also has a bearing on this process: what is it in the group that is conducive to the strong influence of the conductor? In what follows I explore the parameters of the group that are open to the therapist's influence and how this might take place.

Parameters of the group

The psychotherapy group is a very particular kind of group that invites projections and transferences in a largely unstructured space. The lack of structure creates an ambiguous frame in which there are multiple possibilities of projection and interpretation. As Piotrowski (1963) noted in his original studies of projection, the more ambiguous a situation is, the greater the scope for projection. The fewer clues there are in the structure of the stimulus, the more the individuals have to fall back on their inner perceptual bias to make sense of what they see. This is what Murray (1951), the inventor of the Thematic Apperception Test (T.A.T.) called 'apperception'. It is in this complex, unpredictable and ambiguous space that group members look to the therapist for cues and clues as to the direction of the group. They are of course also responding to each other, and their interaction is of paramount importance if the group is to work. But as the leader of the group, the conductor remains a continuing reference point and a figure of speculation throughout. Given the ambiguity of the process, and the many possibilities of interpretation, the therapist's interventions inevitably come from his/her own subjectivity and, given the members' consciousness of the therapist's organizing role, this influences the group in an ongoing way.

Forms of influence

Some writers, including Foulkes (1964) and myself (Nitsun 1996), believe that the conductor in several ways *creates* the group, both practically and psychologically. On a practical level, it is the conductor who initiates the group, selects members, structures the group in space and time, manages the group from session to session and ends the group. At every point there are decisions to be made and these decisions draw on the therapist's subjectivity composed as it is of his/her group template, including the complex shadows of social and psychological heritage which are as much a part of the therapist as they are of every group member. I think it is useful to consider that there is a 'group in the mind' in the same way that Armstrong (2005) postulates an 'organization in the mind'. Each group member will have a group in the mind, as will the conductor. Since the conductor has such a formative influence, his or her group in the mind, with its various attributes and expectations, will influence consciously and unconsciously decisions such as whom he/she attracts to the group and selects for the group, encourages to leave the group and encourages to stay.

Illustration

In a once-weekly group I found myself entangled in a difficult triangular dynamic with two members. One was Terry (42), a white middle-class English man: the other was Fina (39), a black nurse of Caribbean origin. For some months Terry had been critical of Fina for coming late to the group and absenting herself in a haphazard way. While his criticisms were to some extent justified, problems between them escalated when he proceeded to challenge Fina for hardly having worked for years and living on state benefits, including a hefty child allowance to support her four children. This infuriated Fina who felt exposed and shamed. But Terry intensified the challenge, berating her for an attitude of entitlement and dependence. I found myself wanting very much to come to Fina's rescue. I felt indignant at the presumptuous way Terry spoke to her and at least once I confronted him on his judgemental attitude. Silent at first, the rest of the group also began to berate Terry, condemning his insensitivity and intolerance. He in turn felt aggrieved. I suspected that a scapegoating process was afoot and that Terry and Fina might be taking turns in being scapegoat but I felt curiously unable to influence the dynamic.

Over time, the intensity of the conflict lessened somewhat. Eventually, Fina decided to leave. Although she gave good reasons, there was a suspicion that she might be leaving in order to avoid further conflict with Terry.

I remained perplexed about what had happened in the group and my own role in it. I had all along been aware of the significance of my being a white ex-South

African male in a group in which a black woman was under duress from a white male but the awareness fluctuated and did not help me to unravel what was happening in the group. Then, in a flash of recognition, an important part of my childhood in South Africa sprung to life. Like many white children I had been brought up by black nannies. They were very good figures for me, generally warm, playful and affectionate women who brought something soft, sensual and human to my childhood. I realized that in my mind Fina was equated with my black nannies. But it was a painful recognition. I had always, even as a young child, felt a deep sense of shame about the way nannies were treated in apartheid South Africa, their poor pay and conditions and the sacrifices they made in their own lives to work for rich whites in the cities. I realized that I was reluctant to link Fina in any way with these women. I would not have wanted to humiliate her. The black nannies were mainly positive, often loving figures, but the connection was painful. However, I began to understand for the first time why I felt so furious with Terry. I had put into him all the prejudice of white South Africans, associating him in my mind with the worst kind of intolerant apartheid white. But my lack of full awareness of the dynamic at the time, and the repetition of a complex aspect of my childhood, limited my ability to deal with the group problem in a more effective way.

The experience made me wonder whether it was a coincidence that Terry and Fina ended up in the same group. Was there some unconscious acting out on my part, unwittingly reliving a difficult aspect of my childhood past in South Africa by recruiting these two people to the same group? This example illustrates the power of past shadows – the social unconscious – and how they can be embodied in the present: the way the group conductor's own past history can penetrate his/her leadership.

Group leadership

The origins of leadership

The nature of group leadership is a subject to which I can do scant justice in this chapter. But the choice of a preferred group therapeutic approach, including a particular style of leadership, also derives from past experience, beginning with the models of authority and leadership that were prevalent in childhood. As Obholzer (1994) points out, these models become internalized and the basis of subsequent relationships to authority, including one's own representation of authority. This is probably not linear or straightforward. In my own family history, my father's at times authoritarian style of parenting left me with a strong desire not to emulate him. In going the other way, I sometimes found myself floundering in an attempt to be democratic at all costs, only to find that sometimes a firmer authority was needed. Models can have both a positive and negative influence and there may be compensatory attempts to rectify the impact of repudiated leadership. An example is my difficult experience in the sensitivity group during my clinical psychology training that I described above. It is likely that my negative reaction to the leader of the group, whom I perceived as inappropriately active and divisive, was an echo of my response to my father's leadership at the times I perceived him as most dictatorial. I remember what a difficult experience that early sensitivity group was, in a way that has made me deeply aware of the potential for shame and exclusion in a group. I also remember how determined I was not to repeat the mistakes of the group facilitator. With hindsight, I can recognize my own rivalry with these early figures of authority, no doubt fuelling my criticism of them. This all highlights how complex our relationship to group leadership may be. In later years, and especially during the period of my group analytic training, I encountered more positive models of group leadership. But this was not consistent and I remained ambivalent about group leaders. In a previous publication (Nitsun 2009), I explored in greater detail the complex dilemmas facing the group therapist evolving a personally congruent form of leadership.

Models of leadership

The issue of leadership is complicated by the different models of group therapy. A survey of the different group psychotherapeutic approaches reveals how divergent the styles of leadership are that are encouraged within training and practice. In group analysis, Foulkes (1964) and most of his followers espouse a model of democratic leadership that tends towards the passive and the non-interventionist: 'the leader leads from behind'; 'the leader digs his own grave'. In order to understand Foulkes' position more clearly it is useful to briefly examine the historical context in which he formulated his vision of leadership. A refugee from Nazi Germany in the early 1930s, Foulkes (1964) openly acknowledged his deep aversion to the dictatorial style of leadership represented by figures such as Hitler and Stalin. Accordingly, he advocated a form of leadership that was diametrically opposite. But in so doing, he may also have gone to an opposite extreme (Nitsun 2009). Of course, this style of leadership has its rewards, particularly if it empowers the group to generate its own authority and leadership (Hutchinson 2009) and, hence, strengthens the group's agency. But Foulkes' model of leadership has created a culture of idealization around this style of authority that translates with some difficulty into the moment-to-moment requirements of conducting an analytic group with its complex and fluctuating trajectory and its need at times for firmer authority and clearer guidelines (Nitsun 2009).

The visions of leadership cherished and promoted by the different schools of group psychotherapy are no doubt also embedded in a historical past with its own shadows. I know less about the background of non-group-analytic models but a brief glance at some of the better-known approaches reveals just how different their conception of leadership is and how these are also likely to reflect personal and historical influences. Taking, for example, Agazarian and Gantt's (2000) systems-centred approach to group psychotherapy, the leader, in the initial stages at least, takes a very active, interventionist style. There is a strongly didactic element that is used as the basis for group experiments, the leader in a markedly directive role. This can be contrasted with interpersonal group psychotherapy (Yalom and Leszcz 2005), which is perhaps midway between the group analytic and systems-centred approaches. This espouses an active here-and-now leadership style that at the same time encourages spontaneous interaction between members as a key ingredient of the therapy. While there is some research on these approaches, it is insufficient to differentiate the impact and effect of the contrasting leadership styles. Yet, each model tends to make claims for its legitimacy and effectiveness. Until there is more definitive research on these differences, we may conclude that leadership models make sense within the framework of their particular approach and that they reflect cultural and social values, as well as historical influences, that are specific to that therapeutic mode.

Crises of leadership

In my experience, group psychotherapists not unusually go through periods of doubt about the value of their work and themselves as leaders. Some experience considerable uncertainty, generating painful doubts about their capacity to understand and manage groups. While most group therapists eventually work through these difficulties, usually with the help of peers or supervisors, there are some, in my experience, who reach states of such frustration and disillusionment that they decide to withdraw and give up running groups altogether. While these are the minority, their plight is well worth considering, given the cost to them at a personal level, as well as the loss to the profession.

My understanding of clinicians who reach such serious states of impasse or crisis is that they find the leadership role extremely taxing, that they can feel burdened by their groups and that the stress of running groups has come to outweigh the gains. Exploring this in some depth with colleagues in this position, I have been struck by the extent to which past development has been in the background of the problem. The conflicts almost always centre on authority and leadership as reflected in the families of origin and reinforced rather than resolved in later experience.

Illustration

Dermot, age 51, an individual and group psychotherapist, encountered considerable frustration in running groups. This varied from staff groups in public services, where he found participants' motivation and attendance poor, to private therapy groups where he had difficulty recruiting patients and ended up running a group that lasted only four months. He had also applied unsuccessfully for several part-time jobs as a group practitioner, increasingly experiencing failure in a sphere of work for which he had trained for years and once valued. A major part of his difficulty was that he found the role of group conductor exacting. He easily felt overwhelmed by the intensity and unpredictability of the process and frequently felt at a loss in knowing how to exercise authority in the role of group leader. He feared that he might have been responsible for the poor attendance and drop-outs in his groups, as if he lacked the strength of authority and the holding power to maintain cohesion in his groups. As a qualified and experienced individual psychotherapist, he decided eventually to give up running groups and to concentrate on his private individually focused practice.

Exploring a life-long struggle with issues of authority, Dermot recalled a family situation dominated by a powerful father who related to him in a confusing and ambivalent way. He remembered being something of a 'daddy's boy' as a child, sitting on his father's lap and enjoying a playful, affectionate relationship. As he grew older, and particularly with the onset of puberty, his father's attitude changed, becoming distant and critical. The situation was not helped by the presence of a rivalrous younger sister who competed for her father's attention and whom Dermot felt did her best to undermine him. In the background was his good-natured but weak mother, trying wanly to cope with the tensions in the family and to mediate between the combative and rivalrous members.

Dermot himself grew up an ambitious and assertive adolescent, excelling at school and sports, and naturally seeking leadership roles amongst peers. At home, however, this was unacceptable. Any claim on his part to authority was resisted by his father and sister and he not unusually felt put down and humiliated. His views and opinions were almost uniformly disparaged. His mother grew more exasperated and guilty, sensing the difficulty Dermot experienced but unable to offer any real support. When he left home for university in his late teens, Dermot was able to find himself amongst his peers, becoming a popular student with a reputation for clear-headed and fair leadership. However, this made no impact on his family. Although his father and sister seemingly respected his achievements, he never felt included or liked.

First trained as an individual psychoanalytic psychotherapist in his forties, Dermot decided at a later stage to seek group psychotherapeutic training. He was aware of the impact of his family history and how difficult it had been for him to claim authority in the family group. But he had become progressively interested in groups and felt that training as a group analyst was a positive challenge that might help to resolve his tensions around authority. The training, however, was fraught with difficulty. As well as having problems running his own training group and experiencing tensions in supervision, he found his own personal group analytic treatment disappointing. He encountered a charismatic male leader who had his favourites in the group and seemed not to appreciate or recognize him. He felt a mixture of longing to be admired and loved and great anger about being rejected. He appreciated that this was largely transference on his part but felt that the transference dynamic was insufficiently addressed in the group. He became critical of the group analyst but felt that the analyst could not accept his anger: the analyst seemingly grew more distant the more Dermot expressed his disappointment. When he qualified, Dermot was for a while enthusiastic about being a group psychotherapist but then ran into the difficulties previously described.

These observations highlight not only the problematic consequences of a difficult family history and its deleterious impact on a group therapist's functioning, but the way in which this was repeated rather than resolved. This is noteworthy: training and personal therapy, instead of helping to resolve the shadows of the past, can in the wrong circumstances aggravate the problem. The power of past influences, transferences and templates sometimes transcends the good intentions of training and development. Finding one's own voice as an authority, alongside a confident group leadership style, is a struggle that requires sensitivity and care not only on the part of the incumbent but also by those who are responsible for training and nurturing this important skill.

Linking back to the previous section on the analyst's psychogenetic inheritance, Dermot's story reflects the difficulty of living with the shadow of an inimical family configuration. Although he adjusted relatively well in other areas of his life, including his marital relationship and career as an individual psychotherapist, his struggle to become a group analyst was marred by the lingering shadow of family rivalry and rejection and the attacks on his claim to authority and leadership.

The future

This last section completes the trilogy of past, present and future that I chose as a framework for this chapter. I have considered the past and the present, and the links between them, and it is time to look at the future; the future, as a felt sense, of the group psychotherapist in his/her journey through life. I am aware that my interest in this area reflects my own ageing and issues about retirement, also that ambivalence about ending work is shared by many colleagues of my generation. Additionally, I believe, our sense of the future and where we are heading has a bearing on our values and actions in the present. This is as true of the group psychotherapist as of any other, if only because much of our work is long-term, requiring commitment and resilience but also a sense of when and how we end our careers.

I begin with an inspiring statement by a psychotherapist Reppen, contemplating his own ageing and his continuing aspirations:

> We must never stop our studying, learning from the insights of others, not as sycophants, or as ideological dilettantes, but always integrating, enriching, deepening our understanding of what it is to be human. In effect, I am still becoming a psychotherapist now at the age of 70, and anticipate the process will go on for as long as I do.
>
> (Reppen 1998, p. 147)

This hopeful, encouraging statement probably sums up how many ageing psychotherapists feel – or would like to feel. But we know that the fruits of ageing are counter-balanced by the increasing likelihood of ill-health and disability, of greater weariness, weakened memory and the sheer drudgery and depression of being old. There is nothing I can say about this that has not been said. There is also growing interest in the specific challenges facing older psychotherapists, such as when to retire, how to retire and how to say goodbye to a cherished profession and the people who have inhabited it (Junkers 2013). I would like to address more specifically what this means for group psychotherapists. I doubt that group therapists are any different from other therapists in most respects, except for one – that they have usually spent a lifetime working in groups and this does have a special meaning. Working with groups is a privileged way of maintaining links with people and continuing the profoundly meaningful contact with life's many and varied narratives. The challenge in old age of giving up links, of saying goodbye, of a final separation, may be all the more poignant for group therapists who have known this form of connection over many years. There is a danger then of clinging on, of refusing to cut ties. There are many positive examples of psychotherapists working productively into their later years, 70s, 80s, even 90s, displaying the wisdom and intuitive good sense that are the rewards of ageing. But there are also instances of therapists, including group therapists, who have stayed on too long, who not only struggle visibly with encroaching illness and frailty but whose problems of memory and concentration became a source of anxiety and shame for them and their patients.

The greatest challenge of old age, apart from coping with illness and loss of function, is an existential one; the sense of a life lived well, generatively and meaningfully, versus a life that seems to have lacked meaning and purpose. This abiding question is summed up in Erik Erikson's (1980) notion of *integrity vs despair* as the defining parameter of old age. Being a group therapist, in my experience, adds considerably to a sense of purpose and a life lived well, in the social connectedness it provides and in the achievement of a sense of service to the community. Finding one's place in the group as both member and leader, coupled with the potential to integrate the shadows of psychosocial heritage, are key aspects of integrity vs despair: perhaps finally living *with* the shadow as life ebbs and the tide runs out.

Picture 5: 2014

Aged 70, I am still actively conducting groups in a private practice setting, as well as coordinating an NHS group service and teaching and supervising therapeutic group work. I had planned earlier in my career to retire at 70 but find myself still enjoying the work, particularly the groups I run, feeling strong enough physically and mentally to have confidence in my ability to carry on. Yet, I am out of step with friends and colleagues, many of whom have already retired and try to lure me into the autumnal retreat of their lives. I wonder about the defensive aspect of my continuing involvement in the work. Does it protect me from anxieties about retirement, about loss of identity and role, about facing physical and mental decline? How reluctant am I to give up the close attachment I feel to my groups, perhaps fearing isolation and ignominy? And am I trying to evade the lurking shadow of mortality, the darkest shadow of all, increasingly in my consciousness as the years pass by? For the moment, I love this work and feel that it is right to continue, but each day I ponder … for how long?

In one of my groups a male patient has been a group member for fifteen years. The group is hugely important to him. He has been severely disturbed in the past and feels the group has saved him from catastrophe. Recently, when challenged about his dependence on the group, he assertively proclaimed, 'I will never leave this group. The group will always be here and I will always be in it!' I sense that the group as a whole is afraid of losing me and wonder whether members sense my anxieties about losing them, colluding with me in a fantasy of immortality. So, in anticipation perhaps of facing the ultimate shadow, I am aware of how difficult it is for me to give up the fruits of my journey, the long struggle to resolve my own family history and my ambivalence about groups, both as a member and a conductor. Saying goodbye, taking leave of a career, casts its own shadow on our lives.

Summary

This chapter began with the question, 'What motivates us to become group psychotherapists?' and a subsidiary question, 'Why has this subject so rarely been documented relative to the substantial literature on the same theme in individual psychotherapy?' The latter question has so far not been addressed in this chapter. There is perhaps no single answer but possible answers include notions that the group therapy field is more circumscribed, that it is more marginal, that the differences between group and individual therapy in this regard are insufficient to merit special attention. Less obvious answers suggest that there is diminished self-regard amongst group practitioners, that the group field under-represents or even undermines itself through a form of internalized anti-group and that the reasons for choosing group are more complex and difficult to pin down. Whatever the case, this chapter suggests that the time has come for group psychotherapy to stand up and be counted and this includes a thoroughgoing exploration of choice points in the profession, starting with the initial decision to train. As noted earlier, this is not a self-indulgence but a necessary part of professional development at both personal and institutional levels and an aspect of public accountability.

In this initial attempt to get to grips with this complex phenomenon, I have utilized a timeline comprising past, present and future as a framework for understanding the development of the group therapist. There is almost certainly a large degree of overlap between the motivational aspects of becoming an individual and group psychotherapist which touch on strivings as broad as a keen interest in the human narrative, in language and communication and the wish to make the world a better place. But the distinguishing aspects of choosing to be a group therapist have to do with a particular responsiveness to the group and social aspects of one's own and others' histories, as well as an acute wish to understand and repair the primary family group – perhaps, more ambitiously, to heal something of the fractured fabric of the larger community.

I have looked at the impact of past development through the notion of unprocessed trauma, viewed in this chapter as developmental shadows that inhabit our choices and that are integrated to variable degrees in our functioning as psychotherapists. Ideally this leads to *reconciliation* with the past, as a creative and potentially transformative way of living *with* the shadow, which I suggest is implicit in the motivation to train and practise as a group psychotherapist. But, in less favourable circumstances, it can contribute to an anti-group constellation, as well as problematic representations of authority that complicate our functioning as group leaders. The journey I describe is not an easy one. I have highlighted the privileges and rewards of undertaking this work but also the demands of an exacting form of psychotherapy – and the disappointments and casualties along the way. Inevitably, there is an encounter with the anti-group and the particular anti-group configuration the therapist brings to his/her practice will influence both group outcomes and the nature of his/her development as a practitioner. I hope this adds weight to the continuing need for a responsible and in-depth understanding of the forces that shape the group psychotherapist.

References

Agazarian, Y. and Gantt, S. P. (2000) *Autobiography of a Theory: Developing a Theory of Living Human Systems and its Systems Centered Practice.* London: Jessica Kingsley.

Armstrong, D. (2005) *Organization in the Mind.* London: Tavistock Clinic Series.

Bager-Charleson, S. (2010) *Why Therapists Choose to Become Therapists.* London: Karnac.

Billow, R. M. (2011) It's all about me: on the group leader's psychology, *Group Analysis*, 44, 296–314.

Damasio, A. (1999) *The Feeling of What Happens: Body and Emotion in the Making of Consciousness.* San Diego: Harcourt.

Durban, J. (2011) Shadows, ghosts and chimeras: on some early modes of handling psycho-genetic heritage, *International Journal of Psychoanalysis*, 92, 903–24.

Edelson, M. and Berg, D. N. (1999) *Rediscovering Groups: A Psychoanalyst's Journey Beyond Individual Psychology.* London: Jessica Kingsley.

Einhorn, S. (2013) The strange phenomenon of being a group analyst, Paper presented at conference 'Intouchable', March 2013, Gonen, Israel.

Erikson, E. H. (1980) *Identity and the Life-Cycle.* New York: W. W. Norton and Co.

Foulkes, S. H. (1964) *Therapeutic Group Analysis.* London: Maresfield.

Fraiberg, S., Adelson, E. and Shapiro, V. (1975) Ghosts in the nursery: a psychoanalytic approach to the problem of impaired infant-mother relationships, *Journal of American Academy of Child Psychiatry*, 14, 387–421 or *The Psychoanalytic Quarterly*, 45, 651.

Frost, J. C. and Alonso, A. (1993) Brief report: on becoming a group psychotherapist, *Group*, 17, 179–84.

Groesbeck, C. J. (1975) The wounded healer, *Journal of Analytical Psychology*, 20, 122–45.

Harwood, I., Stone, W. and Pines, M. (2012) *Self Experiences in Groups, Revisited.* New York: Routledge.

Hutchinson, S. (2009) Foulkesian authority: another view. Response to lecture by Morris Nitsun, *Group Analysis*, 42, 354–60.

Junkers, G. (2013) *The Empty Couch: The Taboo of Ageing and Retirement in Psychoanalysis.* Hove: Routledge.

Klein, R. H., Bernard, S. B. and Schermer, V. L. (eds) (2011) *On Becoming a Psychotherapist.* Oxford: Oxford University Press.

Lorentzen, S. (2014) *Group Analytic Psychotherapy: Working with Affective, Anxiety and Personality Disorders.* London: Routledge.

Miller, A. (1997) *The Drama of the Gifted Child.* New York: Basic Books.

Murray, H. A. (1951) Uses of the Thematic Apperception Test, *American Journal of Psychiatry*, 107, 577–81.

Nitsun, M. (1996) *The Anti-group: Destructive Forces in the Group and their Creative Potential.* London: Routledge.

Nitsun, M. (2009) Authority and revolt: the challenges to group leadership, *Group Analysis*, 42, 1–23.

Obholzer, A. (1994) Authority, power and leadership: contributions from group relations training, in Obholzer, A. and Roberts, V. Z. (eds) (1994) *The Unconscious at Work.* London: Routledge.

O'Leary, J. (2011) Growing up to be a good psychotherapist, or physician – know thyself! In Klein, R. H., Bernard, S. B. and Schermer, V. L. (eds) *On Becoming a Psychotherapist.* Oxford: Oxford University Press.

Piotrowski, Z. A. (1963) On the Rorschach method of personality assessment, *Psychiatric Quarterly*, 16, 480–90.

Reppen, J. (1988) (ed.) *Why I Became a Psychotherapist.* New Jersey: Jason Aronson.

Schlapobersky, J. (1994) The language of the group: monologue, dialogue and discourse in group analysis, in Brown, D. and Zinkin, L. (eds) *The Psyche and the Social World.* London: Routledge.

Sussman, M. (2007) *A Curious Calling: Unconscious Motivation for Practising Psychotherapy.* New York: Jason Aronson.

Weinberg, G. (1998) The therapist personality, in Rabinowitz, I. (ed.) *Inside Therapy – Illuminating Writings about Therapists, Patients and Psychotherapy.* New York: St. Martin's Press.

Yalom, I. B. and Leszcz, M. (2005) *Theory and Practice of Group Psychotherapy.* New York: Basic Books.

Chapter 7

Falling in love

A group analytic perspective

In this chapter, I present what is probably the most positive and optimistic view of group analytic psychotherapy in this book. It also reflects a change of context. Whereas in previous chapters my emphasis was on the NHS and the problematic environment this constitutes for group psychotherapy, the focus here switches to private practice in central London, a more hospitable and facilitating setting for psychotherapy in general and group psychotherapy in particular, with the benefit of patients who are mostly well-motivated and bring more substantial personal resources to the therapeutic endeavour. Perhaps the very theme of this chapter – falling in love – reflects these differences. These are people whose fundamental safety and security needs can be taken for granted and whose preoccupations are more with development and fulfillment in work and relationships. This is not to say that their problems are insignificant: most patients are struggling with deep-seated emotional problems and longstanding difficulties in relationships, in addition to dealing with the pressures, tensions and sometimes social estrangement of city living. But health is usually on their side and, with it, the potential for growth. Anti-group proclivities, in my experience, are also less pronounced in the private practice setting than in public services, so that less time is absorbed with the group's struggle for survival and more with members' relational and vocational development.

Introduction

Falling in love remains one of the most enigmatic of all human experiences. This is in spite of the many explorations of the theme in drama, literature, philosophy, psychology, psychoanalysis and numerous other disciplines, all of which have in a sense fallen in love with love – and with falling in love – trying to confront and unravel its soaring heights and elusive depths. It is one of the great universal themes in people's lives, across cultures and times, and is both celebrated and lamented in countless love songs, classical and popular, redolent with love found and love lost. The term 'falling in love' itself has vivid connotations. It is an experience of being at one's most alive, most passionately engaged with life, yet at one's most vulnerable. The image of falling expresses a loss of control, of losing ground and hurtling towards the unknown. It is exciting but also dangerous. One could be elevated to impossible heights but also hurled into the depths of despair. It is perhaps the quintessential way in which human beings come out of the solipsistic life of the self into the surrender of self to other. In intensity it may be matched only by religious ecstasy and for many people it is experienced as if close to God, to conversion or transformation – the divine.

The theme of falling in love is of obvious importance in the psychotherapies, particularly psychoanalysis as well as the relationship-focused therapies such as couple and psychosexual therapy, and these psychotherapies have generated their own substantial literature. However, it is a theme with which group analysts have hardly touched base. My own book *The Group as an Object of Desire* (Nitsun 2006) was an attempt to open up the field, although focusing more specifically on sexuality and desire.

The subject of falling in love appears frequently in therapy groups but it is seldom the focus of theorizing or clinical study. In some respects, particularly within group analysis with its predilection for group and social perspectives, it may be too intensely personal, too subjective, too 'individual' a theme to command a theoretical platform. But I emphasize in this chapter that falling in love can be approached meaningfully from a group perspective, that its intense subjectivity has powerful implications for group relationships and that understanding it in these terms is helpful when it comes to making sense of the complex relational processes that underlie this profoundly human experience. In this chapter, I aim to describe what happens in therapy groups in response to the theme of falling in love and I begin to construct a framework within which to understand its interpersonal context: a context which may make the difference between falling in love in a way that is developmental, irrespective of whether love blooms or fades, and falling into an abyss of loneliness and despair.

While I have begun this chapter with the notion of falling in love, my framework is necessarily broader in so far as I put falling in love in the context of relationships more generally and specifically the search for an interpersonal bond that in the longer term satisfies the wider and deeper needs for emotional security and spiritual understanding. Falling in love is usually the beginning of this process, sometimes crystallizing into a relationship that survives and deepens, other times fizzling out in the early or later stages, and still other times lingering in an unresolved state of ambivalence. I will attempt to address both the initial hyper-arousing stage of falling in love and its subsequent journey through the complex landscape of bonding and separation. Falling in love ultimately gains its meaning not just from the intense highs and lows of a sudden, overwhelming experience, but from what happens afterwards, from the question of whether the relationship can withstand the glare of reality, the uncovering of what lies beneath the idealization, and of course what the desired or loved *other* wants. It is a dance of two people, not just one, and the unpredictability of the dance is part of the drama of falling in love.

Relationship outcomes in group psychotherapy

This chapter emerges from one of the most rewarding experiences of my long career as a group analyst: the finding that group analytic psychotherapy can have a facilitating impact on group members' capacity to establish a meaningful relationship with a significant other. This impression is not based on formal research but on my own evaluation of outcomes of people attending psychotherapy groups I have conducted in private practice in central London. The three groups from which these observations are drawn are a twice-weekly psychotherapy group and two weekly groups, all long-term analytically orientated groups of mixed gender. The group of patients under consideration had originally presented with significant relationship problems, mainly not having a satisfactory primary relationship of a sexual and romantic kind but regarding this as a priority in their lives and their hopes for psychotherapy. I found that in most cases there were positive changes in this key area by the time the individuals left group therapy.

The patients were between 27 and 59 years of age. They were relatively well-resourced in terms of education and employment, although several had vocational and employment difficulties. They had a range of associated psychological problems, including depression, which in several cases was moderately severe. Several suffered from significantly low self-esteem. The feature that stood out in all of them, though, was the relationship difficulty. This difficulty took different forms: a long-standing absence of any successful relationship with a partner of the opposite or same sex; a history of short-lived and fragmented relationships; withdrawal from close relationships consequent to the experience of relationship failure; some degree of exploitation or abuse in previous relationships; or a combination of these features. What united them was a wish to make sense of these difficulties, to strengthen hope and belief in their capacity for relationships and ultimately to achieve a satisfying partnership. For members of the group falling in love was important, not necessarily in a grand romantic sense but as a symbol of new hope.

In order to set the scene for a fuller exploration of the theme of falling in love and how it entered the groups, I describe the progress of two individuals, Jean and Marc, who were members of two different therapy groups.

Jean (age 31), a successful professional woman, had become increasingly despondent about her lack of a sustained relationship, having had a few abortive relationships with men, in particular a recent relationship that had left her feeling very disappointed. She felt that she was destined to be a competent high-flyer at work but isolated and lonely in her personal life.

In the family background, her father had died when she was six years old. An only child, she was left with an anxious, dependent mother and little other support. Following her father's death, she became not just her mother's companion but filled in for her deceased father, helping her mother with decisions and taking over part of the household administration. She had increasingly adopted a managerial approach – as if it was her responsibility to maintain control and prevent the unforeseen happening, like her father's sudden death. She had transferred the same wary attitude to her relationships with men and strove to appear strong and coping.

Her interaction in the group was similar. She was liked but members found her cautious and defended, liable to rationalize her own and other people's problems to the nth degree, and frightened of spontaneity. In time, she began to open up, challenging a woman whom she felt was competitive and demanding of her, and softening with some male members who expressed feelings of attraction and affection to her. She developed a wry attachment to the conductor, tentatively expressing warmth and admiration. Having decided early on that she would put all attempts to find a partner on hold, Jean gradually, with the group's encouragement, started dating men. To her own and the group's surprise, she met a man fifteen years older with whom she felt an immediate liking. There were problems: he was going through a divorce and had two daughters who were possessive of him. Also, Jean's mother had developed debilitating medical symptoms. But her relationship strengthened. The group observed her in this relationship trying to manage everyone and all eventualities, appeasing the two unfriendly daughters, keeping her mother happy. She was able to receive and use group feedback, against a background of her increasing recognition that she had sacrificed her own emotional life in order to look after her mother.

In her fourth year in the group, Jean decided to leave. She had gained confidence and was hopeful about her new relationship. Group members thought that she might be leaving prematurely but respected her wish to leave. In particular, she wanted to put more time and energy into the relationship. Before she was due to leave the group, however, her mother became seriously ill. She again felt torn between a sense of filial duty and her own fulfillment. This made it more difficult for her to leave the group than expected. She stayed an extra three months and then left, sad but grateful.

Marc (age 38) was a gay man who joined the group in conflict about his career choice as a graphic designer and lacking a sense of self-worth. He had been sexually abused as a child of nine by an adult male family friend. His mother had walked into room in the house to find him in bed with the friend. This was the only occasion of abuse but it left him with strong feelings of shame and guilt and there ensued a tense, awkward silence between him and his parents that lasted for years and was still unresolved.

He became sexually active with other boys during his adolescence and developed a pattern of promiscuity as he grew into adulthood. He was keen to establish a more substantial relationship but his attempts failed. He felt that he had hardened emotionally through years of disappointment and that he lacked warmth and compassion. In the group, members found him distant and sardonic but noted the odd flash of warmth. He shared with the group the traumatic event in which as a child he had been seduced by the family friend and discovered by his mother. Members noted that he repeated the story a number of times but in a detached way. When a new member joined the group and enquired about the event, not having heard the full story, Marc grew angry and critical towards him. Other members challenged Marc about what seemed like gratuitous aggression: in a sense he had abused the new group member. At first defensive and angry, Marc became tearful and contrite, seeing the connection between his early abuse and what he had symbolically enacted in the group. He spoke for the first time about how cold emotionally the home was in which he grew up as a child and how the family friend who abused him had also been kind and loving.

About two years into the group, Marc started making more serious relationships with other men. The group saw him through a failed first attempt at a partnership that left him feeling bruised and despondent. The group was both challenging and reassuring. Following a period of stasis, he met another man, Dino, through a work contact – he was now in a different job – and started a relationship that almost from the beginning felt right. It was not as exciting as the previous relationship but felt more grounded. After some months, the relationship settled into a partnership and he and Dino decided to live together. This had continued for almost a year before Marc decided to leave the group.

Part of my reason for writing this chapter is the wish to share these encouraging outcomes. I had been aware of the positive way that the groups were dealing with relational issues but perhaps underestimated the changes that were taking place. This is not a scientific finding: there was no control group or other research methodology, but I believe the results speak for themselves. It is especially gratifying that there was improvement in the area of intimate relationships. There is a not uncommon view of group psychotherapy as superficial, lacking depth when it comes to serious emotional problems, helping with overall social functioning but not particularly with intimate relationships. My findings contradict this view.

The group and the romantic journey

In this section I explore aspects of the romantic journey and how this is contextualized within the group, using the examples of Jean and Marc.

In my book *The Group as an Object of Desire* (Nitsun 2006), I emphasized that a psychotherapy group is not just a 'meeting of minds', in the sense of a talking shop about ideas and feelings: it is potentially a passionately engaged group of people struggling with some of the most profound issues of being alive. I also argued, contrary to the belief of some, that it is a useful place in which to deal with issues about sexuality, desire and the longing for relationships.

One of the most striking impressions I have of all three groups is how interested they were in the search for a romantic partner and how much they invested in the struggle to make a committed long-term relationship. This may be surprising given changing preferences in relationships in a culture that tends to vaunt the exciting, the short-term and the experimental. But, as Verhaeghe (1999, p. 2) comments, 'This kind of life-long relationship is still what both young and old are dreaming of'. There was little if any questioning in my groups of the fantasy of enduring love. As the group analyst, I was perhaps the only one who challenged this, raising the question of life's meaning without a partner: how it could still be worthwhile and how pinning all one's hopes on having a 'permanent' partnership might be short-sighted and self-limiting. Group members agreed with me, in principle, if only because some of them might end up without a partner, but remained focused on the desirability of long-term partnerships. Possibly this was because – rather than despite – the fact that we live in a fast-moving, alienating world in which there is the potential for painful separation and aloneness. Living in a large city such as London exacerbates the problem: the paradox of so many people in such close proximity and yet so much social isolation and loneliness. The best antidote may yet be a stable sexual and emotional relationship.

I have a strong impression of the encouragement members gave each other. It was common for members in the throes of a new relationship to update the group on the course of the relationship, how it was going, the highs and the lows, the surprises and complications. Usually this meant describing the would-be partner: symbolically introducing this person, not just by name but as an individual in their own right, with their quirks and vulnerabilities, someone with their own story. The group usually took this person on board. If members failed or forgot to give the group feedback about the burgeoning relationship, someone in the group might enquire, 'How did it go on Thursday night?'; 'Have you heard back from Sam?' Group members seemed genuinely interested, their curiosity reflecting a shared hope. If this relationship succeeded, there might be hope for others.

The value of the group's support was not just in the endorsement of the relationship in an abstract sense but the appreciation of the *embodied* relationship and the presence of *desire* as a force shaping the relationship. Group members were interested not only in the social niceties and observed manners of the couple but in the nature and quality of desire, including sexual desire. This included the *naming* of desire, so that desire and longing were given a voice. Some individuals who are embarking on a relationship may have had very little experience of naming and dealing with their desire, so that tension and confusion can arise simply from the lack of familiarity with intense feelings and desires. The group serves a valuable purpose in helping to give voice to these experiences, to add clarity to the otherwise inchoate and overwhelming. In the case of Jean and Marc, described earlier, this was a useful process. Marc had not had an intimate romantic relationship before joining the group. His first attempt, while in the group, ran aground, largely because he was unable to regulate intense feelings of need and desire. By the time he entered a second relationship he was more emotionally equipped.

My main hypothesis concerns *the support* the group gives the emerging couple. This is crucial for the following reasons. The experience of falling in love, both initially and in subsequent stages, can be socially and emotionally isolating. Falling in love is usually an intense and confusing experience, reawakening past emotional trauma in relationships and fears of re-traumatization. It requires a radical separation from the family group and parental authority and is an important step towards individuation and inclusion on the social register. But at the same time it seeks the approval and support of a group. This applies particularly where individuals have had difficult, if not traumatic earlier relationships. In these situations, the support of a group, their resonances, feedback and advice – the collective wisdom of the group – is invaluable. Even more necessary is the group's support in situations where the new relationship fails. In the previous examples, Jean had been shamed by disappointment in a romantic relationship before joining the therapy group and required a good deal of support and encouragement to open up to another relationship. Marc similarly experienced a major setback in his first serious relationship. With the group's support, he went on to try again. Of course, there are instances in which a patient's quest for a relationship does not get very far. There may be an ongoing sense of disappointment – a common experience in the urban, Internet-driven dating universe. But here too the group can be helpful – by holding the hope that the individual cannot.

The group and the couple – theoretical considerations

These observations lead onto some theoretical perspectives on the relationship between the group and the couple. Whereas this has not been a prominent theme in group analysis, it has been so in the work of Bion (1961), as well as other psychoanalytically orientated writers on groups, such as Kernberg (1995). I add to this my own thinking about the primal scene in group analysis (Nitsun 1994).

Bion's views about pairing are well-known as one of the three basic assumptions. The pair or couple, in his theory, represents the symbolic hope of a Messiah through the generativity of the couple, hence exerting a fascination on the group. Kernberg (1995) offers a more socially focused vision of the relationship between the group and the couple, according the group considerable significance in the vicissitudes of the romantic and sexual journey. He presents two somewhat conflicting versions. In one, the social group celebrates the new relationship, admiring the 'Oedipal' triumph of the couple, offering support and validation of the relationship. In the other, the social group is ambivalent about the relationship. Not only is there envy of the couple but the group seeks to impose constraints on them. This reflects Kernberg's view that social groups are prone to fostering a restrictive sense of conventional morality, hewn from the collective urge to establish social controls and a shared consensus on basic values. This, he suggests, conflicts with the couple's own more personal and private morality. Romantic love and sexuality, he believes, strive for liberation from the surrounding group and its imposed morality. Throughout *Love Relations* (Kernberg 1995), he positions the couple in various respects in opposition to the social group.

While accepting that the group may be ambivalent about the sexual couple, and that the couple can readily evoke envy – a theme to which I return in due course – I find little support in my groups for Kernberg's perception of the group as seeking to repress and restrict the couple. Of course, the difference may be that the groups I describe are psychotherapy groups rather than conventional social groups. This immediately places the group outside of the constraints of typical social groups and in a position in which, as I argue elsewhere (Nitsun 1996), there is the potential to challenge conventional morality. Foulkes (1948) referred to this as 'the group as a forum', a useful concept in my view, in which Foulkes portrays the group as questioning oppressive social mores and counteracting the super-ego rather than conforming to it. In the psychotherapy groups I describe, the couple is welcomed into the group rather than rejected and the morality of the group is a facilitating one rather than an oppressive one.

My own work on the primal scene in group psychotherapy (Nitsun 1994) is relevant here. It emphasizes the centrality of the sexual couple in the dynamics of the group. Based on psychoanalytic notions of the fantasy about parental sexuality, not simply as a split-off sexual act but as a symbol of sexual union, I argue that the fantasy of the primal scene has an implicit hold on the group dynamic and the development of intimacy both inside and outside the therapy group. Returning to Bion (1961), he postulates that the basic assumptions in groups are ways of dealing with the anxiety evoked by a very early primal scene in which the relationship is feared to be aggressive and damaging rather than loving. In my own development of these ideas, I hypothesized that the nature of the primal scene, probably as a shared unconscious fantasy, influences different aspects of the psychotherapy group: intimacy, the atmosphere of the group and the extent to which actual sexual relationships can develop and flourish. The group's preoccupation with coupling may be not just altruistic, in the sense of supporting new relationships, but an attempt at exploring and re-working the symbolized parental relationship, given its influence on individuals' developing relationships. Through their interest in members' developing relationships, the group as a whole explores the sexual subject. Additionally, as have I pointed out, the primal scene is regarded by various writers (e.g. Greenacre 1973; Aron 1995) not solely as a sexual preoccupation but as a way of exploring the origins and purpose of life. I believe this is important in relation to falling in love: the deeper existential aspects that supersede the thrill of romance; the implications of a loving relationship for life as whole, with its many imponderables and mysteries and the need to find anchorage in a sea of the unknown.

> The trauma Marc experienced as a child – being seduced by a family friend and discovered in bed with the man by his mother – suggests a possible inversion of the primal scene. Instead of Marc discovering his parents in bed, they discovered him. We can speculate on what this meant. We know that he saw his parents as cold and unloving, with each other and with him. Assuming an unconscious primal scene, what did he see in the parental intercourse? Was he enacting sexually a wish for intimacy in the family? Was he inserting himself into the primal scene?

Further functions of the psychotherapy group

Love stories

While romantic love is universal, its representation differs from person to person, with myriad variations on the theme. This is the basis of the *love story*, as dramatized in the arts and the media, touching on both the universals and the idiosyncratic twists and turns in every story. Sternberg (1998, 2013) has theorized and researched the notion of the love story. He highlights how we are all exposed to a wide range of stories that convey different versions of how love can be understood and enacted. As a result of our exposure to such stories, and in line with our early relationships in the family, including mythical and unconscious versions of the primal scene, we over time form our own stories of how love may be – and will be – for us personally.

Stories are highly relevant to the group. The narrative basis of group psychotherapy process has been highlighted by a number of writers (Edelson and Berg 1999; Stacey 2003). The story is usually an expression of the person's underlying schema (Young *et al.* 2003) or life-script (Steiner 1990), which tends to have a far-reaching effect on that individual's life. Part of therapy is the challenge, deconstruction and possible reconstruction of the story, particularly where there are elements of disappointment and failure that have become self-fulfilling prophecies. Personal love stories are potent in this regard: the narrative influences relationships in an ongoing way, usually with an imagined denouement and ending. Many stories are only half-realized and, because of elements of trauma and shame, they become encapsulated, unavailable for reflection or sharing. In the group, several constructive processes are mobilized:

- The group acts as a listening post for the different narratives, often giving members their first opportunity to articulate their love stories.
- The group generates a variety of different stories, giving members the opportunity to hear other people's stories and to review their own in the light of others.
- Group processes of resonance and mirroring generate a sense of universality.
- Group members challenge each others' stories and encourage 'restorying' or the refashioning of the narrative.
- As group members begin to evolve different stories, they may start experimenting in relationships in new ways.

The group provides an environment where stories can be told and retold, shaped and reshaped, creating the potential for change and transformation.

Of the two patients previously highlighted, each came with their version of a love story. Jean's story was one of disappointment and hurt, with an assumption that she could never make a satisfactory relationship with a man. An important sub-text was the death of her father when she was six. The group helped her to see that her difficult relationships with men might be an enactment of the loss of her father. Another sub-text was her loyalty to her mother, which meant not making a life of her own or having a relationship of her own. The telling and retelling of this story enabled Jean to realize the impact that it had on her life and to recognize the choices available to her.

The group as a secure base

Implied in the above is the group's provision of a secure emotional base. This function of the psychotherapy group has been elaborated within the framework of attachment theory (Glenn 1987; Marrone 1994), highlighting the value of a stable, consistent interpersonal environment to which the individual can leave and return each week. This acquires additional significance for a group member going through the vicissitudes of seeking a partner, making a connection, dating, risking intimacy and so on.

The group as witness

I (Nitsun 2006) have previously highlighted the function of the group as witness in situations where the individual or couple's isolation has exposed them to conflict, hurt or abuse – or indeed any situation which would benefit from independent and impartial observation. Intimate relationships usually occur in social isolation. The couple retreats behind a boundary into its own privately shared space; the world is kept at bay as the relationship unfolds. But the isolation of the couple, particularly in the absence of friendship or family support, can create problems. The individuals may feel confused and overwhelmed, struggling to meet the challenges of a new relationship. The absence of support, of interested others, creates a vacuum in which the individual may resort to self-protective, defensive and sometimes destructive manoeuvres. The relationship may not survive the strain of the two people on their own struggling with these tensions. The group as witness is able to hear, observe and respond, to offer perspective where otherwise the emotional complexity of the relationship may be overwhelming.

As noted previously, group members usually take an active interest in each other's liaisons outside the group. This is especially important in situations where problems occur in the relationship: where there are unexpected hurts, sudden let-downs or complications such as the discovery that a would-be partner is married, threatened abuse, sexual transgression or the eruption of conflict and aggression: the little and big shocks and surprises that mark the course of a relationship. The individual caught up in these developments is often unable to gain sufficient distance to understand what is happening and how to respond. At these times, the group's function as a witness comes to the fore.

> In Marc's case, the group was helpful in teasing out the difficulties that preceded the break-up of his first relationship while in the group. They helped to clarify his and his partner's different contributions to the problem and bear witness to Marc's grief. This made the break-up more tolerable.

The group as 'third'

The function of the group as a witness overlaps with its significance as a 'third'. Various writers, including Andre Greene (2005), Ogden (1997), and Fisher (1999), emphasize the necessity in emotional development of the third, the person who exists outside the couple and can bring sanity to an otherwise fraught situation. The most common example cited is that of the father coming 'between' the mother and child in early development, helping to moderate the potentially overwhelming impact of the mother and to counter the risk of a symbiotic mother–child relationship. Groups are very good at being 'the third'. This is possibly because there is strength in numbers: the group's position as third is multiplied by its having several different voices. Most of the burgeoning relationships I have witnessed in group therapy have benefited from the presence of the group as third.

> In Mary's case, the group provided the function of a third that was missing in her development due to the early loss of her father. This helped to moderate her over-intense relationship with her mother and facilitate her openness to a heterosexual relationship.

Another version of the third is found in Britton's notion of the triangular space. Linking this to the outcome of the Oedipus complex, Britton (1989) postulates that when the primitive emotions of love and hate for the beloved object can be tolerated in the child's and the parent's minds, there exists the prototype 'for an object relationship of a third kind'. This is a third position from which object relationships can be observed. This creates the capacity for seeing ourselves in interaction with others and for appreciating another point of view while holding our own: a capacity for reflecting on ourselves while being ourselves and for reflecting on others while they are themselves. This triangular space (Britton 1989, pp. 86–7), provides 'the possibility of being a participant in a relationship and observed by a third person as well as being an observer of a relationship between two people'. This more complex psychological skill is very much how groups work: members learn to shift their interpersonal frames of reference and, in so doing, gain a skill which helps them to see themselves and others in a reflexive loop. It is a valuable asset in conducting relationships, helping to avoid a solipsistic position that could put one out of touch with both the loved one and others who have a bearing on the progress of the relationship.

Interpersonal learning

Yalom and Leszcz (2005) regards interpersonal learning as *the* therapeutic factor in group psychotherapy. Much of what I have described above falls into this category: the group's functions as a secure base, as a witness and as a third, all facilitate interpersonal learning. From a self-psychological perspective, the group can be viewed as a *multiple self-object field* (Segalla 1998). The group comprises a variety of different relationships in a single whole, creating a richer interpersonal field than individual therapy and providing opportunities for involvement and feedback from the various group members. As the self-psychologists have pointed out, there are ample opportunities in a group to discover and engage with self-object experiences: mirroring, idealizing, twinship, merging, agency and adversarial needs (Wolff 1988). All these self-object needs are likely to be stirred up in a new relationship and encountering them in the therapy group provides a useful testing ground and rehearsal stage, helping the individual to acquire a stronger sense of self and the capacity to mediate the self-object functions in self and other.

Another way of construing the above is in the light of the group as *a family surrogate*. As is widely theorized and documented, the origins of romantic relationships are in the family, where the quality of early attachment strongly influences the subsequent relationship pattern of the individual (Dinero *et al.* 2008): the sibling configuration also contributes to this process. But the family is usually a cauldron of emotion, of ambivalent relationships with confused boundaries and complicating tensions such as rivalry, envy and hostility. These tensions are of course largely inescapable – they are the warp and the weft of family life. The psychotherapy group has its own tensions but is first and foremost a *stranger group* with a greater capacity for distancing and reflection. It is a group without the a priori emotional intensity of the family but with the ability to process the interpersonal tensions that arise. So, group members may equally experience rivalry and envy but exploration of these feelings becomes part of the currency of the group and is less likely to undermine and sabotage relationships. The group has a holding and containing capacity that is similar to that of the family but without the potentially destructive aspects of unprocessed family relations.

While the group can generate complex relationships, it is important not to ignore more basic and direct interpersonal learning. One fundamental area in relationships is communication: the capacity to communicate feeling states and thoughts in relationship with another. This entails the capacity to *mentalize* the thoughts and feelings of self and other (Fonagy and Bateman 2008). In various ways, these abilities – or the absence of them – can either make or break a relationship. Group psychotherapy provides a unique opportunity to learn and practise these skills, since the process of the group is fundamentally communicational. Foulkes (1964) referred to this as ego training in action. Schulte (2000) highlights the inter-subjective process as germane to groups. Empathic and appropriately assertive interpersonal processes learned in the group add to vital resources needed for relationships.

> Marc entered the group with communication difficulties. A traumatic childhood experience had resulted in his closing up, hiding feelings and using irony to distance people. Alternatively, he would go the extremes of anger and rage. When he first attempted a serious 'outside' relationship, he lurched into an unregulated emotional state, unable to communicate his feelings and needs. The group enabled him to find more effective ways of communicating.

Groups are helpful to members in both big and little ways. Unlike in individual therapy, advice and encouragement are freely sought and freely given. In one group, a male participant realized that he had unwittingly hurt his girlfriend. Worried about how he could make amends to her – common territory for him – he found himself unable to broach the subject at all. Another group member, more experienced in matters of the heart, came up with a simple solution: 'Send her a bunch of flowers.' The advice was acted on and had a positive effect. Here, the patient learned the value of a simple non-verbal gesture, demonstrating the sort of casual but valuable interpersonal learning that is a feature of group therapy.

'Pathologies' of love

I put 'pathologies' in inverted commas as I would prefer to understand rather than pathologize the more serious difficulties people encounter in making relationships. It is necessary to recognize that some of these difficulties may be deep-rooted and problematic but they may also reflect more common if not universal difficulties.

Narcissism

The term 'narcissism' is used in different ways. Popularly, it is associated with a preoccupation with the self, a form of self-love. Fisher (1999), however, points out that it is more about intolerance of the independence of the other, a difficulty in accepting separateness and difference. He suggests that it reflects a paradoxical longing for the other but for an-other who fits a perfect image and is perfectly gratifying – and hence not real.

The diagnostic category of narcissistic disorder is well-established and there is a substantial literature on the nature of narcissistic relationships (e.g. Higgitt and Fonagy 1992; Kernberg 2004). However, what I commonly encounter, rather than examples of 'absolute' or primary narcissism, is the struggle many people have with a narcissistic *part* of their personalities and the tensions this creates in reconciling the needs of the self and the needs of the other. Many people, in even relatively functional relationships, slide between the preoccupation with self as an autonomous, independent entity and the self as dependent, needing closeness and intimacy: in parallel with this, a perception of the other as superfluous and expendable *or* as profoundly needed for emotional sustenance, even existence. The conflict between these opposing perceptions of self and other are what, in my experience, are at the heart of many relational problems and the experience of falling in love. One manifestation is the idealization that is stirred up in the process of falling in love: the loved one is, temporarily at least, the embodiment of all that is desirable and wonderful, and the 'madness' of being in love is an expression of the excitement of discovering the idealized other. But the challenge comes in dealing with the inevitable disillusionment, the discovery that the other is flawed, that one's relationship is flawed, and that there is no perfectly fulfilling other. Whether this can be tolerated, with regret and sadness perhaps, is a touch point in the relational process that makes the difference between a grounded, real relationship and a relationship forever imagined but always elusive.

These are intrinsically human problems and there is no real cure for them: but it is possible to understand and clarify the painful tensions. Group psychotherapy, like most other interventions, does not have an easy answer. However, in my experience, attendance at a long-term psychotherapy group goes some way towards drawing out these issues, sharing them in a way that roots them in universal experience. The discourse may be a lesson in how to stay in communication when the conflict between sameness and difference threatens to tear the relationship apart.

Marc exemplified these problems. A narcissistic tendency towards superiority and self-sufficiency, concealing childhood trauma and vulnerability, was reflected in his promiscuous sex life. His first foray into a serious relationship unleashed intense idealization of the other that exceeded the limits of what was possible in a relationship and led to its dissolution. The group helped him to deal with consequent feelings of disillusionment and despair, eventually facilitating a more realistic relationship.

It is useful to make a distinction between healthy and unhealthy idealization. As the self psychologists point out, idealization is a normal developmental need (Wolff 1988). Similarly, in falling in love, healthy idealization of the other is an intrinsic part of the process. But the idealization needs to yield to compromise, allowing the other their own humanity, flaws and vulnerability.

Narcissistic sensitivity

There is another manifestation of narcissism that is different from the above. This concerns the great sensitivity many people feel about their self-worth: their appearance, knowledge, ability and personality. There may be deep feelings of inadequacy: virtually the reverse of narcissism in its superior and grandiose form. Many coming for psychotherapy have suffered narcissistic injuries in their development through lack of mirroring and failed attunement: lack of being seen, appreciated, encouraged and loved. The consequence may be life-long sensitivity to further narcissistic injury, craving for validation and admiration, and deep vulnerability to slights, rejections and real or imagined insults. This constitutes a problem not only for the person's self-perception and belief but also for their relationships, since there is an exquisite sensitivity to hurt. Such is the sensitivity, that some do not even venture into relationships: others do but remain in a state of heightened sensitivity to imagined or actual rejection.

My experience is that psychotherapy groups are very helpful in the area of narcissistic sensitivity. Although people often fear groups because of the potential for misunderstanding and injury, in reality most patients, I believe, have an affirming experience in the group. Group members are usually generous with their praise and appreciation, but also constructive criticism, and the combination can help a vulnerable ego to strengthen. Seeing others' vulnerability helps to universalize the sensitivity and reduce feelings of isolation and oddness. This is especially valuable in the face of the shame and humiliation experienced consequent to a failed relationship that has occurred within the life-span of the group.

Jean grew up with a confused sense of her self-worth. Becoming a successful professional concealed severe underlying doubts about her attractiveness and likeability. In part, this appeared to be occasioned by the death of her father. Although he had not rejected her as such, in her mind she felt not good enough or lovable enough to keep him. A sequence of failed relationships with men later in life confirmed her fears. In the therapy group, the men's appreciation of her as a woman made an important difference.

The core complex

A further area of disturbance in the development of close, intimate relationships is labeled by Glasser (1979) 'the core complex'. It describes particularly intense ambivalence about intimacy. A deep-seated and pervasive longing for intimate closeness oscillates with a terror of engulfment. A vicious circle is mobilized: fear of *engulfment* alternating with fear of *abandonment*. In some cases, the impossibility of resolution creates a sado-masochistic object relationship, which may be played out with the other (Perelberg 1999). The consensus on the origin of the core complex is that it derives from a primitive engulfing relationship with the mother in infancy in the absence of a 'third', the father, who can intervene and help to regulate the intense cycles of intimacy and anxiety between mother and child (see above for comments on the third).

This pattern of relating is often present in people who attend psychotherapy groups. Their history of relationships says it all. Not surprisingly, these relationships usually break down under the strain of ambivalence. The therapy group is useful in illuminating the pattern, largely because the same pattern is often enacted in patients' relationship with the group. This is reflected, for example, in their mode of group attendance. A period of good attendance, when some closeness to the group may have occurred, is followed by a period of non-attendance. It becomes clear that the patient's erratic attendance hides great anxiety about staying in close contact. Gradually, over time, the pattern can no longer be denied and it becomes possible to explore and understand. People in groups tend to gain insight into this process and show a greater capacity to self-regulate in a relationship, without plunging into either catastrophic engulfment or withdrawal.

Pam was a very erratic group attender. She described an intense alternation between closeness and distance in her relationships. She behaved similarly in the group, going through cycles of opening up and coming very close, then dismissing the group contemptuously and disappearing for periods of time, keeping the group in a constant state of suspension. She initially resisted any challenge to this pattern but gradually acknowledged deep fears of intrusion and began to attend more regularly.

One purpose of the above examples is to illustrate the point that, while there are undoubtedly serious pathologies associated with sexuality and relationships, these problems often reflect the tensions that exist in most relationships. The group helps to universalize problems that otherwise may seem extreme and intractable.

Love *in* and *out* of the group

I have so far emphasized progress in group members' relationships *outside* the group. But this should not exclude the group itself, the way desire and love are evoked and transmitted between members. In my publication on *The Group as an Object of Desire* (Nitsun 2006), I describe the often libidinally charged atmosphere of the group, how this may be just as real as members' relationships outside the group and how this influences their outside relationships.

Many patients come to group therapy looking for love. Not unusually, people come hoping to find sex in the group, a romantic partnership, perhaps even 'the love of my life'. Fantasies about other group members are often sexually tinged: will there be an attractive woman/man to stimulate and possibly satisfy my desires, my deepest longings? Are *you* that person? Given the dissatisfaction people may be experiencing in their own relationships, some degree of emotional or sexual lack, the painful aftermath of a recent romantic break-up, perhaps, or the sense of being stuck in a chronically frustrating relationship, it is not surprising if the level of libidinal need in the therapy group is high. The difficulty then may be in maintaining a boundary between desire stimulated in the group and the rule of abstinence. Although most group members, in my experience, conform to this rule, recognizing that it is there to protect them and the group, there are instances of sexual experimentation and partnership formation outside the group. This is generally very problematic, often enacted in secrecy outside the group but coming to light unexpectedly and placing the conductor in a difficult position. It may require a decision about the protagonists' group membership: do they stay or leave? Does *one* stay and the other leave? These situations usually plunge the group into crisis and it may take months before the problem is resolved, often leaving an anxious shadow in the group.

There is a view that sexual enactments outside the group are the consequence of an inappropriately libidinized atmosphere in the group: that speaking openly about sex and desire in the group stimulates inappropriate acting out. My own view is that the opposite may apply: *not* speaking about sex, and the *pretence* that desire and attraction are not happening, is more rather than less conducive to sexual enactment. My experience is that openness about sexuality and desire in the group is holding and containing rather than over-stimulating and provocative.

There is near universal agreement that relationship formation of members outside the group is an untoward development. But a contrary view, not documented as such, is that outside liaisons are to some extent inevitable and not necessarily a bad thing. I know of several longstanding couples that were forged within a therapy group: members who were attracted, took the risk of meeting outside, discovered a mutual desire for a deeper and more committed relationship, and proceeded to embark on just that. The problem is that for every couple that has achieved this, there are others whose relationship outside the group ran aground, plunged them into difficulty and left them and the group with a painful legacy of disappointment and anger. Group boundaries, in my view, are important specifically for reasons such as this. The opportunistic attempt to establish an extra-group relationship is too vulnerable to derailment, quite apart from the impact it has on the group. The purpose of the group must remain one of facilitating relationships outside the group with *non-group* partners, the group serving to open up the discourse about desire and intimacy, explored openly and non-judgementally, but with a view to strengthening relationships outside the group.

The role of the group therapist

I am aware that I have so far said very little about the role of the group psychotherapist.

The group therapist's role is similar to that in any group. It is essentially a facilitating role, giving the group considerable space to evolve its own culture and therapeutic momentum. But the conductor also has a crucial holding function. The group itself has such an important role in supporting the individual/s going through the storms of falling in love, that the group itself needs close holding. Hence, all the tasks of dynamic administration (Foulkes 1964), such as boundary setting, dealing with breaks, managing entrances and exits to the group, require careful attention. Foulkes (1964) said, 'If the conductor looks after the group, the group will look after the individual'. But the group therapist is not just a boundary manager: he/she is an alive presence with his/her own desires, a person whose own relational history and current intimate relationship/s will influence how he/she responds to the theme of falling in love and the intense emotions stirred up in the process. Further, his/her own differential reactions to group members are likely to be picked up, creating strong sensitivities and rivalries about the conductor's affections. It is important that the conductor is sufficiently in touch with his/her own desires and relational anxieties and how these may consciously and unconsciously influence the group. Above all, the conductor must be open to the narrative of love, in its various guises, as the group may take its cue from the conductor's interest and openness.

An important function concerns the morality of the group and how the group therapist influences this. Matters of intimacy, gender, sexual orientation and sexual fantasy are all intrinsic parts of the contemporary romantic narrative, but all are highly loaded emotionally and challenging of personal and group morality. As I have pointed out (Nitsun 2006), group morality may be an unspoken, implicit but nonetheless crucial variable in the unfolding of the sexual and romantic narrative and I believe that the conductor has major responsibility in influencing this.

The area in which the group conductor is most strongly implicated is in the configuration of transference and counter-transference. This is where the conductor becomes the love object in the group, either for a particular group member or the group as a whole. It is commonly said that transference occurs across the group in a horizontal rather than vertical way, in other words that group members become transference and counter-transference figures for each other and that there is – or should be – less emphasis on the transference towards the conductor (Foulkes 1964). However, there is no doubt in my mind that the group conductor remains a powerful object of transference and is subject to his/her own, often intense, feelings and counter-transference. Transference towards the conductor may or may not always be apparent in the group, possibly because group conductors tend to ignore or underplay it. But, in my experience, idealizing transferences to the conductor, tinged with the romantic and/or the erotic, are common in groups and how the conductor handles them will have a significant influence on the nature of the discourse and the overall group process.

Mann (2003) makes a distinction between progressive and regressive erotic or romantic transference. The 'progressive' view sees erotic transference as healthy, growthful and potentiating development, whereas the 'regressive' view sees it as unhealthy and deriving from primitive, even psychotic, parts of the personality that can undermine the therapy. Ultimately, Mann suggests, there may be both progressive and regressive aspects in erotic transference and that the balance will depend on the particular individuals involved and the psychotherapeutic context. Of course, group psychotherapy alters the context. If it is tricky taking up the erotic or romantic transference in individual psychotherapy, it is a more challenging task in the group, where feelings and behaviours are much more public and exposed. The progressive-type romantic transference towards the group therapist (or for that matter, other members) is easier to manage than the regressive transference. Progressive transferences, in my experience, can be handled by acknowledgement, usually without the in-depth exploration that might happen in individual analysis. This may be enough to contain and facilitate the transference in a way that is validating, without it overwhelming the person or the group. It is possible that this does scant justice to the depth of the transference but there may not be much choice, given how much time fuller attention to the transference would require, and how this might skew the dynamics of the group. At the same time, not taking up the transference at all, in my view, is a mistake. It could fail to mobilize the healthy aspects of the transference, depriving the individual of the validation needed, as well as the spurt in their development. It would also give the wrong signal to the group: that feelings of desire or love towards the group therapist (and other group members) are off limits and not to be expressed.

From what I know of the regressive erotic transference in a group, this is very difficult. It tends to occur in the context of a severe borderline turn in a group member, the erotic aspect linked to a highly aggressive, persecuted and persecutory state of mind. Ideally, with sufficient understanding and patience, it can be worked through. But, equally, it may have a destructive effect on the group. Rather than opening up the sexual or romantic discourse, it may close it down. It may be very difficult, if not impossible, to keep the individual in the group and arrangements for the person to leave may have to be considered.

Lastly, there is the question of the group conductor's erotic or romantic counter-transference. It is important to make a distinction between counter-transference reactions and the conductor's spontaneous desires and feelings that arise in the flow of the group. The conductor, like anyone else, cannot help but feel desire, affection and romantic stirrings towards one or more people in the group. This does not in itself constitute counter-transference. These reactions, as Moeller (2002) points out, occur naturally but unpredictably in groups and, of course, have to be understood and not enacted. Mostly, they are valuable as part of a group culture which encourages the recognition of desire, although the conductor him- or herself is more constrained than other group members in what can and cannot be revealed to the group. Actual romantic counter-transference on the part of the conductor in the group, where the therapist's feelings mirror those of the amorous patient, are in my experience rare, although I give one such example in a previous publication (Nitsun 2006). Where this happens, the conductor potentially becomes entangled in an intense relational process and, in my view, almost always requires additional support or supervision.

Reflections

Contrary to the not uncommon view that relationship problems require the in-depth work of individual analysis, the findings of this chapter demonstrate that the group offers a useful setting and that sharing with others the challenging experience of falling in love can be both supportive and transformative.

The experiences I describe throw some light on the question of the relationship between the couple and the group. This question relates not only to the couple in the psychotherapy group but also to the wider issue of how social groups receive the couple. What I said earlier merits restating. Kernberg (1995) argues that the attitude of the group to the couple is ambivalent, admiring the couple on the one hand but also envying it and wanting to restrain it through making the couple conform and fit into conventional society. My experience is that, while groups can constrain the couple through the kind of conservatism that Kernberg highlights, or make use of the couple as a defence against anxiety and despair, as Bion theorizes, the psychotherapy group in general welcomes coupling in a positive way. Envy, undoubtedly, is stirred up in groups in which one or more group members are enjoying success in a relationship and others not, but overall I have found people to be open about this in groups, in a way which contains rather than exacerbates the envy. If anything, the dynamic of coupling, including the evocation of desire and the promise of fulfillment, has an energizing effect on the group. As I noted in my book on sexuality in groups (Nitsun 2006), Eros, as the organizing principle of love and the erotic, is also a principle of attraction in a general sense, a process of binding (Abel-Hirsch 2001). It is the engine of the psychotherapeutic group, at times challenged by the anti-binding properties of the anti-group – but, as love hopefully wins out, so hopefully will the integrity of the group.

In conclusion, I hope that I have conveyed the powerful interpersonal context that group psychotherapy provides for people struggling with the vicissitudes of seeking a primary love relationship, the impact of falling in love and the challenge of establishing a relationship that lasts beyond the first fires of romance. If I were to sum up in one word the contribution of the group in situations like this it would be *holding* – holding the individual (and symbolically the couple) through the tumultuous and sometimes traumatic experience of falling in love and all that ensues. The experience of falling in love, whether in the full romantic sense of the term or in a symbolic sense, and dealing with the aftermath, triggers not only the excitement and anxiety of the present, but recapitulates earlier experiences of the first 'in-loveness', the longing for the idealized object, the moments of fulfillment and the inevitable periods of frustration and disappointment. Falling in love constitutes one of the greatest psychic risks. The psychotherapy group offers a context that can make the risk more bearable.

A note about the developmental level at which psychotherapy groups function: although I have several times referred to the origins of love relationships in early childhood, group psychotherapy does not generally encourage regression as part of the therapeutic process. Unlike some forms of individual psychotherapy or psychoanalysis, we do not make the assumption that renewed development requires submergence into infantile states. The group usually addresses the adult as an adult, even where there may be a recapitulation of earlier emotional states. I agree with Schaverien (1995) who comments that analysts who concentrate on mother–infant relationship and neglect more mature adult sexual feelings may be abusing their power. By concentrating on infantile relationships, they may discourage growth towards more mature sexuality and relationships. Groups seem to know this intuitively, valuing and striving towards an adult expression of their relational needs. I see this not as defensive or avoidant but reflecting the wisdom of the group.

Finally, while painting a positive picture of the group in relation to the notion of falling in love, I must impart a note of realism. The journey I describe is hard work. It often falters, gets stuck, fails, has to survive disappointment and despair, and recognize its limitations in dealing with the full complexity of relational problems. Not everyone succeeds in forming or maintaining a relationship. Few leave the group in a state of conjugal bliss. Even where the relationship succeeds, falling in love yields to a sense of the ordinariness and struggle of life and the continuing vulnerability of being human.

References

Abel-Hirsch, N. (2001) *Eros*. Cambridge: Icon Books.

Aron, L. (1995) The internalized primal scene, *Psychoanalytic Dialogues*, 5, 195–238.

Bion, W. R. (1961) *Experiences in Groups*. London: Tavistock.

Britton, R. (1989) The missing link: parental sexuality in the Oedipus complex, in Britton, R., Feldman, M. and O'Shaughnessy, E. (eds) *The Oedipus Complex Today*. London: Karnac.

Dinero, R. E., Conger, R. D., Shaver, P. R., Widaman, K. F. and Larsen-Rife, D. (2008) Influence of family of origin and adult romantic partners on romantic attachment security, *Journal of Family Psychology*, 22, 622–32.

Edelson, M. and Berg, D. N. (1999) *Rediscovering Groups: A Psychoanalyst's Journey beyond Individual Psychology*. London: Jessica Kingsley.

Fisher, J. (1999) *The Uninvited Guest: Emerging from Narcissism towards Marriage*. London: Karnac.

Fonagy, P. and Bateman, A. (2008) The development of borderline personality disorders, *Journal of Personality Disorders*, 22, 4–21.

Foulkes, S. H. (1948) *Introduction to Group-Analytic Psychotherapy*. London: Maresfield Reprints.

Foulkes, S. H. (1964) *Therapeutic Group Analysis*. London: Maresfield Reprints.

Glasser, M. (1979) Some aspects of the role of aggression in the perversions, in Rosen, I. (ed.) *Sexual Deviation*. Oxford: Oxford University Press.

Glenn, L. (1987) Attachment theory and group analysis: the group as a secure base, *Group Analysis*, 20, 109–17.

Greenacre, P. (1973) The primal scene and the sense of reality, *Psychoanalytic Quarterly*, 42, 10–41.

Greene, A. (2005) *Key Concepts for a Contemporary Psychoanalysis*. Hove: Routledge.

Higgitt, A. and Fonagy, P. (1992) Psychotherapy in borderline and personality disorder, *British Journal of Psychiatry*, 161, 23–43.

Kernberg, O. F. (1995) *Love Relations*. New Haven, CT: Yale University Press.

Kerberg, O. F. (2004) *Borderline Conditions and Pathological Narcissism*. New York: Jason Aronson.

Mann, D. (ed.) (2003) *Erotic Transference and Counter-Transference*. Hove: Brunner-Routledge.

Marrone, M. (1994) Attachment theory and group analysis, in Brown, D. and Zinkin, L. (eds) *The Psyche and the Social World*. London: Routledge.

Moeller, M. L. (2002) Love in the group, *Group Analysis*, 35, 484–98.

Nitsun, M. (1994) The primal scene in group analysis, in Brown, D. and Zinkin, L. (eds.) *The Psyche and the Social World*. London: Routledge.

Nitsun, M. (2006) *The Group as an Object of Desire: Exploring Sexuality in Group Psychotherapy*. London: Routledge.

Ogden, T. (1997) The analytic third: working with inter-subjective clinical facts, *International Journal of Psychoanalysis*, 75, 3–20.

Perelberg, R. J. (1999) A core phantasy in violence, in Perleberg, R. J. (ed.) *Psychoanalytic Understanding of Violence and Suicide*. London: Routledge.

Schaverien, J. (1995) *Desire and the Female Therapist: Engendered Gazes in Psychotherapy and Art Therapy*. London: Routledge.

Schulte, P. (2000) Holding in mind: intersubjectivity, subject relations and the group, *Group Analysis*, 33, 531–44.

Segalla, R. (1998) Motivational systems and group-object theory: implications for group psychotherapy, in Harwood, I.N.H. and Pines, M. (eds) (1998) *Self Experiences in Group*. London: Jessica Kingsley.

Stacey, R. D. (2003) *Complexity and Group Processes*. Hove: Brunner-Routledge.

Steiner, C. M. (1990) *Scripts People Live*. New York: Grove Press.

Sternberg, R. J. (1998) *Love is a Story*. New York: Oxford University Press.

Sternberg, R. J. (2013) Searching for love: Robert J Sternberg on the stages of his quest to understand what binds us together, *The Psychologist*, 26, 98–101.

Verhaeghe, P. (1999) *Love in a Time of Loneliness*. New York: Other Press.

Wolff, E. (1988) *Treating the Self: Elements of Clinical Self Psychology*. New York: Guilford Press

Yalom, I. B. and Leszcz, M. (2005) *Theory and Practice of Group Psychotherapy*. New York: Basic Books.

Young, J. E., Klosko, J. S. and Weishaar, M. E. (2003) *Schema Therapy: A Practitioner's Guide*. New York: The Guilford Press.

Group analysis and the arts

Group analysis and performance art

My being a painter with a longstanding interest in the link between art and psychotherapy comes to the fore in this chapter. I consider how the two lines of psychotherapy and art are presently converging in unexpected ways. I focus particularly on the overlap between group psychotherapy and performance art, but do so in the wider context of contemporary art, psychoanalytic approaches to art and the range of related approaches such as the arts psychotherapies, using this as an opportunity to explore a rich cultural field that seems relatively neglected in group analysis. I draw a fundamental distinction between psychotherapy as an art and psychotherapy as an art *form* and give some emphasis to play and performativity as concepts that help to create an inter-disciplinary frame for the two fields. The chapter stands in contrast to previous chapters that are strongly clinical in emphasis and that argue for greater rigour in group analysis. This chapter, although different in emphasis, does not detract from the clinical argument but offers thoughts from an alternative perspective.

Background

One aspect of the contemporary world is the increasingly inter-disciplinary nature of cultural progress. Reflecting a world in which many familiar boundaries have disappeared, often with far-reaching consequences, there has been a growing interpenetration of disciplines and schools of thought. As we move further into the twenty-first century, there is a sense of such penetrating change that diverse spheres of thought, action and imagination may be expected to collide in unexpected, even radical ways. The art world is in the forefront of this change, and has been for some decades. Art no longer exclusively concerns the creation of aesthetic objects, opening up instead to a vigorous and sometimes baffling tide of experimentation, generating a plethora of new forms of expression, increasingly recognized as an integral though controversial part of the international art scene (Goldberg 2011). Performance art is at the epicenter of many of these changes, drawing on a multitude of cultural forms and subjects and crossing boundaries with fields as varied as politics, sociology, anthropology, philosophy, theatre, film, literature and music. By contrast, psychotherapy has remained a relatively intact, uniform field, subject to marked variation and conflicting values within the psychotherapeutic community itself, but in essence remaining a largely conservative undertaking concerned with the adjustment of individuals in society and not necessarily stopping to question the grounds for this practice in the light of changing value systems and lifestyles in a technologically and socially transforming world (see Chapter 1). In this chapter I aim to consider areas in which these approaches cross over: how contemporary performance art, in both form and content, verges at times on psychotherapy but presents its ideas in very different ways, and how group analysis in some ways can be seen as reflecting elements of performance art. I also raise the question of what, if anything, performance art can contribute to the 'modernization' and acculturation of the group analytic approach.

The link between group analysis and performance art has a surprising historical precedent. In a tribute to S. H. Foulkes at his 70th birthday, Tom Main (1968, in the Foulkes Archive 2013) recalls how Foulkes, in the days of the Northfield Experiment in the 1940s, was interested not in groups simply for groups' sake, but was keen to get involved in 'group performances'. Main describes how Foulkes, already engaged in very demanding clinical work with soldiers in the hospital, and having trained other staff in group psychotherapy, became less interested himself in 'the therapy of static groups' and more interested in so-called 'group performances'. These included the groups instigated by the resident 'social therapist', groups which reflected the busy cultural life of the hospital, such as the 'stage group' in which there were constant tasks to be performed, including stage and furniture construction, and which created tensions about collaboration and competition. Foulkes is described as an 'action therapist', going into groups at points of trouble and involving the whole group in understanding and dealing with the problem. Main also describes him as an 'opportunist group therapist' on call as a sort of group consultant at times of crisis. This description usefully conveys the origins of crisis intervention and group consultancy in this highly creative time in the history of group and therapeutic communities. It also reveals some early notions of performance as linked to group process, as well as interventions that were spontaneous and short-lived rather than systematized and extended, as is more typical of group analytic interventions.

The idea of psychotherapy as an art has existed for some time. There is also a familiar debate about whether psychotherapy is an art or a science, with proponents on both sides: a highly relevant debate at a time when ambitious research programmes dominate the psychotherapeutic field with their emphasis on evidence-based practice and manualized techniques. There is undoubtedly, in my view, a place for the scientific approach to psychotherapy and a more rigorous evaluation of clinical outcomes, in part to satisfy the criteria of funding that have become more stringent in recent years. But this does not rule out considerations about the aesthetics and meaning of psychotherapy, in settings where the same service pressures might not apply, for the many people who seek psychotherapy as a way of making sense of complex lives, or as a cultural form that occupies an important place in the humanities at a time of escalating change and uncertainty. Psychotherapy, seen this way, is not just a clinical method that provides symptomatic relief and support but a mirror of society as it struggles to cohere in a fragmenting and alienating world, with significant challenges to individuals' identity and ontological security. The 'art' of psychotherapy is consistent with an exploratory, intuitive approach that addresses existential factors in this way. This does not rule out questions of efficacy and effectiveness but recognizes that the psychotherapy of the spirit, the soul, or the psyche in all its complexity, is very different from standardized short-term methods that are offered on a large and growing scale. In any case, the distinction between art and science is by no means a rigid one and in a generative century this may become increasingly blurred.

There is, however, an important distinction to be made between psychotherapy as an *art* and psychotherapy as an *art form*. The former refers largely to the technique of psychotherapy, to the intuitive and imaginative process that underlies the approach, the empathic skills of the therapist and the process of communicating subtleties of meaning, drawn not only from psychotherapeutic theory but from art, literature and philosophy. Although there is some overlap between the two, psychotherapy as an art *form* – a less familiar concept – *concerns the way therapist and patient together create an idiosyncratic cultural process or product* that may be viewed as a subject in itself, to some degree independent of the immediate clinical agenda, even though the 'clinical' in other respects is intrinsic to the meaning of the cultural experience. Where overlap exists between psychotherapy as an art and as an art *form,* it may be in the creation of meaning in the work of the therapy, which in itself can acquire properties of beauty and transcendence, and this may be viewed from an aesthetic or artistic perspective (Bollas 1987; Rance 1992; Nitsun 1996). In line with this perspective, the notion of psychotherapy as an art *form* implies an action or a product that would render psychotherapy, or some aspect of it, identifiable as a *piece of art.* This is where the link with performance art comes in. Psychotherapy can be seen as a performance on the part of both patient and therapist insofar as each plays a role and interacts in both prescribed and spontaneous ways, and it is in the substantiation of this performance, with its intimate textures, social nuances and political sub-texts, that the idea of performance art is relevant.

Group analysis, specifically group analytic psychotherapy, in my view, with its groups of people in interaction, together creating a new, temporary social unit in the cultural field (Jacobson 1989), is especially suited to interpretation as a form of performance art.

Psychotherapy, enactment and performance

The relevance of performance to psychotherapy in general is foregrounded by the growing emphasis on *enactment* as a crucial component of psychotherapeutic process. Whereas enactment was for some time regarded as a problematic aspect of psychotherapy, on a par – and to some degree confused with – acting out, there is an increasing recognition of the inevitability and therapeutic power of enactment in the psychotherapeutic encounter (Steiner 2006; Bohleber *et al.* 2013). More recently, Katz (2014) has built a theoretical framework around this, referring to psychoanalysis as 'the play within a play'. He suggests that in the psychoanalytic process enactment is not just a single overt event but a continually evolving process. Within the 'enacted dimension', concealed or dissociated aspects of the patient's past are not just remembered but relived, creating new versions of existing and past problems and generating the experiential insight that is key to development.

Katz's observations emerge from dyadic psychoanalysis but the argument is very relevant to group analytic psychotherapy. With so many more players in a group, the potential for interpersonal enactments increases exponentially. Given also the more spontaneous process of the group, lacking the constraints of the dyadic frame, there are many opportunities for the re-enactment of past or repressed relationships, as well as the experimentation with new forms of relationships in the here-and-now of the group, which is one of the particular strengths of the group approach. The question is: how comparable is this to performance art?

What is performance art?

Performance art describes a worldwide movement that started roughly in the 1970s but had its beginnings earlier with the Dada and Surrealist movements of the early twentieth century. This new movement sought to break with the established traditions of art, particularly mainstream painting and sculpture, by creating live forms of art that attracted an audience and sometimes encouraged participation between performers and spectators. Performance art from early on adopted an anti-establishment position, challenging a wide range of institutional conventions based on the constraints of the museum and gallery systems. So, assumptions about gender and identity were opened up to investigation: the denial and concealment of the body yielded to the revelation and exploration of the body; and the limits of time, space and materials in art morphed into the investigation of timeless and cosmic phenomena. These are just a few contrasting examples. The form of performance itself is highly varied. It might be a series of intimate gestures or a large-scale semi-theatrical event, a solo performance or a large group of interacting people. It might be fleeting, lasting just a few minutes, to stretching to many hours, days, weeks and even months. It might be performed only once or repeated many times. It may be scripted or unscripted, rehearsed or improvised. It is free-spirited and often anarchic, generally defying categorization and understanding in conventional artistic terms. It frequently embraces and exhibits the body, whether still, in movement, contorted, clothed or naked, but always the site of some social inscription, taboo or expectation. Aiming both to celebrate and confront the human, it from the beginning drew on technology, film and photography, sometimes juxtaposing the human with the mechanical or non-human.

As Goldberg notes (2011), performance art became more and more prominent in the late twentieth century, increasing dramatically as the twenty-first century dawned. With globalization and the breakdown of national boundaries, a new multiculturalism burgeoned and, with this, questions about culture, history and identity proliferated. Performance was well-suited to the representation of these developments, having a long tradition by now of recognizing and deconstructing difference, and responding with vigour to new opportunities to pursue this thread: 'performance was a vehicle that could carry a complex layering of iconographic information regarding the histories and rituals of different nations' (Goldberg 2011, p. 227). In as much as performance had the tools to interrogate these broader developments, it also sought to explore the intimate: the personal, emotional, conscious and unconscious levels of the person, sometimes in the context of the social and the collective. In both respects, the intimate/individual and the social/ collective, it enters similar terrain to group psychotherapy, but generally looking at the field more obliquely, questioningly, sceptically and sometimes satirically. Of relevance also is the exploration in performance art of intense and sometimes extreme states of emotion. Loss and grief are themes that recur in art across the world, the performance providing a medium with which to express, abreact or expiate the emotions.

In many ways, by transcending the barrier between conventional and experimental art, and by subverting the traditional frame of reference, performance art has moved closer to the themes and concerns of psychotherapy: how to live a life, what makes us tick, how we experience our bodies, how we deal with desire, how we relate to each other, how we deal with authority. Beneath the often puzzling and sometimes bizarre presentational forms of the approach, these are the sorts of questions that performance artists are seeking to address. Sometimes, the processes of performance art also are influenced directly by psychotherapy: conversations between people, pseudo- or real therapist–patient dyads, personally revealing group discussions, and so on. In some ways, performance art can be understood not so much within an aesthetic canon, certainly not one that celebrates beauty and harmony in their traditional forms, but within frameworks of philosophy, politics and psychotherapy. It offers strikingly different ways of asking the same questions.

Examples of performance art

With the proliferation of performance art on a global level, there are now so many different forms that it is difficult to choose illustrations. In order to simplify the process, I give examples that to some degree mirror the different contexts of psychotherapy: individuals, dyads, small groups and large groups. At the end of this section there is even an installation that mimics a psychotherapy clinic!

'House with an Ocean View'

Marina Abramovic is one of the most well-known and celebrated living performance artists, often working on her own but inviting participation from the audience. The above cryptically named work was a presentation in the wake of 9/11 in which she sought to embody New York as a city of mourning and repair. For twelve days, Abramovic lived on a remote platform in an art gallery, subsisting only on water, but sharing the space with viewers who came to sit with her, often for protracted periods of time. Although the conditions reflected a sense of despair and desolation, the emotional impact of viewers sitting in silence with her in the aftermath of the tragedy, was, according to many reports, profoundly moving. Here, the performance has elements of the individual (Abramovic on her own), the dyad (viewers sitting with her one by one), the social (the wider audience watching and responding) and the political (9/11 as a symbol of political violence).

'Bus riders'; 'Centrefolds'; 'Complete Untitled Film Stills'

These are the titles of just some of the many collections made by Cindy Sherman, a renowned artist who concentrates on multiple, diverse images of herself in startlingly different guises. Her work spans the last decades of the twentieth century and the first decade of the twenty-first century. Her focus is on the construction of contemporary identity and the nature of self-presentation. Using herself entirely as model and producer, incorporating images from many sources and involving myriad props, costumes and wardrobes, she transforms herself from screen goddess to forlorn socialite to suspected victim of rape to bus ticket collector, to name just a few of the parade of images and characters that inhabit her work. There are also frequent plays on gender, illuminating and challenging the male–female divide. There is a constant play on the fluidity of identity against the stereotypy of identity, mirroring the contemporary struggle to locate oneself – or selves – in society.

'Silver Action'

This is a large-scale presentation by Suzanne Lacy that took place at the Tate Modern Gallery (the Tanks) in London in 2013. Hundreds of women age 65 and over from different social strata across the UK were invited to participate in a live and unscripted performance of staged conversations on the theme of women's political role and the impact of ageing on women's place in society. These were women who had participated in activist movements in the UK during the 1950s to the 1960s and their narratives concerned themes of social and political transformation, the role of personal commitment to these movements and an evaluation of the ensuing changes from an older-age perspective. The performance was based on discussions in groups of four sitting at tables and communicated simultaneously to viewers via photographs, film and sound.

From the examples on page 186, it can be seen that performance art is dealing with issues that are very much the terrain of psychotherapy: identity, gender, loss, mourning, repair, social engagement and ageing. It is also utilizing methods that are akin to psychotherapy: individual self-examination, pair work, and small and large group interaction. It is evident too that it is highly contextual in its design and purpose. Even where individual performance is concerned, this is within a social or cultural context, with political processes seldom far from the picture. Almost always, there is a social critique: the performance is intended to expose, challenge or subvert conventional assumptions and practices. The emphasis on context gives it an affinity with group analysis, which, within the psychological therapies, is one of the more contextually sensitive approaches, dealing with personal issues in the setting of the group and the wider social realm.

It can also be seen that performance art is not meant particularly to please, delight, entertain or soothe the viewer. It has left behind conventional notions of beauty and harmony. Rather it aims to stimulate and provoke thought and this might mean that it is confusing, ambiguous and disturbing. It can of course be moving and enriching but this is usually not without some discomfort. Again, this is not incompatible with the aims and values of psychotherapy.

'Auto-destructive art'

Founded in the 1950s by Gustav Metzger, a Holocaust survivor, auto-destructive art describes a radical movement that focuses on the deliberate destruction of objects (Pollack 2012). In existence for more than half a century, the movement had a renewed spurt following 9/11 and the desire some artists felt to reflect the destructive aspect of both western capitalism and the attacks on western culture. Metzger (in Pollack 2012) described the movement he founded as a challenge to capitalist values and the drive to annihilation. He also described it as reflecting 'the existence of surplus and starvation', a contradictory symbol of capitalist society. Paradoxically, the late composer Stockhausen declared that the attack on the World Trade Centre was the 'greatest work of art' (in Pollack 2012). While referred to as auto-destructive, the process of obliteration can take place in very different ways, large and small, commonplace and extraordinary, and spectators may or may not have a direct bearing on the actions of these works. An example is the performance of South African artist Kendell Geer in which he blew up the wall of a gallery in Antwerp with explosives. The work was purportedly a statement about the violence of his homeland in the post-apartheid era.

This highly radical form of art stands in contrast to those performances that aim at some form of reconciliation and repair. It touches on the psychoanalytic notion of the death instinct and psychotherapeutic approaches that emphasize the recognition of destructive and self-destructive impulses, including notions of the anti-group.

'Sanatorium'

A recent example demonstrates how contemporary art now not only incorporates ideas from psychotherapy, or touches obliquely on psychotherapeutic practice, but actually creates a simulated psychotherapeutic setting, attempting to give it new cultural and social meaning.

An exhibition that took place at the Whitechapel Gallery in London in the summer of 2013, 'Sanatorium' was described as a temporary clinic that provided short, unexpected therapies. Devised by the Mexican artist Pedro Reyes, it was offered as a 'utopian clinic of topical treatments' for inner-city problems such as stress, loneliness and 'hyper-stimulation'. Sanatorium visitors could participate in up to sixteen varieties of therapy drawing on approaches such as gestalt psychology, conflict resolution techniques, psychodrama and hypnosis. Described as 'a secular space for psychological processes', the visitor was required to sign up to sessions and accept the condition that this was not 'real therapy' with a 'real therapist' (the therapists were volunteers who were specifically trained for the event). Each therapy had a performative aspect: there was an introduction, development and closure. A major influence on the exhibition was 'Sociatry', a term originally formulated by Jacob Moreno in 1930 to describe the science and art of healing society (Hare and Hare 1996). This term subsequently fell into oblivion but its spirit was revived in this exhibition, encouraging the spread of brief therapies that address the mounting problems of urban populations.

'Sanatorium' was one of several performances and installations on the London art scene in the years 2012–13 which directly represented or replicated aspects of psychotherapy. Another was Tino Sehgal's large-scale 'happening' in the Tate Turbine Hall in 2012, in which crowds of people came together, in shifting configurations, with those with whom they shared life narratives, the stories spreading haphazardly across the gathering. Contextualized in galleries rather than consulting rooms, these events reflected the absorption of psychotherapy into the wider culture (like 'Sanotorium', above) in a way that might have implications for the practice of psychotherapy in more standard settings. Certainly there was a message to be heeded: psychotherapy is no longer the sole possession of 'the professionals' secreted in their consulting rooms. Access to the therapies, albeit in symbolic or constructed forms, is now possible in the new communities of performance art.

Psychoanalytic perspectives on art

Leaving aside the world of performance art for the moment, I move onto an exploration of psychoanalytic theories of art: what has been said about art 'as we know it' and what implications there are for connecting with more radical contemporary art forms.

Psychoanalysts since Freud onwards have been interested in art, mainly in the dynamics of creativity and artistic expression, but also in the psychohistory of artists and the criteria of 'good' art and 'bad' art. This has been very largely focused on art 'as we know it' or 'have known it', art that satisfies traditional criteria of aesthetic achievement. There is a considerable body of writing on these themes but, for the sake of brevity, I will focus on the contributions of Freud and Hanna Segal, both responding within the 'classical' frame of art, and contrast this with the recent challenge by Adela Abella (2010) addressing the demands of contemporary art and whether/how they can be perceived and understood psychoanalytically.

Throughout his writing, Freud (1905, 1910) understood artistic activity as a sublimation of sexual desires. In 1912, according to Abella, he added narcissistic omnipotence to the configuration, recognizing the element of magic and illusion in art as reflecting a position mid-way between the reality principle and the pleasure principle. Later, Freud included aggression in the unconscious motivational path of the artist but mainly emphasized the sublimation of sexuality as the prime motivational force. However, he also began to question whether the sublimation underlying artistic expression actually succeeded since art increasingly reflected violent and sexual wishes in seemingly unprocessed forms.

Hanna Segal, closely following Melanie Klein, brought aggression more fully into the picture as a force underlying the creative act. Artistic activity, in her view, serves to counter aggression and, more so, to repair and recreate the damaged object. It thus occurs on the axis of the depressive position and is intimately associated with loss and mourning: 'All creation is really a re-creation of a once loved and once whole, but now lost and ruined object, a ruined internal world and self' (Segal 1952, p. 197). The work of art suggests that a process of mourning has taken place and is expressed in symbol formation. Hence, Segal departs from Freud's notion of sexual sublimation as the mainspring of creativity and focuses instead on the confrontation with death in the fantasy of damaging and destroying the loved object. Further, the work of art is seen as a creative achievement in which the ego is enriched and enlivened, restoring the sense of wholeness and integration in the artist.

Segal was very taken with the formal properties of art and emphasized the importance of formal wholeness and harmony, bearing in mind that the source of the artwork might be painful and disruptive, given its unconscious basis in aggression. For Segal, the achievement of order out of chaos was essential in art, a way of repairing and re-integrating the depressive shards of guilt and loss. This was crucial not just for the artist but for the audience, since they would experience the art work through identification with the artist's intentions and should not be left with the lingering shadow of damage or depression.

Segal also expressed strong views on the interplay of the beautiful and the ugly in art. While stressing the desirability of beauty, she argued that the ugly had a very important place. Ugliness, in her argument, represented the damaged and destroyed object in the depressive position that paradoxically has to be part of the art object. Both were essential: 'both beauty … and ugliness must be present for a full aesthetic experience' (Segal 1952, p. 205). In Kleinian terms, beauty represented the life instinct, ugliness the death instinct, and it was in their coming together that art could be born. But it was the transformation of ugliness that was intrinsic to the process.

While Segal's contribution to the appreciation and understanding of art is widely recognized, Abella (2010) challenges its relevance to contemporary art. Departing radically from the criteria of 'art as we know it', with its ideals of beauty and harmony, contemporary art, including performance art, requires a different interpretive framework. Rather than pursuing the canons of classical art, it tends to express the discordant, the difficult and the disordered and this may include unprocessed rawness and ugliness. Both the content and the form of contemporary art may reveal rather than conceal damage. Human vulnerability is almost always writ large but usually without the sublimation and soothing of conventional art. Performance art is also distinguished by its eclecticism and plurality, defying easy categorization, so that achieving a cohesive discourse about it is much more difficult than with familiar 'art as we know it'. Even where it portrays human communication in a sympathetic, collaborative light, such as in 'Silver Action', the project about women and politics described above, it rests heavily on an exposure and critique of social convention.

Abella (2010) draws on the arguments of well-known deconstructionist artists, such as Marcel Duchamp, John Cage and Christian Boltansky, to develop her stance on contemporary art. These figures share a common disdain for the canons of traditional art, maintaining anti-aesthetic positions that vitiate the cultural dominance of 'good taste' and the way, in their view, this has compromised and hidden the more painful truths of existence. Additionally, they question the conventional assumptions about audience participation. Whereas in Segal's view, and that of many other writers, the public is identified with the artist's intentions, passively receiving the aesthetic experience through the hands of the artist creator, in their, more critical view, the public is in danger of being duped, lulled into admiration and complacency. Instead, they believe, audience members should be free to participate themselves, to perceive reality in new ways, to reach meanings which are personal to them and to be stimulated to think and understand in surprising, destabilizing ways.

These alternative views challenge psychoanalytic assumptions about sublimation in art. Both Freud and Segal in their different ways refer to the containment and transformation of primitive sexual and destructive fantasies as a goal of successful art. Integration, harmony and beauty are the ideal achievements. Even though Segal argues that the ugly has a place in art, she sees this as of necessity transformed. But Abella questions this as a valid perspective of contemporary art, suggesting that the raw materials of new art are the situations and fantasies that haunt the human psyche, fantasies of violence and damage, and that this is a necessary confrontation with the 'real'. She argues for the validity of this freer expressiveness:

In a world shaken by barbaric violence and renewed unimaginable destruction, the possibility of a culturally controlled expression of destructiveness is not without value. In this way, contemporary art could be used as a container for primitive and destructive fantasies which rarely find an outlet in everyday life.

(Abella 2010, p. 177)

Performance art has shifted the framework of art from sublimation and reparation to exposure and confrontation. It presents a major challenge not only to art in its traditional sense, and to familiar psychoanalytic critiques of art, but also potentially forges new and different links with psychotherapy. In some respects it gets much closer to the psychotherapeutic process in its determination not to compromise with the defensive aspects of psychological development and instead to lay bare the primitive affects and fantasies, as well as a wide range of human dilemmas of existential and social significance. Art in its new forms no longer seeks to create the pleasing and palliative qualities that made it so acceptable to the public. Whether the public in general – as opposed to a more informed avant-garde – can receive this message is debatable but contemporary art, like it or not, appears to be an inescapable and compelling part of cultural evolution in the twenty-first century.

Group analysis and group psychotherapy

In my view, performance art suggests far greater parallels with group psychotherapy than any other form of therapy. In its frequent use of more than one character as protagonist, and its use of audience participation, performance art invites people to engage directly in collaborative and experimental group processes, encouraging direct communication and interaction in ways that are similar to group psychotherapy. The focus on context, on the individual in a larger social and political landscape, is also congruent with group therapy with its emphasis on the wider configuration of individual–group–society relations. However, group analysis (and group psychotherapy more generally) has so far shown relatively little direct interest in art. This is possibly because it is a newer field than psychoanalysis, struggling to establish a more confident clinical and organizational base before spreading its wings. Also, its applications beyond the consulting room so far tend towards the organizational, social and political rather than towards the arts.

However, there is a sprinkling of publications on the subject, including my own publication 'Artist and facilitator' (Nitsun 1995), which was a response to a paper by Gillian Recordon (1994) linking and comparing the functions and processes of group analytic psychotherapy and art in terms of the creative and integrative intentions of both. Additionally, there has been an attempt to evolve an aesthetic perspective of group analysis. Several writers (e.g. Cortesao 1991; Rance 1992) have described group progress as a movement towards integration, balance and harmony in a way that evokes its own aesthetics of clarity, order and beauty. The idea of transformation is germane to these papers: the transformation of the individual and the group in a mutual movement towards truth and change. However, there is a tendency in these papers towards idealization: towards an idealized conception of the whole, including idealization of both the group process and the aesthetic perspective. I argue that insufficient attention is paid to disruptive factors in the group and that the path to change and transformation necessitates an encounter with the destructive in both the individual and the group. To quote from my paper on art and group analysis (also quoted in my 1996 book), I made the following observations:

> I believe that art is meaningless without some confrontation with the dark side: similarly, that the group experience is incomplete and likely to be superficial without such recognition. Holding together the constructive and the destructive potential is a major requirement of the group therapist, as I believe it is in the artistic process. Sometimes the tension between the two is very great, even unbearable, but usually there comes a point of reconciliation, of synthesis, and a new form emerges. I believe this is also what happens in the group. At every moment the dialogue forms and reforms itself and within this, creative and destructive forms emerge side by side. Eventually, an understanding, an insight, a change, is achieved. Openness to this process is the creative gift of the group analyst to the group – and the gift of the group to the analyst.
>
> (Nitsun 1995, p. 99)

In my presentation of the anti-group, I have frequently referred to the positive value of recognizing and addressing the darker, more hidden, more disruptive aspects of the group: without this, the group might not reach its full potential. In this sense, some of the lessons of contemporary performance art are not far removed. As noted above, however shocking or bewildering the performances may be, they are, through group-related media in a public context, attempting to present the aspects of life, self, other and society that are frequently dissociated or denied in the quest for order and balance – for 'the civilized'. At another level, they frequently appeal to the collaborative strengths of people in groups, as in the 'Silver Action' project, and so, as an art medium, contemporary performance walks a tightrope between the collaborative and the oppositional, struggling with the same dialectic of the creative and destructive that I attempt to incorporate in the concept of the anti-group and that I believe is germane to the development of groups. To what extent performance art might influence group analysis in the future, and to what extent this is desirable, are questions that I consider later in this chapter.

The arts psychotherapies

There are group-based *art therapeutic* approaches that come even closer to performance art than the mainstream group approaches, analytic and otherwise. These approaches emphasize the direct participation of the individual or group in a creative act. In *art psychotherapy* (Wadeson 2010), the emphasis is on visual art, individuals drawing and painting together in the presence of a therapist or therapists. Spontaneous expression of feelings, fears and fantasies, in relation to the art produced, is encouraged. This is usually followed by group feedback and free association, so that the emerging themes are amplified and an atmosphere of resonance and identification is cultivated. *Drama therapy* (Jennings 1997) usually proceeds as a scripted performance almost always practised in a group, with a cast of characters playing out a drama either on their own or with an audience. While the opportunity for free expression is limited by the scripted format, the group often gets in touch with strong emotion and the performance is usually cathartic and therapeutic. *Movement and dance therapy* (Pearson 1996) is usually also conducted in a group, with varying degrees of structure, sometimes closely directed by the therapist, at other times encouraging participants to let go in highly expressive forms that can bring the group alive in intense and energetic ways.

The arts therapies are much closer in spirit and form to performance art than the traditional group therapies. They encourage more bodily involvement and expression, relying less on verbal communication and giving freer rein to imagination and fantasy. They tend to get closer to the free-form emphasis of performance art. In fact, performance art often employs techniques associated with the arts therapies such as dance, art production, dramatic readings and improvised performances, creating a distinct overlap between these domains. One important difference, however, is in the more radical agenda of performance art. Art psychotherapy is usually practised in mental health treatment settings or private practice. While the emphasis is on the expression and understanding of powerful affects and bodily impulses, this is with containment and adjustment in mind rather than a leap into the unknown or the subversion of conventional values, which is more typical of contemporary performance art.

Psychodrama

Even closer to performance art is *psychodrama*. A synthesis of theatre and psychotherapy, psychodrama is a highly participative method in which members use structured dramatization to explore, understand and work though challenging aspects of their lives. Originated by Jacob L. Moreno, psychodrama incorporates theatrical techniques often conducted on a stage, sometimes with the addition of props and lighting, although it can also be practised in freer, less formal settings. Participants are invited to enact real-life situations or inner emotional conflicts, as well as rehearsing for difficult, anxiety-provoking or risky situations in their 'outside' lives. The process usually involves the setting up of a scene incorporating a number of assigned players, such as the protagonist, auxiliary ego and double, each enacting an aspect of the conflict situation. Methods such as soliloquy, mirroring, doubling and role reversal are commonly employed under the guidance of a director. Although much of the approach is structured, the aim is spontaneity and improvisation, valuing surprise as part of the exposition of the problem. Psychodrama is mainly conducted in a group but differs from group therapy insofar as the process tends to focus on one individual, with others in a supportive or mirroring capacity, rather than a group *qua* group where the overall group process is emphasized.

This brief summary indicates that a number of different arts-orientated therapies are inherently performance-based, employing structured situations yet with a premium placed on spontaneity and self-expression. These further confirm the overlap between existing psychotherapeutic methods and the more revolutionary thrust of contemporary performance art.

Play

Another dimension that links the performance arts and psychotherapy is play. Many instances of performance art are playful in intent and form. Cindy Sherman's creation of multiple images of herself, previously described, has a distinctly playful aspect as she sets about reworking her identity in diverse forms, using costumes, make-up and lights. But this is serious art: Sherman is mirroring not only the potential in herself for fluctuating identities but the social construction of identity and the individual sense of self as a creation of class and gender. At the same time, her artistic process is playful, reminiscent perhaps of a girl sitting in front of a mirror trying on her mother's make-up and experimenting with her appearance and identity. One of the main differences between 'art as we know it' and the 'new art', it could be argued, is the element of play. Although the creative process in traditional painting and sculpture can of course be regarded as playful (Nitsun 1995), the play emerging in performance art is bolder, more active, more bodily, more frequently engaging presenter/s and audience in collaborative tasks.

Play as a component of psychotherapy is well-recognized but I draw particularly on the work of Winnicott in order to elaborate this dimension. The relevance of play to psychotherapy in general and group psychotherapy in particular is highlighted in Winnicott's comprehensive statement, 'it is play that is the universal, and that belongs to health; playing facilitates growth and therefore health; *playing leads into group relationships*; playing can be a form of communication in psychotherapy' (1971, p. 48, italics added).

Winnicott (1960), true to his own edict, is famous for the playful technique he devised, 'the Sguiggle'. Here, engaging a child in a cojoint drawing with himself, he produces something similar to Paul Klee's notion of 'taking a line for a walk', in the process establishing a link with the child and learning something about his problems – and himself in relation to the child. This illustrates Winnicott's well-known statement:

[P]sychotherapy takes place in the overlap of two areas of playing, that of the patient and that of the therapist ... The corollary is that where playing is not possible then the work of the therapist is directed towards bringing the patient from a state of not being able to play into a state of being able to play.

(Winnicott 1971, p. 46)

In group therapy, there are of course up to eight or so patients, so that the 'two areas of playing' are multiplied several times over, providing a particularly powerful frame for the emergence of play – especially important where, as Winnicott highlights, there was a prior absence of play or inability to play. In a detailed published analysis of the therapeutic development of a group of adults with serious mental health problems, I noted that play was the crucial marker of progress in the group (Nitsun 1996, chapter 10). I argued there, as here, that this is a particularly important perspective of group therapy: the progress we seek is not simply in verbal communication or rational analysis but in the sphere of play with its more spontaneous and often non-rational quality.

Later writers such as Trevarthen and Daniel Stern have made valuable contributions to the understanding of play in early child development. In Trevarthen's (1998) detailed observations of mother–infant interaction, including the early genesis of the 'protoconversation', play assumes major significance, with imitation, humour and teasing all contributing to the child's development. But the play is not just a solipsistic exercise, as other family members, father and siblings, as well as friends, are drawn into the games and rituals of play. The 'dance of conversation' then becomes a group effort, so reminiscent of what happens in psychotherapy groups when they can come out of the linearity of most verbal communication into the liveliness of play. Stern (2010) refers to the 'proto narrative envelopes' generated by the sharing of parents and children in moments of attunement and lively interchange, so true again of the therapy group at its best. It is for this reason that the anthropologist Victor Turner (1982) emphasizes 'the human seriousness of play'. Play is not trivial: it is intrinsic to communicating beings. This applies at all levels of development, from infancy to old age, and is a greatly facilitating factor in psychotherapy.

But there are also risks in play. Winnicott notes that, for all its positive value, play can engender anxiety, through the excitement that is generated by play and the fear that this might get out of control, as well as through the precarious balance between fantasy and reality that is present in play. Winnicott describes play as 'inherently exciting and precarious' (1971, p. 61). Play often teeters on the edge of violence and can quickly turn into aggression – witness two children playing happily together one moment who the next moment are at each other's throats. These comments are relevant to performance art, which also treads a fine line between play and destruction, sometimes deliberately, as in the philosophy of the auto-destructive artists who set out to destroy all their productions. 'Destructive play', as we may call it, for all its more baffling and disturbing aspects, is an important commentary on the destructive aspect of an instrumental culture that renders objects and people redundant beyond a certain level of use. This includes the art world itself, which is so subject to fashion and fad. At the same time, it reflects the painful reality of the insubstantiality and impermanence of life.

A further aspect of play that merits attention concerns play as preparation or rehearsal. Jacobson (1989) notes that in group therapy, play can serve the function of enabling members to experiment with problems and solutions in advance of their engaging with the problem outside the group. Yalom and Leszcz (2005) and Garland (1982) make similar points about the value of simulation and informal practice in the group. Performance art, through presenting diverse scenarios reflecting real-life dilemmas, similarly offers opportunities for practice, rehearsal and identification. In some respects, much of art, especially theatre and literature, has this function – it is a well-known aspect of classical Greek tragedy – but performance art, through its more direct and visceral style of presentation, often provides a stage for real-life rehearsal.

Performativity

Before returning more fully to group therapy, it is necessary to introduce the concept of 'performativity'. Most strongly associated with the work of Judith Butler (1997), the concept has become an interdisciplinary term to describe the way in which social identity is mediated through action, particularly speech, in the presentation of self. The performative act, however, is not the product of an individual in isolation but an expression of interaction with a larger group. The 'audience' does not simply receive or ratify the individual's performance: it shapes and conditions the performance so as to give it substance and meaning. Butler focused particularly on gender and sexuality as mediated through performativity. Rather than regarding maleness and femaleness, heterosexuality and homosexuality, as intrinsic attributes of people, they are seen as performative acts that have been rehearsed repeatedly in relationship to a society that shapes and mirrors that construction of identity. It is as if the individual has a social script that is enacted over and over again in the consolidation of his/her identity. Although an individual performs the act, the identity belongs to a much larger group (such as 'straights' and 'gays') and depends on even larger groups to reinforce and re-evoke the consensual script. While this may be part of 'natural' social discourse, in which all people are represented through their performativity in one way or another, deriving their identities in interaction with a community, it highlights the power of social groups to constrain – and sustain – identity through hegemonic social conventions and ideologies.

Performance art, not surprisingly, often challenges the process of performativity, highlighting its operation in both subtle and profound ways. There are many possible examples. Cindy Sherman's aforementioned experiments with identity are a form of performativity in which she reveals the power of social categorization and stereotyping. In this case, it is not her voice, the verbal performance, that is uppermost but her constantly reconfiguring facial images – 'the speaking body' (Felman 2003). The many photographic reproductions of her images mirror the ubiquity and range of performative possibilities. As a viewer of her work we join in the public spectacle of witnessing her identity shifts, as if we are the social group that mirrors her efforts, but with the insinuation that we, the audience, are involved in Sherman's programme of exposing the social mechanisms of identity formation. 'Silver Action', a more active type of performance art described above, is also a treatise on the performativity of women whose identities have been reciprocally influenced by the stands they took on political issues in earlier decades. In the current performance in which they participate, they group together in staged discussions that are transmitted via different media to a changing audience. Their earlier actions are thus repeated in new cultural forms that add depth to past experiences, while the performance keeps alive their contributions and the historical context in which these occurred.

Performativity and play overlap in various respects. The performative act of sharing or asserting an identity involves a measure of play, of trying *on* or trying *out* a notion of self in a social context. Both play and performativity relate to what Ryan (1974, quoted in Trevarthen 1998) refers to as 'the pragmatic social context': a social context that to varying degrees both facilitates and constrains the expression of self. In various ways, group psychotherapy can be seen as a pragmatic social context, implicitly constructed to enable the expression of play and performativity in the evolution of the group.

Tying the threads together: the psychotherapy group

Having hinted so far at parallels and links between aspects of contemporary performance art and group psychotherapy, it remains to explore these links in greater detail.

As suggested previously, there is at the outset greater convergence between performance art and group psychotherapy, if only because of the sheer number of people in the group and the strong interactional thrust of the group. Roles and relationships in individual therapy are largely constrained by the hierarchical structure of therapist and patient. In the group, there is greater flexibility. Most contemporary group therapy encourages interaction between members as a key, if not the key, component of the therapy. Not only does this facilitate a more actively interpersonal field, but it allows for the dialectical interchange of roles, in which a member can be both patient and therapist, expressing in varying ways the more hidden and contradictory parts of themselves. They may express their own vulnerability and anxiety but also feel empowered when supporting and helping another patient. This lends itself to a more dramatic field in which there are shifts of role and the unexpected and unpredictable plays an important part, with ongoing elements of surprise, confrontation, conflict and reconciliation. Since the themes that enter the group cover the full gamut of the human predicament, from birth to death and everything in between, this lends itself to a very wide range of conversations and enactments.

The experiential framework of the group could be regarded as a 'theatre of performance'. This would not detract from the real and authentic aspect of group relationships but would add a performance focus, emphasizing the interaction of self and other as active, embodied relationships in a 'pragmatic social context'.

Illustration I

Charmaine was a 31-year-old estate agent in a weekly psychotherapy group. Although most of the other group members were British, she stood out as the 'posh one'. From an upper-middle-class family with parents who were diplomats, she had lived in different countries in her childhood but maintained a fierce Britishness, with all the airs and graces of public schooling and a colonial past. She was very proper in her manner, required exact translations of any reflection or interpretation in the group, and tried to pin members down to precise meanings. She had difficulties in day-to day relationships as well as emotional/sexual liaisons with men and this related partly to her social manner. In the office at work, she felt both superior to her colleagues and painfully excluded by them. She was also prone to exacerbated bodily symptoms of pain and discomfort, for which there was no apparent physical basis. She became angry at suggestions that these might be psychosomatic and said the worst thing anyone could say to her was that she was a hypochondriac.

Although she was a well-liked participant in some ways, group members quickly became frustrated by her intolerance of reflective discussion and her need for exact meanings. She also conflicted with a member who challenged her about her aches and pains and commented that her feared view of herself as a hypochondriac was entirely accurate. Her relationship with the group remained stuck for some time until one of the male members, Tim, started addressing her in a teasing, jocular fashion, imitating her upper-class accent and her insistence on precise meanings. He would address the group in a hoity-toity manner, impersonating her voice, 'Now, that really is not good enough, my dears. We must all strive for clarity and perfection. Where would we all be if we spoke in a muddle and didn't make ourselves clear?' He would sometimes add imagined references to her family or teachers: 'Mummy said the most important thing in life is to speak well, to be very clear.' The group responded gleefully to this mimicry. Charmaine was at first taken by surprise, discomfited, bristling at Tim's effrontery and the group's laughter. But rather than this being cruelly mocking, there was a touch of affection in both Tim's imitations and the group's response and Charmaine began rather nervously to join in with the group's amusement at Tim's parodic play. When she resisted ambiguous or reflective statements in the group, showing her usual inclination to stop the discussion to ask for clarity, group members might intercede, half imitating her manner and turning the frustrating communication into something playful and amusing. The group's interventions teetered between playful teasing and something more aggressive and biting, highlighting Winnicott's notion of the 'inherently precarious' nature of play. Yet, it seemed that it was the 'bite' that really got through to Charmaine.

She became more open in the group. She was able to talk about how strictly she had been brought up as a child, how often she was told that 'children should be seen and not heard' and how difficult she found it to deal with the painful periods of separation from her parents – the loneliness of a diplomat's daughter, travelling from country to country. The group's compassion for her grew and members related more warmly to her. She became more tolerant of ambiguity in discussions, not having to pinpoint every meaning, and she showed an increasing interest in the reflective process. At a later point, when she spoke about how the group had helped her, members commented on how much she had changed. They highlighted her developing openness and how her resistance to psychological thinking had hidden sensitivity and insight.

In this example, Tim's initiating the teasing relationship with Charmaine, in turn adopted by the rest of the group, can be seen as a form of meta-communication. Instead of directly challenging Charmaine's penchant for questioning and undermining the group reflective process – so important to the therapeutic task – they created a comical dialogue in which her habit could be brought into a playful relationship between her and rest of the group. By doing this, they challenged not only her but also the entire cultural edifice from which she emerged, that of British diplomats abroad. In some respects, they were doing this on her behalf as she greatly resented the stuffiness of overseas diplomatic circles and the way they patronized children. Through this venture, she was able to relax to a degree, gradually becoming part of the group and able to use the space more freely and creatively.

Victor Turner (1982), the anthropologist, wrote about the role of ritual and theatre in bringing people together in groups, generating and sustaining what he called 'communitas' as opposed to the sheer physical co-existence of 'societas' (in Trevarthen 1998). In the example of Charmaine, the teasing, humorous and somewhat ritualized challenge to her speech brought her into the sphere of the group, 'one amongst equals'. Possibly for the first time in her life, she felt she belonged and the group itself evolved in this rite of passage.

Illustration 2

This is a weekly group for patients with longstanding emotional difficulties that had a difficult start but is beginning to cohere and become a trusted space. Maureen and Michael have had problems with each other from the beginning of the group. He is prickly and irascible; she is sensitive to slights and any hint of rejection. There are periodic misunderstandings between them. Each feels the other gets the wrong end of the stick. This fuels their mutual irritation and occasionally there are blow-ups. These are usually passed over, leaving a rather uneasy truce. In this session, there is a bigger flare-up than before. Michael has been recalling an episode on holiday with his ex-wife in which the possibility of their having more children came up. Margaret expresses surprise that having children was an issue at a point in their relationship when, according to Michael, they were intending to break up. Michael denies this and gets angry with Margaret.

Michael: What is the matter with you? You always get it wrong! Don't you ever listen?'

Margaret *(furious)*: I did listen and I'm sick and tired of your criticism of me.

Michael: Then why do you keep riling me?

Margaret: I have no intention of riling you and, frankly, there is no point in trying with you anymore. It always leads to this. You keep having a go at me. From now on I'm going to say nothing to you!

Margaret moves angrily in her chair. Tony, another group member, comments that this makes him feel uncomfortable. But Margaret remains angry and questions whether it might be better for her to leave the group altogether. She stays but there is a tense silence in the group, the air bristling with hostility. Geraldine tries to break the ice. She says that she very much likes Margaret's brooch, which is in the shape of a butterfly. Margaret thanks her and they discuss how butterflies are a nice motif in jewellery. 'I love butterfly brooches', says Geraldine. The therapist comments on the evasion: it might be easier to talk about butterflies, he suggests, than talk about the argument that has just taken place between Michael and Margaret, which seems too hot to handle.

Group members then start sharing how they experienced the argument. There is a range of opinions. Some people comment on Michael's very sharp, critical reaction, others on Margaret's over-sensitivity and unwillingness to receive feedback. The hostile atmosphere gives way to a thoughtful discourse as members try to make sense of the conflagration and to express their own views. During this discussion, Michael and Margaret sit back, silently listening to the others, taken with the interest and concern shown by the group. Now Margaret joins the discussion and Michael follows suit.

Margaret: As I've been sitting here, I've realized how much Michael reminds me of my older brother who used to bully me when we were kids. I've never gotten over it – he really had it in for me.

Michael: Come to think of it, Margaret reminds me a lot of my ex-wife Anne. It's not that she looks like her but the kind of argument we had here is exactly what used to happen with Anne and which drove us apart.

The group welcomes these observations and there is a useful discussion about how past relationship difficulties affect present ones. Margaret says that a moment ago she was on the point of leaving the group and never coming back. Members say they are pleased she stayed. Michael agrees and says he can see that he overreacted to her and is sorry. She is more relaxed. The atmosphere in the group lightens and there is a sense of relief and some warmth.

This episode, which had a strong positive effect on the group, can readily be understood in terms of Yalom and Lesczc's (2005) therapeutic factors, 'corrective recapitulation of the primary group' and 'interpersonal learning'. Michael and Margaret's insight into their behaviour and the way this reflected past problematic relationships is the turning point. But it might not have happened without the intervention of the therapist, commenting on the group evasion, and more particularly the group members having a productive conversation about the argument, freeing Michael and Margaret to sit back and think about their own roles in the conflict.

The perspective I want to add concerns the performative aspects of the group. It seems that the strengthening of trust over the previous months in the group enabled Michael and Margaret finally to have an open, productive argument. They are enacting something here of their own past histories with each other and their problematic previous relationships. In order to master the problem they need to perform actions that are different from what they might have previously done in the group. How close this came to being destructive is shown in Margaret's urge to leave – an action that would have symbolized anger and despair rather than reconciliation. But she was able to stay and adopt a different stance. Similarly Michael, rather than escalating the argument and rushing headlong into a divorce, which is what happened with his wife, is able to stop, listen and take a reflective stance. This is in the context of the group performing the function of a reflective chorus. The whole group has taken a therapeutic stance, coming out of their stuck patient roles into that of an engaged group dealing constructively with a moment of interpersonal crisis.

Nothing like this could have happened in individual therapy. The group has a more flexible and richly performative aspect, facilitated by the presence of several people in interacting roles. The psychotherapeutic momentum derives therefore not from the more role-structured process of individual therapy but from the actions of group members emerging in an inter-subjective context, prompting the improvisation of new roles. The group generates an active and productive conversation, thereby allowing the warring couple to come out of their rigid roles into a new way of relating. In some ways, what I am saying is a familiar aspect of group psychotherapy or group analytic process, but I add the notion of performativity as a dimension. This requires a form of negotiation with each other, either explicit or implicit, in the way the rest of the group establishes a thinking space around the conflict, facilitating Margaret and Michael temporarily taking a back seat and witnessing a reflective process through which they come to see themselves more clearly.

The illustration conveys a dramatic episode in the group's life in which there was a creative transformation of relationships in the group as a whole. The group in this episode, as suggested earlier, became a 'theatre of performance'. It approximates Turner's (1980) notion of 'social drama', a social situation which acquires dramatic properties and moves through a process of change. In Turner's theory, the four main components of the social drama are the breach, the crisis, the re-address and the integration. In this example the breach was the tension and lack of empathy between Margaret and Michael, set against the early lack of group cohesion: the crisis was the argument sparked off by the discussion about Michael's marriage and the conflict that ensued; the re-address was the intervention of the therapist followed by the commentary of the 'group as witness'; and the re-integration was the understanding and reconciliation that developed between Margaret and Michael.

It would be possible to understand this group process without drawing on notions of performativity and performance art, but I am trying to look at the material in a way that introduces a performance perspective, wondering whether this is an alternative way of interpreting what happens in therapy groups: a way that brings psychotherapy into the sphere of the arts, with notions of conflict and catharsis as germane to the process.

Illustration 3

Marie is a psychiatric nurse attending a weekly psychotherapy group. She has recently qualified and is finding work as a nurse hardgoing. She feels great demands are made of her and she does not have the energy or inclination to meet them. She also has to suffer less than adequate work conditions: long hours, poor pay, low status and so on. This to a degree parallels her personal life in which she feels unappreciated and unloved.

Members notice how helpful and caring Marie is in the group. She is much more likely to give time to others, to be protective and reassuring, than she is to talk about herself or to ask for help. This confirms a life-long pattern. She was the youngest in her family but the one to whom everyone came with their problems, particularly her depressed father and her chaotic mother. She makes slow progress in the group. Members see her as very stuck in the helper's role, observing her insistence on supporting others and not revealing herself. When one member confronts her impatiently about this, she cries and acknowledges how difficult it is for her. Several members enquire about her anger. Where is it? People have the impression that her helpful behaviour hides considerable anger, even rage. She admits the possibility but goes no further.

In the course of the four years that she spends in the group, Marie's persona as the self-sacrificing nurse is at various times challenged by the other members. They also highlight different sides of her that emerge spontaneously, either in her reports of interactions outside the group or in encounters in the here-and-now of the group. The group is quick to fasten onto these sides, good-humouredly, but somewhat confrontatively, naming these other sides: the 'naughty lady', the 'lazy slut', the 'one who left her parents', the 'angry girlfriend'. This creates verbal referents for Marie's alter-egos and becomes a shorthand for describing Marie's different sides as they manifest in the group. So, at times she can be the naughty lady or the lazy slut and at other times the defiant one who left home. With a provocative male group member who has claimed to fancy her and then symbolically ditches her, she becomes the angry girlfriend. This creates tensions in the group and the male member is aggrieved. But other members feel that this is a breakthrough for Marie as she is able, finally, to express her anger. Through these 'performances', Marie is able increasingly to deconstruct her role as 'the good nurse'.

We see here a possible overlap between the therapy group and the performance art of Cindy Sherman, described earlier. Whereas Sherman embraces diverse identities in her photographs, Marie does something similar, although on a more directly interpersonal level through interactions in the group. It becomes clear that being a nurse, with its associated constraints, is a construct that was created out of necessity in relationship with her family – it was a way of surviving – but that this is open to modification. What happens in the group approximates what Bruner (1996) highlights as human learning through 'anecdotal inter-subjectivity'. Marie's problem is tackled not through the therapist's interpretations or cognitive challenges: it happens through interactive play.

Discussion

Drawing the parallel between performance art and group psychotherapy, it could be argued that group psychotherapy be envisioned as a form of performance art. This might seem tendentious, given that the aim of psychotherapy, on the face of it, is very different from that of art. Psychotherapy, group or otherwise, exists to provide psychological help with emotional problems, to alleviate psychic suffering and to strengthen the functioning of the individual. Art has no curative aim as such. 'Art as we know it', the term I use throughout for conventional art, exists to stimulate, please, entertain, amuse, enlighten, edify, but is not primarily designed as therapy. On the other hand, with the breakdown of familiar boundaries in art and the way in which contemporary art has opened a range of bolder psychological possibilities – and invited us to reconsider our aesthetics – the argument for seeing psychotherapy as a performance art may be relevant. Certainly, group psychotherapy, with its greater interactional and expressive range, comes close to this redefinition.

Pursuing the idea of group psychotherapy as a performance art, and looking at the above examples in their entirety, we can see processes that might satisfy the criteria of either or both conventional theatre and contemporary performance art. From a theatrical point of view, we see the build-up of tension in at least two of the examples, the conflict between two protagonists leading to a dramatic climax that reaches its peak and then dissolves. As mentioned, it satisfies the criteria of Turner's (1980) notion of 'social drama', with its four-stage process of breach, crisis, re-address and re-integration. The group has a crucial function in witnessing the drama and encouraging a constructive outcome, acting as a community in which the protagonists are re-integrated. Were this transposed to a public space, with looser boundaries and more direct audience engagement, we could see it qualifying as a piece of performance art which might be very resonant to viewers and possibly have a therapeutic aspect as well.

The aspect of performativity I introduced into the description of the therapy group has connotations not only of the presentation of self in interaction with others but also of the body and expressive movement. Much of group therapy is theorized and practised in verbal terms and there is relatively little emphasis on the body and physical movement (Nitsun 2006). Yet, in some of these group illustrations, it is clear that communication is expressed dramatically via the body and actions, either in reality or in intention. When Margaret in the second example, for instance, becomes enraged with Michael, she not only says this, but moves angrily in her chair and at least twice threatens to leave the group altogether. When Marie conflicts with a provocative male group member, he gets up and goes. These are relatively common occurrences in therapy groups but point to the importance of bodily movement (or inhibition) as a major expresser of emotion in the group. We know this intuitively, of course, but to what extent can we respond to the challenge of performance art, which often embraces the body in movement, and make this a greater focus in our work – or at least include it more fully in our theorizing?

Pursuing the analogy of art further invites questions about the broader nature of art, discussed earlier in terms of the dimension of the raw and unprocessed versus the processed and the integrated. This antithesis was explored earlier in the chapter in the section on psychoanalytic views about art. I drew the distinction there between classical art, or 'art as we know it', espousing notions of beauty and harmony, and contemporary art or 'new art' as eschewing traditional concepts of beauty in favour of the incidental, accidental, the raw and undisguised. The distinction was also reflected in the contrast between traditional psychoanalytic renderings of art as represented by Freud and Segal on the one side and a contemporary writer Abella on the other. Freud and Segal emphasized art as sublimation or transformation, whereas Abella argued for the ugly, the raw and the unprocessed as true ingredients of art and as embodied particularly in contemporary art forms. This touches on the debate about the value of the inchoate, the unexplained and the not-understood as inevitable components of the therapeutic frame vs the primary need for greater coherence and integration as a requirement of psychotherapeutic progress.

I suggest that the group examples above illustrate the presence of both the raw and the unprocessed *and* the movement towards integration and harmony. Certainly, the second example illustrates this quite vividly: the raw, spontaneous confrontation between Margaret and Michael is tentatively processed by the other members, encouraging further processing by the two protagonists themselves and leading ultimately to a sense of integration and greater harmony – cohesiveness – in the group. But it is touch and go: the outcome could easily have been fragmentation and a derailment of the therapy. As psychotherapists we work towards greater resolution and the 'beauty' this may produce in the sense of understanding and transformation. But this usually requires the exposure of the raw and the unprocessed, the inchoate and the fragmented. This lurking or even surface chaos is so often part of emotional disturbance, particularly where severe. The lessons of contemporary art, therefore, mirror and reinforce the necessity of allowing and encouraging the emergence of the darker and disruptive aspects of self and others, especially in groups where there is a hovering anti-group process which might otherwise pre-empt spontaneous expressions of discord and disorder. How much emphasis we give this in psychotherapy is a matter for debate and personal choice. But this is one reason, I suggest, to pursue the linking of contemporary art and group psychotherapy: to throw a different light on what it is that fuels the therapeutic momentum of the group.

Conclusion

I have drawn a complex tapestry, linking the threads of contemporary and classical art, psychotherapy, the arts psychotherapies, play and performativity, but with an emphasis on the way performance art per se has moved in a direction that overlaps with group psychotherapy. Since psychotherapy appears increasingly to be appropriated as a cultural 'possession', as illustrated particularly in the public installation 'Sanatorium' described earlier, there is a need to examine the areas of convergence that are increasingly apparent. I have speculated on the possibility of re-envisioning group psychotherapy within the sphere of performance art, drawing on various aesthetic traditions and utilizing frameworks such as Turner's 'social drama'. The chapter highlights the active, embodied dimension of psychotherapy, especially group therapy, which contrasts with the largely verbal approach of most therapies, and invites a greater emphasis on the presentational and performance aspects of our individual and social selves.

It is tempting to try to forge an integrative model in which the different strands unite but in this chapter I have mainly laid out the broad pattern of the two main approaches, group psychotherapy and performance art, and their possible areas of convergence. In any case, neither art nor psychotherapy is a static form that lends itself to easy categorization. Both are likely to transform in the coming decades, in the ever-changing cultural context in which we live. I suggest that keeping an eye on both, and their areas of overlap, is a promising direction for the future.

References

Abella, A. (2010) Contemporary art and Hanna Segal's thinking on aesthetics, *International Journal of Psychoanalysis*, 91, 163–81.

Bohleber, W., Fonagy, P., Jimenez, J. P., Scarfone, D., Varvin, S. and Zysman, S. (2013) Towards a better use of psychoanalytic concepts: a model illustrated using the concept of enactment, *International Journal of Psychoanalysis*, 4, 501–30.

Bollas, C. (1987) The transformational object, in *The Shadow of the Object: Psychoanalysis of the Unthought Known*. London: Free Association Books.

Bruner, J. (1996) *The Culture of Education.* Cambridge, MA: Harvard University Press.

Butler, J. (1997) *Excitable Speech: A Politics of the Performative.* New York: Routledge.

Cortesao, E. L. (1991) Group analysis and aesthetic equilibrium, *Group Analysis*, 24, 271–7.

Felman, S. (2003) *The Scandal of the Speaking Body.* Stanford, CA: Stanford University Press.

Freud, S. (1905) *Three Essays on the Theory of Sexuality*, SE 7, 130–243. London: Hogarth Press, 1953–74.

Freud, S. (1910) *Leonardo da Vinci and a Memory of his Childhood*, SE 11, 63–137, London: Hogarth Press, 1953–74.

Garland, C. (1982) Taking the non-problem seriously, *Group Analysis*, 15, 4–14.

Goldberg, R. (2011) *Performance Art: From Futurism to the Present.* London: Thames and Hudson.

Hare, A. P. and Hare, J. R. (1996) *J L Moreno. Key Figures in Counseling and Psychotherapy.* London: Sage.

Jacobson, L. (1989) The group as an object in the cultural field, *International Journal of Group Psychotherapy*, 39, 475–98.

Jennings, S. (1997) *Dramatherapy: Theory and Practice.* London: Routledge.

Katz, G. (2014) *The Play with a Play: The Enacted Dimension of Psychoanalytic Process.* Hove: Routledge.

Main, T. (1968) In honour of the seventieth birthday of Dr. S. H. Foukes, from the Foulkes Archive, Group-Analytic Contexts, 60, 20–5.

Nitsun, M. (1995) Artist and group facilitator: thoughts on paper by Gillian Recordon, *Group Analysis*, 28, 97–9.

Nitsun, M. (1996) *The Anti-group: Destructive Forces in the Group and their Creative Potential.* London: Routledge.

Pearson, J. (1996) *Discovering the Self through Drama and Movement.* London: Jessica Kingsley.

Pollack, B. (2012) Under destruction, *Art News*, June.

Rance, C. K. (1992) The aesthetics of group analysis, *Group Analysis*, 25, 171–81.

Recordon, G. (1994) Creativity: aspects of common ground between artist and facilitator. *Group Analysis*, 27, 329–37.

Segal, H. (1952) A psycho-analytical approach to aesthetics, *International Journal of Psychoanalysis*, 33, 196–207.

Steiner, J. (2006) Interpretive enactments and the analytic setting, *International Journal of Psychoanalysis*, 87, 315–20.

Stern, D. N. (2010) *Forms of Vitality: Exploring Dynamic Experience in Psychology, the Arts, Psychotherapy and Development.* Oxford: Oxford University Press.

Trevarthen, C. (1998) The concept and foundations of infant inter-subjectivity, in Braten, S. (ed.) *Interpersonal Communication and Emotion in Early Ontogeny.* Cambridge: Cambridge University Press.

Turner, V. (1980) Social dramas and stories about them, *Critical Inquirer*, 7, 141–68.

Turner, V. (1982) *From Ritual to Theatre: The Human Seriousness of Play.* New York: PAJ Books.

Wadeson, H. (2010) *Art Psychotherapy.* New Jersey: John Wiley.

Winnicott, D. W. (1960) String, *Journal of Child Psychology and Psychiatry*, 1, 49–52.

Winnicott, D. W. (1971) Playing: a theoretical statement, in *Playing and Reality.* London: Pelican.

Yalom, I. B. and Leszcz, M. (2005) *Theory and Practice of Group Psychotherapy.* New York: Basic Books.

Chapter 9

Rebel without a cause

Authority and revolt as themes in the cinema

The medium of film, in addition to its enduring appeal and entertainment value, is a rich repository of the cultural narrative in its many and varied forms. While psychoanalysis has established a lively discipline of film studies and has produced some outstanding reviews and reflections on film (Gabbard 1997, 2001; Sabbadini 2007), group analysis has so far not in any substantive way embraced the challenge. There is great potential to do so, to explore what the movies tell us about the worlds they depict, both past and present, to examine the psychological dramas enacted in the stories, and to consider how group analysis can illuminate our understanding and appreciation of the many facets of the movies. In this chapter, I adopt the theme of authority and revolt as a focus for reviewing four well-known films: *Rebel without a Cause, If...*, *One Few Over the Cuckoo's Nest* and *The White Ribbon*. I am interested in the films not only as powerful portrayals of human psychological dilemmas but in the cultural ethos surrounding the films and what it tells us about social history both in the substance of the story and in the temporal and environmental contexts in which the films were made. In this chapter, I am specifically interested in the different representations of authority and rebellion and how the narrative of each film resolves (or not) the universal struggle with power and what it is to be powerless. In so doing, I aim to link intra-psychic, social and political contexts in my first attempt at 'group analysis goes to the movies'.

Gabbard (1997), in a well-known psychoanalytic treatise on film, observes that psychoanalysts have adopted several approaches to the understanding of film. These include the film as representing a developmental moment; the film as reflecting the film-maker's unconscious; the film understood as dream material; the film from the perspective of the spectator or viewer; the film as an illustration of psychoanalytic insights; the film as explicating a particular character or characters in a parallel way to the analysis of an individual/s in the clinical setting; and the film as a dramatization of mythological themes. While potentially drawing on any of these approaches, in this chapter I will focus mainly on three perspectives: the developmental moment; the analysis of character/s that are caught up in the human drama; and, particularly, the film as representing a theme from underlying cultural mythology. As clarified by Paul (2011), the latter approach, which emphasizes the cultural narrative, derives from Levi-Strauss' notion (1975) that myths are 'transformations of fundamental conflicts or contradictions' that are germane to a cultural era and that in reality cannot be resolved. In the same way that dreams provide wish-fulfillment, so the narratives of film offer solutions to human problems that are otherwise unattainable or illusory. This is what gives films their power: the dramatization of themes of human conflict that find their resolution (though sometimes not) in ways that are sufficiently credible to believe in and that leave a sense of mastery over the difficulty, if not impossibility, of the human struggle. In pursuing the theme of authority and rebellion in the four designated films, I test out this idea as a central organizing motif in the film narrative, exploring the different ways the conflict issue is resolved, or not, in the unfolding of the drama.

If group analysis has anything to offer the abovementioned approaches to film study, which are already complex and reflect several directions that are compatible with group analytic interests, it is in the understanding of group processes as revealed in the film narrative which are linked to the drama and the destiny of the characters; as well as the context of the narrative and the making of the film in time and space – when the film was made and where. The possibility emerges of a newly configured appreciation of the movie that takes account of these interacting domains.

The theme of authority and revolt

My interest in this subject is reflected in the Foulkes Lecture I presented in London some years ago (Nitsun 2009). The mainspring of the lecture was my difficulty with the widely accepted Foulkesian conception of authority in the analytic group as a largely passive form of leadership (Foulkes 1964). While recognizing and appreciating the democratic vision underlying this view, and the value to the group of facilitating, non-impinging leadership that recognizes the strengths of the group, I at the same time argued that the complex dynamics of authority relations were over-simplified in this formulation. As I saw it, there are aggressive aspects of the relation to authority, including rivalry and conflict, as well as injustice and cruelty, that could be marginalized and lost to view – and hence modification – in a culture which insists on the benign and facilitating aspects of leadership. This is not meant to imply that leadership should deliberately provoke aggression and rebellion but that conflict-laden responses to authority are so common in intra-psychic and social representations of authority that this deeper ambivalence and the potential for revolt should be an integral part of the theory rather than a hindrance that is avoided. Otherwise, we might cultivate an incomplete version of authority as a major social and historical touch point and this would also delimit the scope for dealing with the psychological complexity of authority dynamics in the analytic group.

I referred in my 2009 lecture to examples of the intense conflict surrounding leadership and authority in events in history and literature, illustrating the narratives with images from art history. I also highlighted the issues of authority surrounding Foulkes' death in 1974, when he collapsed and died in full view of a group of the next generation of group analysts. I suggested that there were deeply unresolved anxieties about competition and leadership succession, that Foulkes' death occasioned considerable guilt and that the mourning of his passing has been ambivalent and incomplete. I went further to suggest that the failure to deal with Foulkes' death may have impacted the progress of group analysis and the development of theory and practice. My sense was that these views were ambivalently met: some recognition and resonance but also some unease and denial on the part of group analysts, generating uncertainty about my observations, albeit that they were speculative and hypothetical and not meant as a definitive treatise. In the present chapter, I welcome the challenge of a different medium, film: the possibility of generating a group analytic approach to film studies generally; and, specifically, the potential for an alternative approach to the theme of authority and revolt as represented in the powerful and illuminating art form of the cinema.

Cultural narrative in films

Exploring the subject of cultural myth as generating the film narrative, I draw from the paper by Paul (2011), which gives a clear and very useful account of the subject. Citing both Freud's analysis of the Oedipus myth, not so much as a study of an individual but as the symbolic representation of a dynamic conflict with universal overtones, and Levi-Strauss' notion of myths as cultural representations of common human themes and longed-for solutions, Paul undertakes an analysis of films as cultural schemas that offer fantasy solutions and hence satisfy collective longings. Within this frame, he focuses particularly on the 'succession scenario' and the tensions inherent in the western patriarchal construction of leadership succession. The main conflict area and contradiction in this scenario, as it applies to male succession, concerns the requirement, in fantasy at least, that succession entails murder. To succeed to senior status, a 'junior' male must kill a 'senior' male; to prevent this from happening, a senior male must kill a junior male; at the same time, to allow succession to proceed, a senior male must *not* kill a junior male; and in order to avoid guilt and a possible death sentence, a junior male must *not* kill a senior male (Paul 2011, p. 456). Using this contradictory perspective, that recognizes both assertion and innocence, Paul highlights the award-winning film *Slumdog Millionaire* (Danny Boyle, 2005) in which the main character Jamal Malik rises from a slum child literally covered in shit to the heights of fame and fortune, involving a triumph of succession over several rivals and adversaries. He shows how, through a series of narrative twists involving several characters, the plot successfully manages the inherent contradictions of succession. So, the hero ultimately achieves a virtually impossible dream: winning fame through a public contest (the television quiz), a fortune of money and a gorgeous girlfriend to boot. However, Paul makes the point that the strength of a cultural myth is its universal relevance: that it applies not only to males in a traditional conflict over authority and power, as in succession, but to other configurations of the human drama that embody similar tensions. His conclusion is that the popularity of particular films derives from the profound resonance of their themes, including their symbolic solutions to human dilemmas. He suggests that, in addition to its entertainment value, film generates insights into the 'underlying cultural dynamics of our society' (Paul 2011, p. 454). In other words, film not only borrows themes from the wider culture but throws a beam of understanding on these themes.

Paul's observations are relevant in this chapter for several reasons. Firstly, his analysis of the cultural meaning of film is close to the thesis I develop in the chapter, helping to understand the great impact that movies have on the popular imagination. Secondly, the theme of succession, and the way Paul addresses it, is close to the subject of authority and revolt that is the focus of my approach to the movies, especially when viewed in the light of its aggressive components. Thirdly, Paul highlights the difficulties of currently relying on a 'patriarchal' interpretation of cultural progress, for example the Oedipus complex, when the role of men generally, and fathers specifically, has changed so much in the 'post-paternal' era (Laurent 2009). He recognizes that there are similar reservations about Freud's notion of a primal crime, the slaying of the father by the sons, as the basis of human social organization. The patriarchal assumptions of this myth do not sit comfortably within a post-feminist culture. But in a separate paper, Paul (2010) examines the thesis of the primal horde more closely from a phylogenetic point of view and concludes that overall it retains considerable plausibility as an evolutionary account of group development. I am inclined, with no more than intuitive resonance, to agree with this view.

In my own analysis of film, I aim at a broader cultural perspective than either the Oedipus complex or the primal murder of the father but these interpretations, controversial and hypothetical as they are, remain, in my view, an indispensable frame of reference for the understanding of cultural mythology and the cultural artefacts of our age, such as film. I do not utilize the intricate dynamics of the succession scenario as represented in film in the way Paul does, but the general point about the cultural narratives underlying seminal movies, and the entrainment of solutions, hoped-for solutions and quasi-solutions to mythic human dilemmas, provides a valuable frame of reference.

Authority as a theme in film

It is impossible in this chapter to do justice to the full historical sweep of the cinema and the extraordinarily rich and varied cultural representations of film from its early beginnings to the present day. But what can be said is that within the vast pantheon of movies there exist some pervasive themes that recur in different narratives across the eras and genres of cinema. The theme of authority and revolt is a natural choice of subject for film: it has all the elements of drama, with powerful themes of justice and injustice, conflict and reconciliation; it represents a universal dilemma in so far as most societies and institutions have an authority structure which not unusually provokes rebellion or revolt; it is also central to the individual human struggle to assert the self and personal rights, often against an oppressive authority. Additionally, film is an excellent medium in which to explicate the subject of authority and revolt. The screen provides a powerful frame for the scenes of conflict and (sometimes) resolution that are inherent in the drama. It is not surprising therefore that the theme appears frequently in the cinema and that it takes centre-stage in some of the most influential and successful films of all time.

A quick dip into film history reveals the theme of authority and revolt as dominant motifs in a range of different categories of film. It is the leitmotif of early classics such as *The Battleship Potemkin*, 1927; *Mutiny on the Bounty*, 1935; and *The Caine Mutiny*, 1954. These films share the specific context of mutiny as a form of revolt but they convey fairly complex issues about authority and leadership, often posing searching questions about moral responsibility and accountability. In contrast to these films is the treatment of authority in the popular tradition of Biblical movies, such as *The Ten Commandments* (1923, 1956), *Samson and Delilah* (1949), *The Robe* (1956) and *Ben Hur* (1963). In these films, authority is vested in the absolute power of God, unquestionable and unshakeable, and the purpose of the narrative is to show how justice and deliverance are meted out to those who are on the side of God and punishment to those who are not. Authority is divided between good and bad with little if any place for questioning, doubt or ambivalence. Another category in which authority and revolt are prominent themes are biographical films that portray renowned leaders who must deal with substantial challenges to their authority – and face their own internal crises of conscience. These include 'biopics' of famous leaders such as *Ghandi* (1975) and, most recently, *Lincoln* (2012). These films usually show leadership at its quintessence: triumphing over doubt and resistance and contributing to civilized progress.

As is evident from the above, the representation of authority, leadership and revolt in film depends very much on the context, value system and philosophy that underpin the narrative of the particular film or set of films. The point in cinema history which I choose as the departure point for this chapter is the post-World War II body of films, which more openly than before question establishment values and social norms, touching on both deeply personal dilemmas and wider social processes such as the early Civil Rights movement in the USA. In this period, against the lingering shadow of a devastating world war, authority at a social level is put under severe duress, while at the same time there is growing self-reflectiveness about the individual's personal authority and responsibility. A psychological perspective becomes part of the genre, psychoanalysis and psychotherapy now embedded more firmly in the culture and providing a reference point for both the narrative themes of these films and their implicit meanings.

From a large number of relevant films, I have chosen three vintage films – *Rebel without a Cause* (1954), *If...* (1967), *One Flew Over the Cuckoo's Nest*

(1975) – and a much more recent film, *The White Ribbon* (2009). I have chosen these films because they are widely known, highly influential and emblematic of the sorts of themes I postulate as fundamental to a discourse about authority and rebellion. Unlike some of the other film categories mentioned, they do not offer the representation of an idealized authority commanding unambivalent respect. Rather they present authority as flawed, oppressive and generally problematic and the relationship to authority as complex and ambivalent. They offer no easy solutions. This makes them different from the category of films that Paul describes as providing symbolic solutions to universal dilemmas. The films I consider either suggest no solution or offer only partial solutions, which, I suggest, is closer to the reality of our lives than the wish-fulfilling endings of the more up-beat, popular films. In this sense, it may be necessary to differentiate films which offer solutions from those which do not and to consider what this means for the art of the cinema as well as the perspective of the viewer.

These films also illustrate some of the points I seek to emphasize when exploring the group analytic representation of authority. There is of course a large gap between the cinema and the consulting room and the insights of one may not transfer to the other but I attempt later to examine what, if anything, we may learn as group analysts from an understanding of the particular films I have chosen.

Rebel without a Cause (Nicholas Ray, 1955)

I begin with an iconic American film of the mid-1950s about teenage moral confusion and violence that is often described as having altered American culture (Biskind 1983). By the time this film was released, the theme of authority and revolt was already well-established in the cinema, given its archetypal status. But *Rebel without a Cause* invites attention because of its iconic status and more specifically because it dramatizes the cultural preoccupation at the time with 'juvenile delinquency', the term then used to describe anti-social youth behaviour in the context of a communication breakdown with the parental generation. The film's impact was such that in 1990 it entered the list of distinguished films deemed by the US Library of Congress' National Film Registry as 'culturally, historically or aesthetically significant'. Critic Emmanuel Levy (2005) describes it as 'the most influential youth picture in American history' and McKelly (2005) as 'an inaugural cinematic artifact of a postmodern culture of rebellion'.

Briefly, the plot concerns the arrival in town of troubled, delinquent teenager Jim (played by James Dean) who has a tormented relationship with his parents, a weak-willed, indecisive father and a highly dominant, critical mother. The parents' relationship is itself fraught with conflict and in an early scene Jim cries out, 'You're tearing me apart'. In spite of his attempts to stay out of trouble, Jim is soon drawn into conflict with the local gang of bullies who threaten him, lure him into a knife fight and goad him into a dangerous car chase which ends in the death of his main rival who hurtles headlong over a cliff into the sea. By now, Jim is not alone in his increasingly desperate misadventure. Judy (played by Natalie

Wood), a pretty, lost fourteen-year-old whose relationship with her father has broken down, comes to his side in a dawning romantic attraction, and Plato (played by Sal Mineo), a deeply troubled younger adolescent separated from his parents, attaches himself to Jim in a strongly idealizing way. These three, now in a closely aligned group, are being hunted by the local gang in revenge for the death of their car-driver leader as the action moves in the torrid night to a shadowy, derelict palatial home. This is the scene of the eventual tragedy: in a shoot-out with the police, Plato, now crazed with fear, is shot dead. Jim falls sobbing over his dying friend. Suggesting some hope of reconciliation between the generations, Jim's father comes to his side and the two embrace as father and son.

The film has been the subject of considerable commentary. The themes I focus on here are authority and rebellion, the way this is generated in family relationships and what this says about American, and probably western, society at the time. Perhaps the most striking feature of authority in the film is the *absence* of authority in the conventional family. Jim is desperate for direction from his weak father but gets none. Twice, early on in the drama, he seeks his father's advice on the extent to which he should consort with the local gang – which is his eventual nemesis – and both times he is given a non-committal response. In parallel, Judy tries to get close to her father who contemptuously spurns her affectionate approaches on the grounds that she is 'too old' for 'this stuff' (film commentaries suggest that the father is probably anxious about his own incestuous desires) but this is done in a cruelly casual way that denies any parental responsibility. Plato is an abandoned adolescent who shows his rage and despair early in the film by killing a litter of puppies. The film makes it clear that it is no accident that the teenagers are so lost, angry and vulnerable: they are deprived of parental care but, more so, of any vestige of appropriate and constructive authority. More than almost anything else, the film is a critique of the breakdown of parental authority and the consequent loss of trust between the generations.

The absence of authority (or distortion of authority in the case of Jim's shrill, critical mother) appears to be an intrinsic part of several dysfunctional families shown in the film. None of the families appears to be working as a family, other than in spurious ways, and the protective shelter of family life is missing. In line with my own formulation and reflected in my concept of the family as anti-group (Nitsun 1996), these are anti-group families: there is very little respect, affection and authority in the group. Plato's killing of the litter of puppies is a disturbing symbol of his hatred of the family, the litter of puppies representing the family that he has lost, which he mourns but also hates. He is the 'enemy of the family' (Meltzer 1973). In a sequence that I find very telling, the tightly knit triangular group-on-the-run formed by Jim, Judy and Plato, becomes an idealized surrogate family. Plato a number of times openly says that he wishes Jim was his dad and, as the relationship of Jim and Judy also intensifies, there is a palpable sense that this threesome represents father, mother and child. They grow very close physically, intertwined as if one. For a brief idyllic period in the strange shadowy garden of the abandoned house, suspended in time and space, there is a sense of a deeply contented family group. But then comes the sacrifice. Plato dies and the illusion of the family is once more shattered.

What is striking is that the young people's confusion and violence in the film is the product not of a strict, oppressive authority but of a largely absent authority. In this sense, the rebel without a cause can be seen to *have* a cause: not to overthrow a crushing parental authority but to shake into action a nebulous, non-existent or neglectful parental authority. This aspect of the film is sometimes criticized for being conformist (Biskind 1983): Jim's problem, the film can be interpreted as suggesting, could be resolved by his father playing the traditional role of dominant, assertive father and his mother the role of accepting, submissive wife. If this were achieved, the suggestion goes, family cohesion would flow, Jim would have a stronger base for his adult development and suburban harmony would be restored. But this criticism is offset by a view that the film's message about authority is a contradictory one (Fujiwara 2005): neither that youth's reckless defiance is desirable nor that the propping up of patriarchal hegemony is any sort of solution; rather that the urge to rebel and the urge to conform exist side by side in a state of paradoxical tension. This is a meaningful interpretation: it touches on the universal ambivalence about authority, the desire and need for it and the hatred of it.

The message of the film, seen in this way, illustrates the theses I develop in my own view of authority: that there is a developmental need for a clear authority that provides a secure moral frame but is also strong enough to be challenged and potentially undermined; that problems with authority are associated with ambivalent and sometimes violent impulses; and that the analogy of a realistic and perhaps necessary relationship with authority is one of *wrestling* with authority – like Jacob and the Angel in the biblical story (Nitsun 2009). This highlights the importance of engaging with authority rather than resorting to the extremes of either attack or submission. I suggest that *Rebel without a Cause* is a classic and influential film because it embraces these issues in an unflinching way and is not afraid to look deeply at the anxiety, longing and violence that are intrinsic to our relation to authority.

What of the wider social issues reflected in the film? Looked at from a larger group perspective, we see a society sharply divided between the generations: an anxious parental generation and a disaffected youth generation, with a vast chasm of understanding between them. This might be the first time in cinema history that the generational split is represented so strongly, vividly and tragically. Given that historically the medium of film is by now reaching millions of people, the message transmitted to audiences is that parental authority has broken down and that youth is in revolt. It is probably this aspect that is pivotal in the film's reputation as having changed American culture. From now on, there can be no pretence that the family as an institution is sacrosanct or that authority is intact. It seems important that, time-wise, the film is wedged between World War II and the Vietnam War, the devastation and horror of Hiroshima still sending shockwaves around the world and battles in Korea raging. Given the later protest movements of the 60s and 70s, American youth was getting ready for a massive resistance to the authority of the elders that propelled the country onto these killing fields. While the rebellion in *Rebel without a Cause* takes place in small-town, suburban middle-class America, it symbolizes the far wider and greater rebellion to come.

Some last points about the film, in some ways tangential but important nonetheless, concern the young stars who played the three leading characters. James Dean, giving a career-defining performance as Jim and becoming a cult figure of the twentieth century, created a great impact, the anti-hero who influenced a generation. But, almost in the realm of the bizarre, were the subsequent violent deaths of all three stars at a premature age. Sal Mineo was murdered in New York at the age of 37: Natalie Wood died aged 43 in an as-yet unexplained boating accident; and most strikingly, James Dean himself was killed aged 25 in a car crash shortly before the release of *Rebel without a Cause* in the USA. He was speeding at more than 100 miles per hour in a racing car on a Californian highway. Besides killing himself, he seriously injured two others – an uncanny replay of his 'chicken run' in the film. There is a story that just two hours before the fatal accident, Dean was ticketed for speeding. Apparently, his response was, 'So what?' before driving to his death (from *The Film Guide* 1996). If ever there was a blurring between art and reality, this was it.

In the film, there is some hope of redemption through the tragic loss of Plato. In reality, in James Dean's own life, there was none.

If... (Lindsay Anderson, 1968)

Described as 'a landmark of British countercultural cinema' (Rotten Tomatoes cinema reviews) and as 'one of the key texts of the 60s revolutionary sentiment' (*The Film Guide* 1996), *If...* tells the story of a violent and destructive rebellion in an English boys' public boarding school. The film is often regarded as a satire but its message is razor sharp and, like *Rebel without a Cause*, it made an impact worldwide.

The main protagonist is Mick (played by Malcolm McDowall), one of three allies returning to boarding school after the summer recess. A period of freedom and immersion in London's alternative culture during the break is followed by re-entry into the viciously oppressive school system. A weak headmaster and indifferent staff have devolved authority to the brutal school prefects who bully and humiliate the younger boys, extracting sexual and other favours. Mick, however, is no walkover: smart, lippy and sardonic, he has no truck with the prefects' rule. He has consistently resisted their arbitrary and capricious power. Now the group of three friends engages in some petty rebellions, like a forbidden excursion into town, a late-night drinking party and an affair with a local girl in the town. This falls foul of the sadistic head prefect who, on the boys' return, arranges a prolonged and vicious beating in the name of school spirit and decorum. Mick comes in for particularly savage treatment.

At boiling point, Mick and his allies decide to go to war. The film moves into surrealistic territory as they mount an attack on all the staff and visitors at a

'Founders' Day' ceremony. First snuffing the crowd out of the school hall with a fire and asphyxiating smoke, Mick and his guerilla band of supporters climb the roof of the school building and, standing astride, proceed to pummel the crowd with guns and grenades. The last scene shows the crowd disintegrating under the rain of fire. The scene freezes as the film title *If...* is blazoned across the screen in large red letters. The irony of the title now deepens: it comes from Rudyard Kipling's valedictory poem about strength and courage in the face of adversity and turmoil, echoing a jingoistic schoolboy mentality that takes a perverse twist in the events of the last part of the film. There are many possible readings of the narrative; a parody on schoolboy mentality and adventure stories (*The Film Guide* 1996); a critical attack on the English public school system; a wider attack on British society with its rigid hierarchies; and an even wider comment on the state of the world in the late 1960s. Film commentators regard it as no accident that 1968, the year of *If...*'s release, was the year of the French student uprising which sparked uprisings in various countries and is often regarded as the beginning of the worldwide student protest movement. *The Film Guide* (1996, p. 314) also describes the film as 'unmistakenly concerned with the Vietnam War and its ideological underpinnings', an interesting analogy given that *If...* is such a British film in content and context, yet revealing how widespread its significance might have been. The world was in ferment in the face of a further war and student groups and others were no longer prepared to comply with the culture of war-mongering. *If...* plugged into the mood of these cultural and political movements. Like James Dean in *Rebel without a Cause*, the main actor Malcolm McDowall became identified culturally with youth rebellion, turning up as the sadistic Alex in the violently anti-establishment film, *A Clockwork Orange*. Unlike Dean, however, he survived and went on to develop a career as an actor.

If... makes a useful comparison with *Rebel without a Cause*. The films are similar in one respect. Both, in representing the struggle with authority, portray the *abnegation* of authority on the part of senior figures. In *Rebel*, it is Jim's father who is unable or unwilling to exert a form of realistic, constructive authority, while in "*If...*, it is the headmaster and senior staff who delegate authority, unchecked and unregulated, to the school prefects. In both cases, this appears to be the condition for a violent enactment of perverse authority. In *Rebel*, the gang leader assumes a bullying, provocative authority; in *If...*, the prefects institute a reign of terror which in turn triggers the revenge attack on the school as a whole.

Where *If...* differs from *Rebel* is in the scale of the revolt and its social consequences. In *Rebel*, the revolt is at a domestic level: there are two tragic deaths, both of young people, but the community remains intact and there appears to be a reconciliation between father and son. Even if the cultural symbolism of the film, as I have suggested, far exceeds the small-town suburban context, the devastation we see is at a domestic level. In *If...* there is an assault on the entire school community. We do not see the outcome of the attack, but the impression, whether factually- or fantasy-minded, is that there is mass destruction. Although I have linked the narrative to the student uprisings of the subsequent decades, there is a further association: the school killings that became a feature of gun culture in the last few decades of the twentieth century and early decades of the twenty-first century, particularly in the USA. These murders, usually on a mass level, are mostly the responsibility of a single individual, usually a crazed, alienated, angry young person, almost always male. The causes of these attacks have been analysed in various ways but the blame is usually put on the individual and, to an extent, the family. But, in the light of the above commentary, we may wonder to what extent the violence is a reaction to the failure of authority at a social level: the curious mixture of abnegation and enforcement of authority in arbitrary ways that creates confusion and lack of containment and triggers the upsurge and enactment of violent impulses. The message is that it is not authority per se that provokes rebellion but *ambiguity* in the implementation of authority, where the boundaries of leadership and responsibility are unclear and the moral framework absent.

One Flew Over the Cuckoo's Nest (Milos Forman, 1975)

One Flew Over the Cuckoo's Nest is one of the most celebrated films of the 1970s and possibly *the* definitive cinematic rendering of the link between psychiatry and mental health. The themes of authority and power – and the abuse of both – are controversial political and philosophical issues in the history of psychiatry and this film is widely appreciated as a compelling statement about these issues. It is also widely known for the brilliant, Oscar-winning performance of Jack Nicholson playing the main protagonist of the story, Randle 'Mac' McMurphy, and the complementarily strong performance of Louise Fletcher as his formidable adversary, Nurse Ratched (whose name is widely used colloquially as an exemplar of the stern, unflinching face of authority).

The film is set in a ward in a psychiatric institution typical of mid-twentieth-century state institutions. Randle 'Mac' McMurphy (Nicholson) is a recidivist criminal serving a prison sentence (for the rape of a fifteen-year-old girl) who is transferred to the institution for evaluation, partly through his own design as he prefers the prospect of hospital to the harsh prison conditions. Playing mad, manic, provocative, demanding, ebullient, impulsive, Mac quickly becomes the leader of the group of male inmates, each of whose characters is vividly delineated in the story, including highly anxious stutterer Billy, delusional Martini, paranoid Dale and 'Chief' Bromden, an imposing American Indian whose enduring silence is taken as a symptom of his being deaf and dumb. The ward is presided over by Nurse Rached (Fletcher), a stickler for order and control whose efforts at suppressing opposition and rebellion on the ward are 'ratcheted' up in proportion to Mac's increasing determination to overthrow her rule and claim freedom for himself and the other men.

Mac takes the men through a series of adventures designed to embolden them, including a baseball game and group deep-sea fishing on a stolen boat. This has an empowering effect and, in a moving scene, the 'deaf and dumb' Chief begins to speak, breaking the silence of decades. But Mac's rehabilitative efforts increasingly collide with Nurse Ratched's regime and her efforts to suppress Mac and the men become more and more draconian. This includes shock treatment delivered to several of the inmates following a brawl. But the final denouement comes after a wild party arranged by Mac to include two up-for-it girls, alcohol and general disinhibition, which leaves the men wasted and the ward wrecked. Billy participates in a sexual liaison with one of the girls, at Mac's instigation, and while this has a liberating effect on him, Nurse Ratched announces her plan to expose him, specifically to his mother. This panics Billy and he kills himself. Mac, enraged with Ratched, nearly chokes her to death.

For some time now Mac has been aware that the institutional authorities plan to commit him indefinitely and this unleashes a powerful urge to escape. But his near fatal attack on Ratched is bound to provoke a serious backlash and he is subjected to the ultimate weapon of psychiatric control – a lobotomy. In the concluding scenes, 'Chief' reacts with horror when he realizes what has happened to Mac – he sees the lobotomy scars on Mac's mask-like face, now denuded of expression and life. In a gesture of determination not to let Mac endure a living death – an act of mercy – 'Chief' smothers him to death with a pillow. He then manages to do what Mac could not do – to break out of the hospital. Smashing a grated window by hurling a massive object through it, 'Chief' climbs through the window and in the dawning light of morning escapes to freedom. The men on the ward wake up to see his flight.

One Flew Over the Cuckoo's Nest has been the subject of extensive and varied commentary. The film touches on several compelling themes: the line between sanity and madness; the control system of psychiatry; the power of institutionalization; and the impact of the rebel leader on the group. The issue of sanity vs madness is mostly vested in the character of Mac (Nicholson), who teeters between sanity and madness, echoing the plight of Shakespeare's Hamlet and the way his feigned madness morphs into real madness, creating uncertainty about where the one ends and the other begins. But this raises the wider question of traditional psychiatry's construction of mental illness. Cuckoo's Nest was based on the best-selling novel of the same name that was published in the 1960s and that was part of the growing anti-psychiatry movement. This was paralleled in the UK by the critical voices of Ronald Laing and his associates at the Philadelphia Association. These protestors also echoed the brilliant writing of Thomas Szasz on The Myth of Mental Illness (1962). In Szasz's view, resolutely presented over several decades, psychiatry was responsible for the widespread pathologization of behaviours that were no more than the idiosyncratic expressions of human beings living their lives in their particular ways. By abusing their own authority, the argument went, psychiatrists sought to diagnose and control these behaviours using medicalized systems, often in institutionalized contexts, thereby posing a fundamental threat to human rights, freedom and dignity. These views were heavily underscored in the writing of Erving Goffman in Asylums (1961), which became a key text in the increasing move towards deinstitutionalization. Goffman formulated the notion of the 'total institution' in ensuring conformist and predictable behaviour by the enforcement of 'guard' and 'captor' roles in ritualized ways. The institutionalized are systematically stripped of their sense of themselves and are suppressed, negated and routinized.

The ward system in *Cuckoo's Nest* very much reflects Goffman's observations. Everything about the demoralized male inmates, forgotten by society, trapped in the institution, living bleak, colourless lives, and equally everything about Nurse Rached, in her grim determination to maintain order and control by all possible means, smacks of the total institution. Mac's entry onto this dehumanized stage marks the possibility of liberation from the oppressive regime but he can do so only by outright rebellion, by attacking the foundations of the institutionalized system. In so doing, he sacrifices himself but brings a glimmer of hope to the inmates and the message of freedom that ultimately gives 'Chief' the courage to break free. Although 'Chief' is a lone figure at the end of the film, running into the night, he symbolizes the universal vision of freedom from oppression.

As a narrative concerning authority and rebellion – and the metaphor is very apt – authority is very much represented by Nurse Fletcher and the ward system, and rebellion/revolt by Mac. Although the film has many comic moments, it ultimately is a serious statement about the power of oppressive authority and the difficulty, if not futility, of opposing it. This was a crucial message for psychiatry. By the time *Cuckoo's Nest* was released, the programme of deinstitutionalization in numerous countries was already underway but the culture of control of 'mental illness' was to some degree alive and well. Although the anti-psychiatry movement was in time criticized for its excesses, for denying the difference between 'real', severe psychological disturbance and inappropriately pathologized human behaviour, there was a growing recognition of the oppressive dynamics of medicalization and institutionalization. The psychiatry of the twenty-first century, thanks largely to these changes, mostly differs from its predecessors. Although still criticized, it tends more to recognize the risks of its diagnostic and treatment strategies. I emphasize this point in order to highlight how important a contribution *Cuckoo's Nest* made to the counter-culture of the time, reinforcing my point about the cultural narrative underlying film as reflecting universal concerns and how this can contribute to social change. The solution the film offers to the cultural dilemma, once again, is bleak, in terms of Mac's fate and that of the inmates, but the possibility of hope in the face of oppression, symbolized by 'Chief''s escape, is an inspiring and enduring message.

Some final comments about the nature of group leadership as portrayed by Mac. In terms of the group analytic ideal of relatively passive and largely non-interventionist leadership, Mac is anything but. He seizes the opportunity of leading the inmates in a highly pro-active way, galvanizing and prodding the men into action and risk-taking that has been dormant for years. Of course, this is in direct competition with Nurse Rached, who is repressive and punitive. They represent two opposites: the repressive and the liberating: the controlling and the anarchic. This defines a fundamental relation to authority that, once set in motion, can only escalate. In the film, destiny holds that there can be no compromise and it is this lack of compromise that fuels the narrative and makes it the tragi-comedy that it is. However, the question arises of whether this could be different in a different context at a different time. In some ways, in group analytic leadership, we run the gauntlet of these two approaches, the controlling and the anarchic, both in the dynamics of our groups and the way we construct and present ourselves as leaders. While supporting the value of democratic leadership in group analytic terms, I nevertheless argue that the extremes of leadership, as revealed in *Cuckoo's Nest*, are not just attributable to the heroes and villains of the fictional world but reside in each of us, in a state of fluctuating potential. This is important not only at a theoretical level but in terms of the way we conduct our groups, how much of the archetypes of leadership we can engage with and what freedom there is in the group to explore both sides of authority, the benign and the malign.

The White Ribbon (Michael Hanecke, 2009)

The next film, Michael Hanecke's highly acclaimed *The White Ribbon*, requires a substantial shift in time and place. It is a twenty-first-century film set in Germany in the years 1913–14, directed by an Austrian film maker and released in 2009. I have missed out several decades of film history along the way – purely for reasons of space, as there are numerous examples of the authority–revolt theme in films of these decades that I would have liked to include. My selecting *The White Ribbon* may be surprising, given its setting in the early twentieth century – when my other choices have all been within the later twentieth century and highlighted social issues relevant to the time. But I chose *The White Ribbon* for the vivid, often chilling way it depicts a whole community in the grip of a destructive process in which the enforcement of authority, inter-generational tension and rebellious enactments have brought the community to its knees, illustrating social and large group processes that are in turn related to political and historical developments. The film takes place on the very edge of World War I, raising important points about what this community tells us about the catastrophe to come and beyond that, to the further catastrophe of World War II. The director Hanecke (2009) has himself related the themes of the film to the roots of fascism and to the origins of evil, radicalism and terrorism. In this sense, I aim here to broaden the frame of authority and revolt and to locate it in both the historical and contemporary spheres. Authority and revolt are key themes throughout history, but *The White Ribbon*, in my view, offers a remarkable mirror onto the psychological tensions that fuel human lives, their communal enactments and their reverberations in the larger spheres of society and history. The film's narrative in the period 1913–14, exactly 100 years ago from now, is a contextual crossover that highlights the tensions underlying the main themes and their relevance to both subsequent and contemporary society.

The setting is a remote village in northern Germany, filmed with the precision and authentic sense of detail for which Hanecke is famous. It is a rigidly ordered society in which everyone knows their place. There is a strict hierarchy of authority: the baron presides over the village in feudal fashion; the farmworkers are yoked unquestioningly to their roles; the pastor is the moral authority, similarly enforcing order and control. He is a severe disciplinarian who insists on his own children wearing the infamous white ribbon, an act of humiliation for wrongdoing, to be rescinded only when the children are 'cleansed'. There is an educated bourgeoisie that keeps the community functioning: teacher, doctor, midwife, all bound by their identities. But this outwardly placid society is inwardly repressive and dysfunctional and there is an escalating series of vicious but mysterious acts in the village. Malice, spite and hostile retaliation begin to fester like sores, but under a shroud of secrecy and denial.

Some of the mysterious events include the doctor being thrown from his horse by a trip-wire that is suspended between two trees; the young son of the baron abducted, abused and badly beaten with a cane; and a disabled boy violently assaulted and almost blinded. In addition to these unsolved crimes, there are violations that are more obviously perpetrated by a known individual or individuals, such as a farmhand, embittered by the punitive behaviour of the baron, who destroys a crop of cabbages. There are also acts of domestic violence happening behind closed doors. The doctor humiliates the woman with whom he is having an affair, goading her to commit suicide as the only solution to her troubles and his distaste for her. The pastor institutes a reign of terror against his children. Any attachment or affection between these people is submerged under the twisted fabric of unequal power relationships. The only person seemingly exempt from these vices and hypocrisies is the teacher, who from the beginning tells the story in recall as an old man. But he can neither extricate himself from the horrors, nor influence people for the good – nor, in his narrative recall, make sense of the sinister developments that increasingly engulf the community.

Children play a particularly prominent part in the unfolding drama. Some of the tenderest moments in the film are enacted by the children, such as when the pastor's youngest son tries to reach his stern father emotionally through the plight of a bird in a cage. Similarly, the doctor's tiny son asks his first big existential question about the meaning of death. But, apart from these moments, there is a sense that the children in the village are banding together in a sinister mission. More and more it seems possible that these children, who have been at the end of the line of repression, cruelty and humiliation, are seeking their revenge. There is a growing sense that, in the face of their helplessness, there is no solution other than to act cruelly to others: the objects of their displacement. While vigorously denying the accusations that come their way, especially after the attack on the disabled child, the evidence points more and more in the children's direction. Hanecke himself, apparently, preferred to keep the responsibility for all the attacks ambiguous, leaving the audience with the challenge of not knowing or making their own sense of the mystery, almost as if the viewer is drawn into a judging or conspiratorial role.

As the film draws to a close, the village is on the verge of collapse. Several people flee, leaving questions unanswered about their responsibility or complicity. The streets are deserted, the shutters closed, the community fragmented. There is a sense that the old order has been destroyed. Then comes World War I.

There have been many searching commentaries on *The White Ribbon*. One area of debate concerns the children and their part in the village atrocities, not only how far they are culpable in the present but to what extent they represent the generation that is to come, specifically the generation that becomes the Nazis. Hanecke, in a published interview (2009), backs out of this particular link, saying he would prefer to leave the question open, partly because the film aims to make a statement at a broader level of significance. However, most commentators favour the premise that everything that happens in the village in the film foreshadows not just World War I but an embryonic Nazi Germany. In this view, the village is a microcosm of Germany about to descend into massive conflict and then to repeat history in 1939, this time with even greater force and violence. Picking up Hanecke's point about the film as a narrative of evil, what does the village tell us about the operation of evil? In various ways, we see the swell of evil, not only in the individual incidents but also in the sense of something deeper, more fundamental, more poisonous, more intractable, in the dark heart of the community.

In Hanecke's interview noted above, he describes the film as a narrative of evil: 'the origin of evil' (Hanecke 2009). Picking up on this theme, I use the term 'evil' here not in a way that supports the idea of 'original' evil but as a broad description of malign forces that we more commonly understand from a psychological perspective. Several psychoanalytic writers use the term 'evil' in this more discursive way. Amongst these, Zaltzman (2007) raises important questions about individual and group responsibility and comes down strongly on 'evil' as a collective phenomenon that supersedes individual psychopathology. She also suggests that, unlike individual disturbance, evil is impervious to the strategies of understanding and treatment. She emphasizes the sobering possibility that evil is a constant, immutable and intractable aspect – a 'dark zone' – of civilization. It involves profound regression, a state she describes as the 'the triumphant advance of a collective cultural regression'. At the same time, the regression does not just recreate an old situation: it produces a previously non-existent state, a new social formation. Evil therefore has its own perverse creativity; it is generative and regenerative of evil. However, Zaltzman questions the assumption that these acts are *inhuman*. She argues that the acts are human by virtue of the fact that humans commit them. It would be consoling if a clear distinction could be made between human and inhuman, evil and innocent, but this denies that the so-called 'inhuman' springs from all of us. Nazism and other forms of extreme fascism belong shockingly and inextricably to the human register (Villa 2010, p. 672).

Returning to the film, we see the creation of 'evil' in recurring formations in the community, in the way that Zaltzman postulates the generativity of evil. Each act of abuse has its own perverse character and consequences. We also see how this all happens within the human register. The perpetrators are seemingly ordinary people living ordinary lives: the children go to school, play; the adults work, they go about their daily business, as in all communities. But the destructive violence does not just arise in a vacuum. The hierarchy of power in the village is so set and so unyielding, that something is bound to give. The enforcement of authority is so relentless, the humiliation so deep and the shame so corrosive, that the acts of retaliatory violence are hideously understandable. The further point, and this highlights the overriding perspective of my argument, is that there is *no possibility of rebellion or revolt* in this community. Any hint of rebellion on the part of the children is firmly suppressed and punished. The white ribbon of the film's title is not just a ribbon attached to an individual's sleeve: it is a collective symbol of the shame and repressed rage that strangle the community. When the children commit their heinous crimes – assuming that the children are responsible after all – *they mainly do it to other children, in fact the youngest children amongst them.* A scapegoating process is afoot: the victims are the most innocent, powerless and vulnerable figures in the community. This suggests a complex response: at one level, a form of identification with the aggressor in so far as the children who have been aggressed become the perpetrators (Kernberg 1992); at another level, an identification with the helpless children being abused; and at a further level, an attack on the parents and the social order that suffocates the community. It is important that these are not just random acts of violence. They are the expression of extreme humiliation and rage in the face of an intransigent authority: there is no solution in this community other than the secret enactment of violence: the revolt has gone underground; scapegoats must be found; hatred must be expiated.

What of the mystery that surrounds the acts of abuse? Even as the perpetrators become more obvious towards the end of the film, there remains a miasma of confusion. But how much is this real confusion and how much is it a *wish not to know*? If the latter, it would fit in with processes of denial and dissociation generally in the village where there is repeated blindness to questions of responsibility. This suggests the powerful operation of 'turning a blind eye', a defence against acknowledging reality, culpability and guilt (Steiner 1985). This in turn normalizes betrayal and violence, producing a moral void, a situation akin to what Hannah Arendt (1963) described as 'the banality of evil'. She observed that at the point at which thought concerns itself with evil, there is frustration because there is *nothing* – no raging sadism or passionate hatred – which makes it difficult to observe and grasp the roots of evil. It may be that the film maintains confusion about responsibility until the end so as to drive home this point: the swell of 'evil' is greater and more insidious that we can comprehend.

Finally, I offer some thoughts about the anti-group components of the community. The group processes of the village community in this film are so striking and so implosive that an anti-group perspective is highly relevant. If we judge the presence of the anti-group in terms of the destructive outcome of a given group conflict or denouement, then the violation and fragmentation of the community as a whole strongly invites an anti-group interpretation. While we follow the individual acts of attrition as the story progresses, we are aware that this is a community turning against itself in an unstoppable way. Hanecke himself refers to this as 'civil war', not necessarily civil war in the way we know it, but 'the daily war that goes on between us all. All the big wars can be traced back to all these small ones between all of us' (Hanecke 2009). The village community is in the thrall of a war against itself. The suggestion is that Germany's twentieth-century wars are a continuation of this 'group disease', to utilize a term of Bion's (1961), but on a larger scale. The stage is set for the quintessence of the anti-group: the atrocities of World War II.

Another feature of the community is the lack of an 'outside' enemy. Although the baron in the film employs some Polish estate workers, there is seemingly no Jewish or other outsider group on whom the community can focus its fear and hatred. Had there been so, this might have enabled the community to cohere, to project its hostility outwards. Instead, the villagers are consumed by the enemy within: the true state of the anti-group. The paradox is that at the end of the film, Germany is about to plunge headlong into war, this time with a distinct enemy in tow – and with the fierce nationalist pride that unites them once again.

Further reflections

It remains to draw together the main impressions generated by the four films under consideration, particularly regarding the theme of authority and revolt, how this impacts on a group analytic understanding of leadership and the further question of whether group analysis has a distinct contribution to make to the study of film. Taking the four films together, all seminal films that were both critical and popular successes, there is an overriding sense of the importance of the authority–rebellion–revolt theme and support for the thesis that the theme has a profound significance in both our cultural consciousness and unconscious mythology. Its significance extends from the psychological struggles of families dealing with post-war inter-generational tensions in *Rebel without a Cause*, to the severely institutionalized authority of schools and state hospitals in *If...* and *One Flew over the Cuckoo's Nest*, and to the contamination of an entire community in *The White Ribbon* and its premonitory significance for the wars of the twentieth century. The theme is played out over and over at many levels of the individual, group and collective psyche. We might suppose that it has an archetypal significance – in the belly of the human struggle for survival, assertion and transformation.

What the films collectively demonstrate is the great difficulty in resolving the tensions between those in authority and those subject to authority. They suggest, as I have argued in my treatise on group analytic leadership, that the urge, need or requirement to rebel or revolt may be a common aspect of social development and that this tendency is intensified by the institutionalization and enforcement of authority in ways which undermine individual and social freedom. This produces a shame-based constellation of humiliation and rage that deepens the urge to rebel and ignites the act of rebellion or revolt. In turn, this reinforces the determination of those in authority to control and repress revolt, setting the stage for a continuing cycle of attack and retribution – until, as in all four films, a point of no return is reached. Then, almost literally – as in *If...* and *The White Ribbon* – all hell breaks loose. The consequences are destructive at both individual and social levels. Of course, these themes are dramatized in the movies in order to intensify the emotional impact on the viewer but they can do so because the underlying narrative resonates so deeply with audiences.

My argument stands open to the charge of bias when it comes to the choice of films. This is true: I have chosen films that illustrate my thesis. Possibly different conclusions would have been reached had the choice of films been different. In theory, I could have chosen films that deal seriously with the same theme but that illustrate a constructive, transformative relationship with authority. However, these films are in the minority. Further, if these films do exist, they do not have the same iconic status of the films I have reviewed: they are not generally as well-known, successful or familiar to screen audiences. There may be reasons for this too. The resolution of conflict with authority, or indeed the absence of conflict, does not have the same dramatic charge as the intense struggle with authority, particularly if it leads to open, escalating conflict, with the possibility of violence, which, like it or not, invigorates the narrative. This raises the question of whether there is something about the archetypal authority-rebellion theme that satisfies the popular imagination, probably as the enactment of a wished-for but repressed impulse to rebel, to take revenge against a hated authority, animating the construct of oppressive authority in the viewer's imagination and experience. If this is the case, it particularly speaks to the importance of this narrative in cultural mythology. The films chosen are successful and popular for a reason: they resonate deeply with a universal struggle with authority and a wish to rebel. Very possibly, this stems from childhood development when the individual is dependent on adult authority and ultimately has little option but to submit; but the sense of frustration, of smallness and shame, is repeated again and again in development and the emotional backlog is seldom resolved.

It is instructive to assess the outcomes of the rebellious struggles that feature as themes in the films at hand. These are not 'happy endings' in the sense associated with most Hollywood or other films. These films challenge the notion that the movies serve to provide wished-for solutions to cultural dilemmas that are otherwise insoluble – the reason Paul (2011) advances for the popular success of films like *Slumdog Millionaire*. Outcomes like Plato's death in *Rebel* and Mac's death in *Cuckoo's Nest* are not ideal solutions. Equally, the mass attack on the school in *If...* and the destruction of a community in *The White Ribbon* are hardly optimistic endings. Possibly, though, these endings resonate with a different aspect of the audience mentality: recognition of the fateful outcomes of universal struggles that do *not* have easy or ideal solutions. More so, the presentation of a destructive or tragic solution or non-solution may have a cathartic value: the exposition of such scenes on the screen is a vicarious expression of the longed-for overthrow of authority that is concealed in the civilized imagination.

What are the implications for group analysis, specifically around leadership? To generalize from the world of film to the consulting room is questionable – these are such different domains – but assuming the cultural 'truth' reflected in these movies, the lesson to be learned, in my view, is that the group analytic emphasis on democratic leadership in a largely passive sense misses the complexity of the authority–revolt relationship. Film after film demonstrates the human need to challenge – and the tragic consequences of smothering rebellion. The problem of this omission for group analysis is not so much, or not only, a theoretical one but a problem, in my view, about clinical practice. Without an adequate framework for understanding authority relations, and with a passive representation of leadership, which must affect the way the conductor runs the group, much of the challenge of leadership and the associated working through may be lost. Group members, I suggest, may not have the opportunity to rebel, contest, *wrestle* with authority in the way I have suggested facilitates a developmental solution to the problem (Nitsun 2009). The self psychologists (Kohut 1977; Wolff 1988) argue that rage and aggression are 'bi-products' of distorted and unhealthy relationships with authority figures: the engendered shame triggers the rebellion. If this is the case, there may be an argument for stripping group leadership of its more contentious, active or provocative aspects, in line with the group analytic value system. I see the argument but am not convinced. Passive leadership may invite conformity and good behaviour. Firmer, stronger, more active leadership gives group members something to contest, to oppose, and possibly emerge stronger in the process.

Some remaining issues warrant comment. One is the powerful emphasis in these films on male authority and male rebellion. The females in the plot are usually in supportive roles – mothers, sisters, lovers, but not primary figures in the clash between authority and revolt. The one exception is Nurse Rached in *Cuckoo's Nest*, who is very much identified with the oppressor. This emphasis on the masculine and de-emphasis on the feminine in relation to narratives of authority and revolt is typical of most other films in the genre, an interesting finding given the ascendance of female authority in the twentieth century – contrasted with the diminution of the male. This applies not only to the cinema of the twentieth century, which is where three of my films reside, but to present-day cinema as well. As various writers comment, assumptions about male prerogative and hetero-normativity have lost ground in the contemporary social landscape, challenging classical Oedipal dynamics and cultural representations of authority (Paul 2011). But the medium of film appears not to have caught up with these changes: it may require another generation before the change is fully reflected in the symbolic arts, such as the cinema. Alternatively, it may be that the masculine version of the authority–revolt configuration is so deep-rooted that it maintains a powerful hold on the imagination of film audiences and the cultural ethos.

The group analytic perspective

One of my remaining tasks is to consider ways in which group analysis as a discipline may make a contribution to film studies. In many ways, the overall approach in this chapter is group-analytic. The notion of cultural mythology as a framework for understanding cinematic themes is consistent with a group analytic perspective, emphasizing wider social and collective processes. Additionally, we could consider specific aspects of Foulkesian theory as benchmarks or frameworks within which to explore film narratives. Foulkes' (1964) notions of the four levels of the group – the current level, the projective level, the transference level and the primordial, for example – is congruent with the approach already outlined and may constitute a fruitful addition. We, for example, could regard the starting point of the film narrative as representing *the current level*; the distribution of roles and their attributes, particularly if viewed symbolically or as fantasy constructions, could illustrate the *projective* level; the relationships between the main characters, especially in so far as they recapitulate unresolved tensions of the past, could constitute the *transference level*; and, very importantly, the cultural myth or fantasy underling the narrative represents the *primordial level*. Similarly, the dual concept of the foundation and the dynamic matrix (Foulkes 1964) could be usefully applied. Evaluating the background canvas of the story, in cultural and psychological terms, as the foundation matrix, and the development of the narrative, through plot and character change, as the dynamic matrix, could generate insights about the overall process of film and its cultural significance. All four films reviewed in this chapter are open to this analysis. These approaches could be complemented by the core group analytic concepts of mirroring and resonance. Mirroring operates at several levels of film: in the unfolding communication between characters; the cultural resonances in the narrative itself; and the mirroring relationship between the film as artistic medium and the viewing audience. In my last thoughts below I attempt to develop the mirroring analogy still further.

Last thoughts – and a hypothesis

My final hypothesis draws on the concept of the organizational mirror (Nitsun 1998a, 1998b) in which I develop a schema for understanding organizations in the dimensions of time and space with an emphasis on the mirroring processes that bind the organization into a meaningful, though often dysfunctional, whole. I argue that within this matrix there is usually some underlying mythological theme that influences, and is influenced by, the organizational process. This is conceptually close to the notion of the cultural fantasy or narrative as structuring the themes of movies that I have developed throughout this chapter. Drawing together the concept of the organizational mirror and the notion of the cultural basis of film, I extend the analogy to look at the totality of the film in its multi-layered context. This draws together levels of the film as varied as the different aspects of production, the stars and the behind-the-scene politics, in addition to the film itself, its predominant narrative and its function as a mirror of a particular society at a particular juncture in time and place. By doing so, I hope to create a vision of the film as a complex cultural product that is both influenced by the surrounding ethos and influences it in return, affecting not just the life of the film but the lives of those who are intimately associated with it – and the public beyond. We all know how when a film is released, and in the run-up to its release, particularly if it is a film of some consequence, there are stories about the making of the film, the casting, the lives of the stars, the controversies the film sparks off and the impact it has on audiences. What I am suggesting is that this can be understood as an integrated whole: not just as separate fragments but as a kaleidoscopic mirror that reflects disparate elements in a meaningful configuration. This may be particularly the case with films that have unusual stature, such as those I have reviewed in this chapter. I further suggest that the totality happens not by accident or chance but by a symbolic thread that links the theme of the film and its cultural context. In some respects, we get close here to the notion of *art and life:* where the two meet.

In order to illustrate this point, I return to the first film explored in this chapter, *Rebel without a Cause.* I commented earlier on a particular aspect that remains a puzzle in Hollywood lore – the death of James Dean. As mentioned before, Dean, driving at breakneck speed, died in a car crash in which two other people were killed, shortly before the release of the film in the USA. In the film the character Jim, as we know, is a tormented teenager in conflict with his parents and himself. One of the pivotal events in the film is the dangerous car chase in which his main rival crashes to his death. Was it just synchronicity that James Dean died in a car crash himself shortly after the film was made? And that amongst his last words to a traffic cop were 'So what?' – almost as if he was speaking in the voice of Jim, the film character? This striking link highlights that Dean, Hollywood's newest star, was himself a complex, restless, rebellious individual, according to reports (McCann 1992), struggling with his homosexuality at a time when this was anathema not just in society at large but in the film studio system with its obsession with public image and approbation. When Dean is offered and accepts the role of Jim (his namesake), how much does this set the scene for his own destruction? How much does his identification with the character, Jim, confused and self-destructive, entangle him psychologically? Is it that, like Jim, he cannot rebel successfully and instead turns his rage inwards? Are Jim the 'rebel' and James Dean the 'star' symbolically one? In the film, the tragic fall-guy is Plato but in reality, the world outside the cinema, it is Dean, hell bent on destruction as he speeds to his death and that of two others on a Californian highway. Following the accident, Dean became one of Hollywood's great posthumous heroes, an icon of his age, forever the rebellious youth. His fame assured his immortality. I offer this as a further aspect of the unconscious impact of the movie and its cultural meaning – suggesting that in the failed rebellion, symbolically, there is a form of sacrifice. Mac in *Cuckoo's Nest* is a parallel example – fighting for the freedom of his cohort of institutionalized men, he is symbolically robbed of his own life. Through the trial by fire, the failed hero is sacrificed and immortalized in the process. In case of James Dean, art and life come together in one fatal event. The film *Rebel without a Cause* went on to become one of the highest-grossing films of its time and a cultural legend, James Dean, was born in the process. I suggest that this was not just coincidence: that the star's iconic status and tragic destiny mirror the deep cultural significance of the film, the link between art and life and the theme of authority–revolt in particular.

Lastly – the time in which this happened. I have previously referred to *Rebel* in the light of post-World War II history. James Dean died in 1955, approximately ten years after the war, but also at the end of the Korean War (1950–53), and near the beginning of the Vietnam War (1955–75). Many thousands of young men died in these wars and thousands would die in the wars to come. The link with the film is tangential but it is interesting to connect the suburban tragedy of *Rebel* with the wider historical context. Was *this* the stifled protest: the rebellion *with* a cause that would be played out again and again in the landscapes of war? This is a metaphorical interpretation. I am not suggesting that failed late- adolescent rebellion accounts for the massive events of war. Obviously, there were major geo-political forces that shaped these wars. However, I am suggesting that unresolved cultural processes of authority and revolt may be enacted through the plunge into armed and dangerous combat.

The description above is an example of how I suggest we can see film in its broadest and deepest meaning as an expression of a cultural narrative that mirrors events in the 'real' world: that it creates a matrix of signifiers that has a transcendent and sometimes transformative function. This interpretation accords the medium of film powerful significance in the lives of millions of people across the world, as a mirror of our lives and the struggles we share as human beings. It is also consistent with the group analytic perspective, highlighting the expanded matrix of film that links art to life, symbol to society. In this way, film's impact is amplified and, with it, the screen's greatest asset – the rich, complex and sometimes dark world of the cinema itself.

References

Arendt, H. (1963) *Eichmann in Jerusalem: A Report on the Banality of Evil.* New York: Viking Press.

Bion, W. R. (1961) *Experiences in Groups.* London: Tavistock.

Biskind, P. (1983) *How Hollywood Taught Us to Stop Worrying and Love the Fifties.* New York: Henry Holt.

Film Guide, The (1996) Rebel without a Cause, p. 570, London: Virgin Books.

Foulkes, S. H. (1964) *Therapeutic Group Analysis.* London: Allen and Unwin.

Fujiwara, C. (2005) The Rebel, *The Boston Globe,* 30 October (Globe Newspaper Co. 2006).

Gabbard, G. O. (1997) The psychoanalyst at the movies, *International Journal of Psychoanalysis,* 78, 429–34.

Gabbard, G. O. (2001) *Psychoanalysis and Film*. London: Karnac.

Goffman, I. (1961) *Asylums: Essays on the Social Situation of Mental Patients and Other Inmates*. New York: Anchor Books.

Hanecke, M. (2009) Interview on *The White Ribbon, Time Out*, November 2009 (author Dave Calhoun).

Kernberg, O. F. (1992) *Aggression in Personality Disorders and Perversions*. New Haven: Yale University Press.

Kohut, H. (1977) *The Restoration of the Self*. Madison, WI: International Universities Press.

Laurent, E. (2009) A new love for the father, in Kalinich, L. J. and Taylor, S. W., *The Dead Father: A Psychoanalytic Inquiry*. Hove: Routledge.

Levi-Strauss, C. (1975) *The Raw and the Cooked: Introduction to a Science of Mythology, vol. 1*. New York: Harper and Row.

Levy, E. (2005) Review of *Rebel without a Cause* (Nicholas Ray), Cinema 24/7 e-reviews. Online: www.rottentomatoes.com/m/rebel_without_a_cause/ (accessed 13 August 2014).

McCann, G. (1992) *Rebel Males: Clift, Brando and Dean*. London: Hamish Hamilton.

McKelly, J. C. (2005) Youth cinema and the culture of rebellion, in Slocum, J. D. (ed.) *Rebel without a Cause: Approaches to a Maverick Masterwork*. New York: SUNY Press.

Meltzer, D. (1973) *Sexual States of Mind*. Perthshire: Clunie Press.

Nitsun, M. (1996) *The Anti-group: Destructive Forces in the Group and their Creative Potential*. London: Routledge.

Nitsun, M. (1998a) The organizational mirror: a group-analytic approach to organizational consultancy, part 1 – theory, *Group Analysis*, 31, 245–67.

Nitsun, M. (1998b) The organizational mirror: a group-analytic approach to organizational consultancy: part 2 – application, *Group Analysis*, 31, 505–18.

Nitsun, M. (2009) Authority and revolt: the challenges to group leadership, *Group Analysis*, 42, 1–23.

Paul, R. A. (2011) Cultural narratives and the succession scenario: *Slumdog Millionaire* and other popular films and fictions, *International Journal of Psychoanalysis*, 92, 451–70.

Rotten Tomatoes (undated e-cinema reviews) Review of *If...* (Lindsay Anderson). Online: www.rottentomatoes.com/m/if1968/ (accessed 13 August 2014).

Sabbadini, A. (2007) *Projected Shadows: Psychoanalytic Reflections on the Representation of Loss in European Cinema*. Hove: Routledge.

Steiner, J. (1985) Turning a blind eye: the cover-up for Oedipus, *International Review of Psycho-analysis*, 68, 69–80.

Szasz, T. (1962) *The Myth of Mental Illness*. New York: Secker and Warburg.

Villa, F. (2010) Review of Zaltzman, N. (2007) L'Esprit du Mal (The Spirit of Evil), Paris: Editions de l'Olivier, *International Journal of Psychoanalysis*, 91, 667–674.

Wolff, E. (1988) *Treating the Self: Elements of Clinical Self Psychology*. New York: Guilford Press.

Zaltzman, N. (2007) *L'Esprit du Mal (The Spirit of Evil)*. Paris: Editions de l'Olivier.

Summary and conclusions

Journeying through the landscape of the twenty-first century, it is evident that there have been profound changes since the twentieth century and that seismic change at all levels of society and social process is ongoing. I have tended to emphasize throughout this book the anxiety arising from these changes, including anxiety about survival and continuity at personal, social and institutional levels, anxiety that in some form has always been there and that forms the substrate of our lives, but that is heightened by the accelerating speed of change and the uncertainty arising in the current world. I have considered change as fundamental as the loss of society, the collapse of time, the destruction of the environment and the whole question of what it means to be human in an increasingly technological age. I have also emphasized changes within psychotherapeutic culture that challenge some of the traditions we most value and that may require revisions of theory and practice. These visions of a future that is unravelling before us may seem dramatic, even dystopian, but I, for one, prefer to have a grasp of the precarious, of the outer limits of what we might have to countenance, than go blindly into the future. However, I hope I have similarly conveyed the enormous creativity that parallels these changes. In many ways, we would not be facing such an uncertain future had it not been for the immense technological and medical advances that mark our age, as well as artistic and cultural transformations across many domains.

Group analysis is inevitably challenged by these changes and I have raised questions about its future as a psychotherapeutic form in the twenty-first century, within the same frame of analytic psychotherapies that may be under threat. But, at the same time, I have hinted at the considerable potential there is for group analysis to make its mark in the twenty-first century, assuming society does survive in a recognizable form. As we know, a time of crisis is often a time of opportunity and it is on this note that I want to make some concluding points.

Perhaps the most important contribution group analysis can make in the evolving future is in the area in which we already have considerable experience and expertise – the facilitation of communication in embodied groups of people. If this is important at present, it becomes all the more important in an ever-expanding technological universe in which people are drawn increasingly into virtual communities and disembodied forms of communication. In some ways, nothing less than the human encounter is at stake. The group analytic excursion into small, median and large groups, each representing overlapping but also different social contexts, different forms of anxiety – and different potentials – equips us well to offer a framework for the strengthening of *real group relationships* in the coming decades. However, this requires adaptation on the part of group analysis: a reconsideration and revision of theory in line with social changes that radically alter our understanding of the group matrix, including Foulkesian concepts of the foundation and dynamic matrix, and the fundamental notion of the individual as a nodal point in a social network – a vision which becomes hugely transformed in the emerging networks of the Internet. Group analysis will have to consider the meaning of the intensifying social media and virtual communities that are at the heart of the Internet and what this implies for the future dynamics of human groupings. Established schools of thought or those in the process of being established, such as group analysis, are often reluctant to open up to new and different perspectives, given the institutional investment in identity and continuity. But the need for theoretical development can be seen as a positive challenge and offers valuable opportunities for creativity and innovation.

When considering the challenges to group analysis as a psychotherapeutic form, this book has highlighted the dramatic changes in clinical services since Foulkes originated group analytic therapy. The changes include the increasing diversification of the population, particularly in urban areas, the greater range, depth and complexity of psychopathology than previously existed, and the vastly increased demand for psychotherapy at the same time that public funding has visibly shrunk. This means that competition between the psychological therapies has sharpened and that survival more than ever depends on meeting criteria for what constitutes accountable practice.

The fact that all the changes I highlight are social 'through and through' throws into relief the increasing social emphasis in the theoretical development of group analysis: a potentially creative convergence. The social emphasis of group analysis is one of its most distinctive and generative features. At the same time, I have expressed reservations about the development of a theoretical social perspective, including a generalized notion of the social unconscious, in separation from empirical grounding in clinical and other 'practical' applications of group analysis. Group analytic psychotherapy has particular needs to strengthen the theory–practice link and to ground theory-building more fully in the empirical realm of evaluation and research. There is a long way to go, but in line with Greene's (2012) proposals, there are creative opportunities here too, including the potential to incorporate research in everyday clinical practice rather than turn research into an unreachable goal and an impossible burden.

Part of the challenge to group analysis stems also from cultural shifts in the appreciation of psychological change, how this comes about and what time-span is permissible and realistic in an age of rapid evolutionary change. That short-term behaviourally orientated psychological therapies have become the order of the day is a product not only of funding pressures, seemingly backed up by effectiveness research, but of an entire zeitgeist that encourages rapid transformation and accelerated change. Group analysis needs to address this, possibly at the level of discourse concerning social values but also in terms of opening up to different ways of working. There are suggestions (Lorentzen *et al.* 2014) that shorter-term group psychotherapy has equivalent outcomes to longer-term approaches and, while this may be unwelcome news to some diehard practitioners, it also suggests a flexibility in our approach that can be seen as an asset rather than a liability. It is for similar reasons that I suggest modifications of technique in group psychotherapy services for more disturbed and inaccessible populations, such as in the NHS, where notions of safety, rest and refuge are more relevant than analysis. Further, I argue for the value of opening up to other models of psychotherapy, such as CBT, where I discover greater commonalities with group analysis than is commonly assumed, where there are novel perspectives and opportunities for dialogue, cross-fertilization and joint working that would strengthen the group analytic presence in public services. Above all, I argue for openness and appreciation of difference in the psychotherapeutic field and against dogma, self-idealization and self-regarding defensiveness.

Another area of challenge is in the area of leadership. Undoubtedly, this will constitute a major focus in the coming age, against a background of the disillusionment and mistrust in leadership that emerged in the economic and political crises of the last decades. This is one reason, in my view, why it may be important to revisit group analytic notions of leadership, which in their democratic emphasis and appreciation of leadership from within the group, have much to offer in and outside psychotherapy, but suffer from sufficiently detailed attention to the leadership process, particularly when leadership is under fire. Linked to this are unresolved questions about authority – what represents the most facilitating and effective authority – that have an important bearing on the development of the group and anti-group, given the impact of leadership on the formation of both functional and dysfunctional groups.

I attempt in this book to make a contribution to the subject of leadership through focusing on the professional development of the group analytic psychotherapist, highlighting how marginal this area of interest has been until now, but how important the person of the group therapist is in the evolution of a leadership role and style. This includes the therapist's own representation of authority and how this is mediated in the group. Unmanaged problems in this area, I suggest, generate crises in both the group and the conductor and lead to disaffection in work as a group analytic psychotherapist.

A creative challenge in the developing century emerges in the possibility of widened inter-disciplinary collaboration. I am referring particularly to the arts and the sense of increasing convergence between the arts and psychotherapy in general and group psychotherapy in particular. Forays into the world of music, the visual arts and the performing arts are already beginning in group analysis and I see much further potential. In this book, I have considered a link between group analysis and performance art, as well as the application of group analytic thinking to film studies, which may bring fresh perspectives to the world of the movies and in turn illuminate some of the complex human dramas that we struggle with in our own field of work.

It remains for me to consider the place of the concept of the anti-group in all the above. The theme has woven through all the chapters in this book. It is in the spirit of the dialectic of creativity and destruction that I want to position the concept of the anti-group at the close of the book. The exploration of group processes in several domains confirms the need for a critical principle of group life that facilitates recognition of the darker, disruptive side of groups and the ambivalence towards groups that marks western culture. We have seen this process weaving through contexts such as:

- the wider social order in which the struggle for group integration is continually undermined by the pull towards fissure and fragmentation;
- the shadow side of technological change reflected in alienation and loss of embodied intimacy;
- the obverse of 'progress' more generally in the social disorganization and loss of familiar cultural beacons consequent to technological change;
- the destruction of organizational life through internal and external conflict and competition;
- the valorization of individuality, self-creation and personal gain, at the expense of communal responsibility;
- the continuing exploitation of the natural environment and the denial of responsibility for consequences;
- the healthcare environment in which the healing motive is undermined by a coercive and punitive culture as well as political intrusion;
- the clinical sphere, in which attempts to establish group psychotherapy as a primary therapeutic mode are undermined;
- the implosive aspect of psychotherapy groups in public services, particularly in environments such as the inner city with its high level of social isolation and fragmentation;
- the family in which the requirements of group containment and protection are challenged by neglect, aggression and abuse;
- the impact of leadership failure on groups, suggesting a link between dysfunctional authority and anti-group processes;
- the group analyst/therapist's struggle with his/her own anti-group reactions in the face of problematic group developments.

These are some of the main anti-group processes I have explored in this book. However we explain these processes, it seems to me essential that we recognize and strive to understand them and that our love of groups, our belief in the collaborative and creative strengths of people in groups, should not blind us to our destructiveness and self-destructiveness and the way this may be expressed and enacted within and between groups. Getting *beyond the anti-group*, as the book title suggests, first requires getting into it, getting to grips with it – and surviving it.

References

Greene, L. R. (2012, July 9) Group therapist as social scientist, with special reference to the psychodynamically oriented psychotherapist, *American Psychologist,* advance online publication; doi: 10.1037/a002914.

Lorentzen, S., Ruud, T., Fjeldstad, A. and Hoglend, P. (2014) Comparison of short-term and long-term dynamic group psychotherapy: a randomized clinical trial, *British Journal of Psychiatry,* 203, 280–7.

Postscript

There are several important group-related themes that I have barely touched on in this book. One concerns Bion's notion of the basic assumptions and its applications in the group literature; the second, the violence and destructiveness of groups on the geo-political stage of national and international conflict. To a degree, the omission is purposeful. Both are complex themes in their own right and, given the range of subjects already covered in the book, it would have been impossible to do justice to these themes as well. Yet, the themes reverberated in my mind while writing the book and in this last section I propose to address them, if not in depth then at least in recognition of their significance and their relevance to the subject of the anti-group.

First, Bion's theory of the basic assumptions. In my original book on the anti-group (Nitsun 1996), I made clear the influence of Bion on my thinking. Bion's appreciation of the darker, disruptive and regressive aspects of group functioning was immediately resonant and largely congruent with an anti-group perspective. Additionally, Bion's metapsychology of the group and the way he understood the individual's ambivalent relationship to the group reflected the concerns that led me to formulate the anti-group. His well-known comment on the individual being a 'group member at war with himself for his groupishness', and his assertion that for an adult membership of a group may be as complex as the relationship to the breast is for the infant, emphasized that group membership is fraught with difficulty and ambivalence – again very much in the spirit of what I was attempting to say in the anti-group. We cannot assume that belonging to a group, although desirable if not essential, comes easily, readily and naturally to all people. There is a pervasive tension between wanting to belong and wanting not to belong, to remain unfettered, unattached, an 'individual' in the customary sense of the word, whether one sees this as arising from an illusory wish for separateness, an anxiety about merging, fears of attack, loss of identity, envious and competitive impulses, a narcissistic retreat, or simply a wish for singularity.

Additionally, I was attracted to Bion's understanding of group process. His notion of group mentality as a reservoir of individual and group introjections and projections, with powerful stirrings of anxiety and primordial fantasy, accords with my own understanding of group process and experience, reflected in some of my theorizing about both the anti-group and my concept of the organizational mirror. That the anxieties Bion posited may be dealt with in regressive and destructive ways, undermining the group purpose and task, is also consistent with my viewpoint. My attraction to this aspect of Bion's thinking throws into relief some of my difficulties with Foulkes' theories, notably the striking absence of any coherent account of aggression in groups and towards groups.

Where I depart from Bion is in the weight of his pessimistic viewpoint and what Hoggett (1992) refers to as the lack of a 'positive, creative and constructive force' in Bion's account of group life. It was for this reason that I sought in formulating the anti-group a way of reconciling Foulkes' relative optimism and Bion's relative pessimism: the anti-group, in my view, is not a static or isolated aspect of group identification but part of a dialectic in which group-supportive and group-antagonistic processes emerge in constant interplay, eventually in 'good enough' conditions leading to greater, if fluctuating, integration of positive and negative group identifications.

The other aspect of Bion's approach with which I have difficulty is his theory of the basic assumptions per se. His three-fold categorization of the basic assumptions of dependency, flight-fight and pairing is widely known and influential, each assumption representing a regressive mode in the face of intense anxiety stirred up in the group. These three basic assumptions have been added to over the decades by other writers: a fourth basic assumption of "oneness" postulated by Turquet (1975), a reformulation of the fourth basic assumption (as I understand it) as "aggregation- massification" by Hopper (1997): a fifth basic assumption of "me-ness" (Lawrence, Bain and Gould 1996); and a sixth basic assumption suggested by Roth (2013) that reflects the violent and murderous propensities of groups that arise in relation to heightened threat to the integrity and survival of the group. Roth highlights Bion's omission of actual violent destructiveness in groups (as opposed to impulses and ideation) and makes a convincing case for this most egregious aspect of human group behaviour to be incorporated in any psycho- or group-analytic understanding of groups. But I have difficulty with the whole notion of the basic assumptions in so far as it, in my view, posits an intervening variable (the basic assumption) that is not adequately explained and that it unnecessarily categorizes the group response, creating a quasi-mechanical notion of shifts between group polarities which in turn generates a numerical order of hypothetical basic assumptions. Already, there is some confusion and overlap, as I see it, between different versions of the assumptions – and, in any case, why should there be *three* basic assumptions, or for that matter *four* or *five* or *six*? Why not rather have a notion of group defensive or regressive behaviour, based on faulty expectations or hopes, and linked to the intense anxiety stirred up in groups, that can take a variety of forms in different groups and different circumstances, rather than a set of fixed polarities? Whatever the answer to these questions – and I am sure this is worthy of debate – I recognize my own difficulty with the formulation of basic assumptions (I do believe our attraction to some theories and not others is largely personal) while at the same time appreciating that the literature on the basic assumptions is resonant with ideas that are very relevant to understanding groups.

In my earlier book (Nitsun 1996), I postulated that the basic assumptions could be re-interpreted as different expressions of the anti-group. All three, four, five or six basic assumptions mentioned here reflect a fundamental difficulty in accepting and relating to the group as a group in the sense of belonging and differentiation. They all in different ways, whether consciously or unconsciously, mainly seek to subvert, fragment, collapse, extrude or destroy the group, all arising from the fundamental anxiety and ambivalence noted earlier about group membership. Looked at in this way, it may be unnecessary to postulate a gathering series of basic assumptions. A more parsimonious explanation is that groups usually generate anti-groups and that the shift between group investment and group repudiation, reflected in varying processes of group cohesion and fragmentation, generates different ways of seeking to resolve the tension, some constructive, some potentially destructive as in the basic assumptions, but with the potential for transformation once the source/s of group anxiety and hatred can be located. This does not rule out the likelihood of there being more complex social processes that underlie these developments and influence group outcomes – as the literature on the basic assumptions amply suggests - but a simplified approach may make it possible to generate clearer operational definitions of the basic assumptions, putatively linked to the anti-group as a common thread. This may have more heuristic value in day-to-day group work and group studies than a series of abstract propositions that argue appropriately for the urgencies of group development but can teeter between confusion and somewhat mechanical categories of group dysfunction.

The second area of my omission in this book is the phenomenon of violent destructiveness enacted on the world stage. I referred briefly to fundamentalism and terrorism in Chapter 1 but the larger issue of social violence merits further consideration in anti-group terms. I am influenced here by Roth's (2013) challenging paper in which he reappraises Bion's contribution and finds it lacking in this particular area, suggesting that Bion's war experiences led him to avoid rather than incorporate what he saw – killing on a mass scale. Roth highlights the great difficulty psychoanalysis in general has had in addressing the mass genocides of the two world wars in the twentieth century, including the phenomenon of Hitler's cataclysmic leadership, which is inadequately understood in conventional psychoanalytic terms. Rather, Roth suggests, these are large group phenomena which entrain pathological leadership but must be understood fundamentally in group terms.

This challenge takes on added significance in the current century, and the present time, when we are witnessing ongoing and unstoppable social violence and murder, epitomized at the time of writing this book by the brutality of the protracted Syrian conflict etched against relentless murderous hostilities in other parts of the world. Roth refers to the work of Kaes (2007) in trying to make sense of mass destruction of this sort. My interpretation along anti-group lines of this writing derives from a paradoxically positive view of social groups as providing ongoing functions of safety, protection, satisfaction of dependency needs, defence against malignant internal group developments and containment of fears of isolation and loneliness. The equilibrium maintained by groups providing these functions, however, is fragile. Aggressive and competitive tensions within group, impulses to transgress agreed codes of conduct, and hostile and violent propensities, threaten to implode and destabilize the group. Shifting alliances within the group add further to the tension and destabilization, necessitating a sometimes urgent solution that may enable the group to survive and continue. Although 'healthy' groups can usually generate constructive actions within-group to strengthen safety and continuity, dealing constructively with transgression and conflict and pre-empting a latent or emergent anti-group of a destructive sort, less healthy groups can manage within-group safety only by creating/maintaining a repudiated group as destructive 'other'. This 'other' group may be a split-off sub-group of the larger group or an outside group which is readily invested with hostile identifications as the 'enemy', with characteristics ranging from despicability to dangerousness, depending on the historical context of inter-group relations and the nature of counter-group identifications and projections. The outcome of this process also varies considerably, from minor, barely tolerable inter-group rivalry to catastrophic group destruction, as in world wars and other more local but intense political and social clashes.

Of course, in large-scale violence of the sort that is most troubling, the inter-group dynamics are complicated and many-layered, with profound geo-political considerations and significant leadership considerations that I can only mention here. But what I am attempting to highlight is the anti-group component of these dynamics, notably the transition from *intra*-anti-group to *extra*-anti-group developments, which can turn out to be lethal. This argument reinforces my often-stated view that the anti-group arises when survival is at stake and that the projection of hostility onto the 'other' group provokes fears of counter-attack, thereby perpetuating the state of survival anxiety that generates the split in the first place. It also highlights the importance of recognizing inherent anti-group tendencies within groups so that they may be reconciled in a way that minimizes the impulse to project the hostility onto an/other group/s.

Coming back to the main contents of this book, which have been more focused on clinical and organizational concerns, alongside developmental and aesthetic considerations of group life, I wish to end on a note of the ubiquity of anti-group phenomena and the way the difficulties in groups we see in clinical settings mirror wider and deeper processes at a global level. In this way, I end echoing the start of the book that foregrounded the question of survival in the twenty-first century – but also the creativity demonstrated time and again in ensuring and protecting our survival.

References

Hoggett, P. (1992) *Partisans in an Uncertain World*. London: Free Association Books.

Hopper, E. (1997) Traumatic experience in the unconscious life of groups: a fourth basic assumption, *Group Analysis*, 30, 439–70.

Kaes, R. (2007) *Linking, Alliances and Shared Space: Groups and the Psychoanalyst*. London: International Psychoanalysis Library.

Lawrence, W. G., Bain, A. and Gould, G. (1996) The fifth basic assumption, *Free Associations*, 6, 28–55.

Nitsun, M. (1996) *The Anti-group: Destructive Forces in the Group and their Creative Potential*. London: Routledge.

Roth, B. (2013) Bion, basic assumptions, and violence: A corrective reappraisal, *International Journal of Group Psychotherapy*, 63, 525–43.

Turquet, P. (1975) Threats to identity in the large group, in Kreeger, L. (ed.) *The Large Group: Dynamics and Therapy*. London: Constable.

Index